Acting-In

3rd Edition

Acting-In

Practical Applications of Psychodramatic Methods

Third Edition

Dr Adam Blatner

Foreword by J. L. Moreno

FREE ASSOCIATION BOOKS/LONDON

Published in 1997 by
Free Association Books Ltd
57 Warren St, London W1P 5PA

Copyright © 1996 by Springer Publishing Company, Inc.

ISBN 185343 367 5

A CIP catalogue for this book is available from the British Library

Produced for Free Association Books by
Chase Production Services, Chadlington, OX7 3LN
Printed in the EC by J.W. Arrowsmith Ltd, Bristol

To David and Alisa, my son and daughter,
whose natural childhood play helped me understand
Moreno's insights regarding spontaneity and creativity.

Contents

Foreword to the First Edition

In 1921, I created psychodrama out of the earlier work I did with group psychotherapy, sociometry, and improvisatory theatre. Since then I have written numerous books and scores of articles on the subject. Dr. Blatner's book, *Acting-In*, will be a good adjunct to my writings. This is an excellent work on the subject.

I am especially pleased that Dr. Blatner notes the theological basis of the method of psychodrama.

I have always tried to show that my approach was meant as much more than a psychotherapeutic method—my ideas have emphasized that *creativity* and *spontaneity* affect the very roots of *vitality* and spiritual development, and thus affect our involvements in every sphere of our lives. Furthermore, I have always wanted to have people attend to the processes of health, as well as to the problems of illness; thus I am glad Dr. Blatner has noted the applications of psychodrama in the home, school, and world of business.

When I first met Dr. Blatner in 1968, he was a resident in psychiatry at Stanford University. At that time he showed me a collection of writings by others in the field of psychodrama, along with a few additions of his own—a syllabus he had assembled entitled "Practical Aspects of Psychodrama." I encouraged him to continue his interest in psychodrama and to do more of his own writing. Apparently, he has taken my advice.

I am further pleased with the different audiences to whom this book can be addressed: for those who are interested in learning about psychodrama, it can be an introduction; for those who are practitioners, these materials can comprise a useful handbook; and for the serious student, *Acting-In* is an up-to-date and extensive resource for references and background materials.

I wish the author every success in this undertaking.

— J. L. Moreno, M.D., 1973

Preface to the Third Edition

Since its first publication 23 years ago, *Acting-In* has now become one of the major introductory texts in the field of psychodrama and a significant adjunctive resource for psychotherapists and others who use role playing or action techniques in their work. So far, it has been translated into Spanish, Dutch, Swedish, Japanese, Chinese, and, I am told, Arabic, which speaks for how psychodrama is now internationally recognized. There has been a tremendous expansion of its use all over the world, and a corresponding development of theory and integration of the method with analytic and other approaches.

I have significantly revised this edition, seeking to clarify various processes. In 1988 I wrote *Foundations of Psychodrama: History, Theory & Practice* as a complement to *Acting-In*, designed to offer more in the way of background material, not only regarding the way psychodrama can be integrated with other therapies, but also the philosophical and even spiritual basis of Moreno's work. And although *Acting-In* is designed for students, I've included recent developments in theory and technique which can also be informative to experienced practitioners. One of the other functions of this text is to provide a more scholarly basis to our work, and to this end I've updated the references which reflect the varieties and depth of applications of psychodrama in many fields of endeavor.

Psychodramatic methods have now become integrated into drama therapy, drama in education, sociodramatic explorations of community issues, personal growth programs, men's and women's groups, organizational development, consulting to business, various recovery and self-help groups, and many other contexts aside from psychotherapy. And within the fields of psychotherapy, these approaches are further integrated with a wide range of other methods—imagery, cognitive, behavioral, bodywork, family therapy, and programs of systematic eclecticism. This not only reflects the potential of these methods to facilitate a wide range of exploratory and therapeutic processes, but also to aid in the development of more cost-effective treatments in a time of increasing economic constraints.

Also, a number of procedures which had once been utilized primarily in the clinical context are now being modified for application in educational and spiritual dimensions of life, and not only for young people, but throughout the life cycle. Psychodrama should be viewed not as a separate school of thought, but as a complement to the growing understanding of human nature and the human potential. This was Moreno's vision, one that attempted to offer specific methods which could achieve the noble goals of fostering creativity, spontaneity, self-expression, and community spirit.

Finally, I want to acknowledge with the deepest appreciation the inspiration and support of my muse and wife, Allee.

Adam Blatner, MD, TEP*
Austin, Texas

* A note about my name: In many citations regarding the first (1973) edition, I'm listed as H. Blatner, but in 1977 I changed my first name to Adam. Incidentally, this shift in identity was stimulated by Zerka Moreno who, in a workshop, had the group talk about how we felt about our names and whether we would choose a different one. At that time I had remarried, so the idea of a new identity seemed right, and after a few months of playing with the idea, we found a name more to my taste. To my delight, the psychodrama community and others were very supportive of this change!

Introduction

Many of the most powerful active approaches in contemporary psychotherapy and education are derived from the method of psychodrama, in which a person is helped to imagine and enact a problem instead of just talking about it. Psychodrama and its associated methods of sociodrama, role playing, and sociometry were invented around the 1930s by Jacob L. Moreno, M.D. (1889–1974). The purpose of this book is to introduce some practical applications of the psychodramatic method to readers from a variety of disciplines.

The psychodramatic method integrates the modes of cognitive analysis with the dimensions of experiential and participatory involvement. Actually "doing" the interaction, engaging one's own physical body and imagination as if the situation were unfolding in the present moment brings into consciousness a host of ideas and feelings not generally accessed through simply talking about that situation. The nonverbal elements of communications not only act interpersonally, but also as inner cues, so that, for example, behaving in a more angry or frightened manner will evoke an awareness of emotions which may have been otherwise repressed.

Action approaches are especially useful in therapy not only with patients who have little capacity for intellectual and verbal exploration (e.g., children, psychotics, delinquents, etc.), but also for those who tend to overintellectualize their experiences. One of psychodrama's most significant advantages is that it converts the participant's urge toward "acting-out" into the more constructive channel of "acting-in."

ACTING-IN versus ACTING OUT

Expressing feelings and ideas in action is a natural tendency because the physical experience of embodying a role lends a greater degree of fullness, is a stronger expression of will, and more completely affirms the sense of self. In other words, when an idea is embodied in a form that can be both witnessed by others and kinesthetically processed in one's own being, it becomes "more real." This important theoretical concept has significant implications for therapy and education (Schwartz & Schwartz, 1971). Moreno called this tendency *act hunger*, and noted that people need to do more than simply talk about their reactions and desires (Moreno, 1985).

If act hunger is frustrated, people will often impulsively "act out," their activity expressing their needs outside of awareness (Kellerman, 1984; Ormont, 1969). This dynamic has been well described by psychoanalysts, but what hasn't been appreciated is that this same inclination can be harnessed in service of greater self-awareness (Rubin, 1981). In psychodrama, the action is played out and even exaggerated, linked to its original settings and to other modes of expression. Because it operates in the interpersonal field, witnessed by the director and audience, it also evokes the protagonist's own "witnessing" function. Psychodrama converts behavior intended to avoid awareness into behavior which promotes insight and a greater capacity for self-reflectiveness (Bromberg, 1958; Fingarette, 1969, Zeligs, 1957).

For this reason, I've given the name *acting-in* to the sublimation of act hunger as a vehicle for therapy or for personal or group development. Acting-in (or what Davies in 1976 called "acting-through") uses the dramatic context to generate "role distance" through which actors can figuratively step back and witness their own performances. Role distance is the essential component of imaginative play and the basis for the most natural way to learn. Simulation learning processes have applications not only in therapy, but in many types of training where a more complex understanding and skill development is needed, from the rehearsal of dance to astronaut training.

In addition to the task of clarifying emotional conflicts, the psychodramatic method can be applied to the challenge of developing human potentialities. Through acting-in, the individual can be reintroduced to many dimensions of personal experience that have been neglected in our contemporary, overintellectualized society: creativity, spontaneity, drama, humor, excitement, vitality, playfulness, ritual dance, body movement, physical contact, fantasy, music, nonverbal communication, and a widened role repertoire. Western civilization has relegated many of these pursuits to childhood, the theater, or mythology, and in so doing has drained our souls of their richest treasures. It is essential that we learn to recognize the vitality that can only grow within the context of play, and to cultivate and refine play so that we can preserve the spirit of childhood in our adult lives (Blatner & Blatner, 1988). Such activities also ground the individual in a truly wholesome and relatively resilient sense of authentic self. Because of this, integrating the experiential worlds of feelings, sensation, and imagination into our existences may become a major goal of contemporary education and psychotherapy.

PSYCHODRAMA IN CONTEXT: AN OVERVIEW

I do not view psychodrama as a separate school of thought, but rather its methods and principles are complementary to a multimodal and integrative approach to psychotherapy or personal development. Psychodrama may further be adapted to nonclinical contexts, as role playing in education or business and industry, in programs for spiritual development or community building, and even as ways of problem solving and recreation in everyday life. Although it is most powerful when used within a group context, in modified form psychodramatic techniques can catalyze family therapy processes, couple therapy, and even individual therapy (Blatner, 1994; Stein & Callahan, 1982). And aside from the techniques, the principles associated with psychodrama add a great deal of richness to the general understanding of individual and social psychology. Psychodramatic methods have been incorporated into many other approaches, including behavioral, cognitive, "body therapies," family therapy, and Gestalt therapy. In Europe and South America, psychodrama and psychoanalysis have been integrated far more than in the United States, but the last decade has seen increasing understanding of the way experiential and analytical methods may operate synergistically.

I use a number of metaphors to illustrate my view of psychodrama's place in treatment. Sometimes I suggest that the action methods presented in this book are to therapy what the introduction of electric power tools were to carpentry: One has to have reached a fair degree of competence in the craft to use them, but the new tools add greatly to the ease and range of tasks. Or they may be likened to the introduction of woodwind instruments to the orchestra, which vastly extended and deepened the range of effects that were possible. The mixture of two technologies is often synergistic, that is, it leads to a new form that is more powerful than simple addition can predict. So, too, does the addition of psychodramatic methods to conventional verbal forms extend the power of psychotherapy. Verbal and nonverbal forms need not be at opposite poles, for it is quite possible to interweave the aspects of cognitive and experiential, objective and subjective, and other polarities of human experience (Blatner, 1968).

During the second half of the 20th century, the technological-philosophical pendulum began to swing back again toward an incorporation of the dimensions of emotion, sensation, and imagination into the world of personal experience. Psychotherapy is no longer being restricted to the modes of dyadic or group verbal discussion. Eclecticism (which includes more active approaches to psychotherapy) is being increasingly accepted (Arkowitz, 1993).

The importance of these phenomena was foretold in the first quarter of the twentieth century by Jacob L. Moreno, a Viennese psychiatrist who developed the methods of sociometry and psychodrama, as well as being a major contributor to the evolution of group psychotherapy. In an effort to reintroduce the spirit of growth-through-play into our lives, he emphasized ideas about spontaneity, creativity, action, self-disclosure, risk taking in "encounter," importance of the present moment (he coined the term here-and-now [Moreno, 1923]), the significance of touch and nonverbal communication, the cultivation of imagination and intuition, the value of humor and the depth of drama. The psychodramatic method and its derivatives are the primary vehicles by which people can learn to develop these potentialities in themselves.

CAUTIONS

At this point, I wish to note some cautions for the reader. Psychodrama is no panacea: Any romanticizing of a single approach is dangerous, as it blinds one to the limits of that approach and the values of other methods. Psychodramatic techniques can be very powerful, but mere technique is not enough. It behooves the practitioner to develop skills with humility and commitment. With creativity and sensitivity, the practitioner must learn to know and work with the psychological dimensions of a client's life.

I strongly encourage the reader to obtain some supervised training in the use of psychodrama before attempting to apply any but the most elementary methods. (How to get the training is discussed in Chapter 10.) The mastery of psychodrama itself requires a significantly greater degree of training than can be provided in any one book. One cannot learn these approaches through "cookbook" reading, any more than one can learn art or music solely from a text. Nevertheless, I hope that the reader may be stimulated to use some of the methods and to continue to explore the theories and applications of an eclectic approach to psychotherapy and education. I further emphasize the importance of supplemental readings from the bibliography at the end of this book.

In summary, therefore, I am presenting this book as an introduction to the theory and practice of using the psychodramatic method in a wide variety of psychotherapeutic and educational settings. I believe that the applications of these methods can do much to facilitate the reintroduction of the elements of spontaneity and creative empathy into human experience.

REFERENCES

Arkowitz, H. (1993). Integrative theories of therapy. In D. K. Freedheim (Ed.), *History of psychotherapy: A century of change* (pp. 261–303). Washington, DC: American Psychological Association.

Blatner, H. A. (1968). Comments on some commonly held reservations about psychodrama. *Group Psychotherapy, 21*(1), 20–25.

Blatner, A. (1994). Psychodramatic methods in family therapy. In C. Shaefer & L. Carey (Eds.), *Family Play Therapy.* (pp. 235–246). Northvale, NJ: Aronson.

Blatner, A., & Blatner, A. (1988). *The art of play: An adult's guide to reclaiming imagination and spontaneity.* New York: Human Sciences.

Bromberg, W. (1958). Acting and acting out. *American Journal of Psychotherapy, 12,* 261–268.

Davies, M. H. (1976). The origins and practice of psychodrama. *British Journal of Psychiatry, 129,* 201–206.

Fingarette, H. (1969). Self deception. In R. F. Holland (Ed.), *Studies in philosophical psychology.* New York: Humanities.

Kellerman, P. F. (1984). Acting out in psychodrama and in psychoanalytic group therapy. *Group Analysis, 17*(3), 195–203.

Moreno, J. L. (1923). The philosophy of the here and now. (In German). Berlin: Gustav Kiepenheuer. (Also noted on pp. xix–xx in Moreno's 1953 2nd edition of *Who Shall Survive?*)

Moreno, J. L. (1985). *Psychodrama, Vol. 1* (p. 65–6). Ambler, PA: Beacon House.

Ormont, L. R. (1969). Acting-in and the therapeutic contract in group psychoanalysis. *International Journal of Group Psychotherapy, 19,* 420–432.

Rubin, T. I. (1981). Foreword. In G. Schattner & R. Courtney (Eds). *Drama therapy: Vol. 2. Children.* New York: Drama Book Specialists.

Schwartz, L., & Schwartz, R. (1971). Therapeutic acting-out. *Psychotherapy: Theory, Research & Practice, 8*(3), 205–207.

Stein, M. B., and Callahan, M. L. (1982). The use of psychodrama in individual psychotherapy. *Journal of Group Psychotherapy, Psychodrama & Sociometry, 36*(3), 118–129.

Zeligs, M. A. (1957). Acting-in. *Journal of American Psychoanalytic Association, 5,* 685–706.

1

The Basic Elements of
Psychodrama

Psychodrama involves the staging of a problem in life as if it were a play, and so certain terms are used which are derived from theatre: *protagonist, director, stage, audience,* and the like (Moreno, 1946). Moreno developed some terms specifically for psychodrama, such as *auxiliary ego* (nowadays more often called simply *auxiliary*.) And other terms have come into use as derivatives of psychodrama or Moreno's role theory, such as *role playing* and *sociodrama*.

Although psychodrama was first developed as a type of group therapy, it quickly was applied in creative forms, as an integral part of what is today called *milieu therapy* in hospitals; with couples and families; and even with individuals, using only one or two cotherapists. As *sociodrama* it also addressed group issues that dealt with the general roles in the group, beyond any focus on the individual, and further was applied in community settings to reevaluate not just the group, but the larger social network.

All these settings and situations have in common an appreciation that problems may be analyzed and worked with as if they were a kind of play that could be creatively revised. We are encouraged to think of ourselves not, as Shakespeare said, "merely players," mindlessly playing out our life scripts, but rather also as the playwrights and codirectors of our life's dramas. To meet this challenge, psychodrama makes available to us the rich methodology that is used in the theatre. Thus, people can be helped to present, for example, not only what actually happened in a given situation,

1

but more important, they can explore all the statements that were never made, although they were thought, or feared, or remained at the subconscious level.

Psychodrama thus opens the way to exploring possibilities inherent in a situation, various aspects of the minds of each of the players, and the richness of the interpersonal and cultural field. And, as mentioned in the introduction, these explorations can apply not only in psychotherapy, but also in many other settings where one might want to encourage a greater understanding of the complexities of life or to develop or practice strategies for being more effective.

BASIC TERMINOLOGY

As mentioned earlier, Moreno named five basic elements of psychodrama: the protagonist, director, auxiliaries, audience, and stage.

The *protagonist* is the person who is the subject of the psychodramatic enactment. Whether acting as a client, patient, student, trainee, group member, or other form of participant, in the act of portraying a personal life situation a person becomes the protagonist. (In this book, because complex situations are described which demand pronouns that refer to a single person, and in order to avoid the linguistic sexism yet prevalent in much professional literature, I will generally refer to the protagonist as a "he" and the director as a "she.")

The *director* is the person who orchestrates the psychodrama to help the protagonist explore a problem. In therapy groups, the director takes on the role components of both director and therapist, although, for example, in hospital groups, a patient's individual therapist might also be present.

In personal development or other types of groups, the leader's role may be more flexible. In a training group, the director of an enactment may be one of the group members. If the person who is most frequently in the role of group leader needs to deal with her own issues—either related to other aspects of her personal life or regarding some interactions in the group itself—then another person serves as director and the previous leader/director shifts into the role of protagonist. These psychodramatic roles—protagonist, director, audience, auxiliary— are not fixed assignments. They can shift, and an individual might play each one of them in turn over the span of several enactments. However, to accomplish more than relatively simple forms of role playing, the director role does require a complex of skills which go beyond the ordinary training of most psychotherapists or group leaders.

The *auxiliary* (formerly also called the "auxiliary ego") is Moreno's term for anyone besides the protagonist and the director who takes part in a psychodrama. Usually the auxiliary portrays someone in the protagonist's life, such as a spouse, employer, or "another part" of the protagonist. More than a "supporting character," an auxiliary might play a bridge in a dream, a nameless sense of pressure pushing on one's back, or even the protagonist's unspoken feelings. This last mentioned role of the auxiliary is given a specific term, the *double*. Use of the technique of doubling is the subject of Chapter 3.

The term *audience* refers to the others present during the psychodrama. The audience is the group in which the enactment occurs and may be a psychotherapy group, a seminar or class in school, or participants at a workshop in management training. Being an audience implies more than simply being in the group because when the psychodrama is going on, the director uses the audience as part of the process. For example, the audience may give feedback, be a source of auxiliaries, or serve as a Greek chorus. After the psychodrama is over, the group ceases functioning as an audience and becomes more like a conventional group with a more interactive discussion dynamic.

THE STAGE

The *stage* is the area in which the enactment takes place. The stage may be a formal platform for psychodrama; it may be the area off to the side of a group or the actual locus of the conflict *in situ* (e.g., the reenactment and exploration of a conflict between children on the playground where it was occurring moments earlier). There are some props and structures, however, that can make the dramatic function even more effective.

In the original form of psychodrama, Moreno and his colleagues used a specially constructed stage, such as that shown in Figure 1.1. The three levels, lighting arrangements, balcony, and design were all empirically developed to facilitate the power of the enactments. Any of these components can be useful if included (Enneis, 1952). Modifications of this design have also been used, such as having part of the stage sunken, as was done at the St. Louis State Hospital (Moreno, 1971, p. 497).

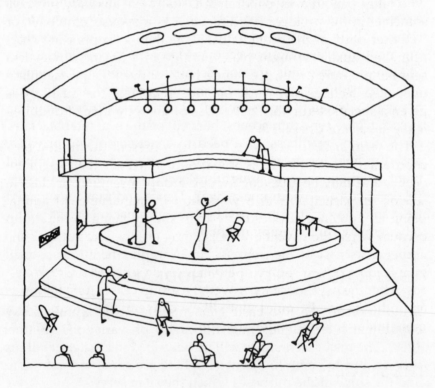

Figure 1.1

The main stage should be at least 12-15 feet in diameter. A raised platform that can easily be stepped onto is helpful in subliminally establishing the "as-if" set in the participant. (The Greeks used the device of the proscenium arch to mark the border of the stage—when people cross the arch they enter or exit from the world of the drama.) As a protagonist and auxiliary ego move toward the stage, their stepping upward indicates to all concerned that they are entering the psychodramatic reality.

On the stage there may be a few props: Some lightweight chairs and a simple table are most often used. Pillows, a mattress, and a variety of other props can also be useful. The chair is not only for sitting on, but, when empty, can "hold" any fantasied or projected figure. It can also become a barricade, a platform, or an indicator of height, authority, or status. The *table* can become a building-top, a desk, a judge's seat, a breakfast-room table, or a cave in which to cringe or hide. Pillows and foam rubber bats can be used for fighting, pounding, beating, protection, or perhaps to be held as a baby.

More elaborate aids are not essential but can provide remarkable effects. Special lighting, for example, may be used to evoke many moods: red to represent hell, a bistro, or an intense emotional scene; blue for death scenes, heaven, or the sea; total blackness for isolation, loneliness, or a need to enact something privately; and dim light for dream scenes. Music, either skilled accompaniment or emotionally meaningful recorded songs, can be a powerful adjunct to psychodrama as well. Dance and movement activities can be integrated into psychodramatic enactments, as well as other creative arts therapy methods.

THE TECHNIQUES OF PSYCHODRAMA

In addition to the five basic elements, there are scores of psychodramatic techniques and hundreds of variations (Blatner, 1988). The major techniques will be described in greater detail further on, but to begin to orient you, here are some of their names and the some of the purposes which they can serve.

- In order to *clarify a protagonist's feelings*, the techniques of *the double, soliloquy, multiple selves,* and *monodrama* are used.

- For heightening and facilitating the *expression of emotion*, the director may use *amplification, asides,* and the *exaggerations* of nonverbal communications, along with exaggerations of the dimensions of height, space, and position.

- The protagonist may be aided in becoming aware of personal behavior *(self-confrontation)* through the use of techniques such as *videotape playback, role reversal, behind-your back, audience feedback, chorus,* and *nonverbal interaction* exercises.

- Goals and values may be clarified through the use of the *magic shop* or the *future-projection* techniques.

- *Support* can be given with the techniques of *ego building, sharing,* and the judicious use of physical contact, such as hugging or holding.

- Issues of group process can be clarified through the techniques of the *spectrogram* and *sociometry*.

- Finally, there are many special techniques that can be used along with psychodrama, such as *hypnosis* and *guided fantasy*.

Through the use of the above techniques, the director can help the protagonist to enact a broad range of experiences: scenes from everyday life, as well as dreams, memories, delusions, fears, and fantasies.

AN OUTLINED DESCRIPTION OF A TYPICAL PSYCHODRAMATIC ENACTMENT

I. The Warm-up (see Chapter 4)

A. The director warms herself up.

B. The group discusses goals, roles, fees, limits, time arrangements, and so forth.

C. Getting acquainted; exercises are used that introduce group members to each other.

D. The director leads the group in action exercises that build group cohesion and spontaneity.

E. This often leads to a discussion of what the participant experienced in the warm-up exercises, which in turn leads to the emergence of a theme of common interest to the group, or to an individual's problem.

F. One of the group members is selected to be the protagonist, who will enact his own or the group's problem.

II. The Action (see Chapter 5)

A. The director brings the protagonist to the stage, where the problem is briefly discussed (Schramski, 1979).

B. The conflict is redefined in terms of a concrete example—one that could be enacted.

C. The director helps the protagonist to describe the physical surroundings in which a specific action occurs, thus setting the scene.

D. The protagonist is instructed to play the scene as if it were occurring in the here-and-now.

E. The director brings other members of the group forward to take the parts of other significant figures in the protagonist's drama—these people then become the auxiliaries.

F. The opening scene is portrayed.

G. The director helps the auxiliaries to learn their roles by having the protagonist change parts with them (reverse roles) for a brief period during which the protagonist then portrays the behavior of the other figures in his drama. As the auxiliaries learn their roles, the protagonist gives them feedback until he feels that the scene is being enacted in an essentially similar way to the way he pictures it in his mind. This "molding" activity furthers the warm-up of the auxiliary egos and the protagonist himself.

H. The scene continues with the director introducing other psychodramatic techniques that function to elaborate on the feelings being expressed (e.g., soliloquy, the double technique, asides, etc.).

I. As the enactment unfolds, the director uses a variety of other techniques in order to explore different facets of the protagonist's experience.

1. Ambivalence is explicitly demonstrated through the use of several individuals (auxiliaries) on the stage, each portraying a different part of the protagonist's psyche.

2. Empathetic or projected feelings of the protagonist can be enacted through role reversal.

3. Self-confrontation for the protagonist may be utilized through the mirror technique.

4. Significant past memories are reenacted.

5. Future plans, hopes, and fears can be symbolically realized and explored.

6. The protagonist's suppressed emotions—guilts, resentments, fears, yearning—can all be expressed using a variety of facilitating techniques.

J. The action may be carried to a point where the protagonist experiences a sense of having symbolically enacted those behaviors that had been suppressed—fulfillment of act hunger.

K. The protagonist is helped to develop other adaptive attitudinal and behavioral responses to his situation—this is called working through (see Chapter 6). (In role playing contexts, this process may become the predominant task of the group.) Some specific techniques used in working through include:

1. Repeat role playing of the conflict, with the protagonist trying a different approach with each attempt.

2. Modeling by other group members, who show how they would deal with the problem.

3. Role reversal between the protagonist and his auxiliaries—the other figures in his enactment—so that the protagonist can discover, through actually experiencing the other person's situation, some clues as to what behaviors might achieve the desired effect.

III. Closure (see Chapter 6)
  A. Following the main action, the director helps the protagonist to receive some supportive feedback from the other group members. Rather than encouraging an intellectualized analysis of the protagonist's problem, the director encourages the group members to share with the protagonist the feelings they had related to the enactment.
  B. The director may proceed to use a variety of supportive psychodramatic techniques.
  C. Further discussion by the group ensues.
  D. Finally, the director either goes on to the process of warming-up to another psychodramatic enactment with a different protagonist, or moves toward terminating the group, possibly using a variety of closing techniques.

MAJOR FORMS OF PSYCHODRAMATIC ENACTMENT

Finally, there is the terminology regarding the meaning of psychodrama itself. In fact, there is a fair amount of crossover in how the terms are used, and some degree of cultural politics and semantics associated with the various words. In some locales, *role playing* is much preferred, as the prefix *psycho-* seems to suggest something that's either too psychoanalytic or too criminally insane, while the suffix *-drama* for many people still carries an aura of phony theatrics, hystrionic emotionality, and manipulativeness, as if a background voice could caution, "Now don't get dramatic!" So some directors are using different words to communicate the essence of this most valuable group of methods, such as *action techniques* or *clinical role playing*.

One thing that psychodrama is *not*, however, is merely a psychologically infused dramatic novel or theatrical piece. Nor is it a similarly psychologically loaded and rather dramatic event in the news, although such phenomena have been termed "psychodramas" in magazines, newspapers, and other media. This point must be emphasized, because what are generally and erroneously so described always lack the essential element of the psychodramatic method: This approach is a context in which the participants are enabled to suspend their habitual reactive patterns and reconsider how else they might choose to respond. Psychodrama is a method aimed at creativity, healing, and wisdom, not a blind playing out of some tragic pattern of self-deception. I hope the readers of this book will help to correct the misuse of the term by enlightening journalists who may not know of the constructive power or even the existence of psychodrama as a methodolgy.

Role playing has been a term used as an equivalent to psychodrama by some leaders in the field, such as Kipper (1986) or Corsini (1966). In other settings, this term is used a little more specifically to refer to enactments in which the goals are more limited. For some, role playing avoids any exploration of the personalities of the players and focuses only on a deeper understanding of the role—and this meaning is closer to the idea of "sociodrama," to be discussed in a moment. For others, role playing refers to an even more superficial or behavioristic approach, focusing on the task of rehearsing a behavior, or finding the best specific response strategy. Originally, Moreno used the term, *role training* for this latter purpose. In these more task-oriented senses, the term role playing blends into other simulation forms of learning or exploring, astronaut or flight training, military exercises, situation tests, and other approaches which have become widespread in our culture.

SOCIODRAMA versus PSYCHODRAMA

Sociodrama refers to an exploration of a problem that involves a role or a role relationship, a theme which might be relevant to a group of people. Moreno wrote about people of different racial or ethnic backgrounds meeting to attempt to resolve their differences. Some other examples are:

- Nurses attempting to understand more about their feelings about patients with AIDS
- Teenage boys and girls meeting to explore expectations in dating and attitudes about sexuality
- Seminary students exploring common religious issues

- Physicians, nurses, administrators, lawyers, and others in the community exploring problems of medical ethics

- New parents sharing feelings about the stresses and strategies of dealing with the first year of the baby's life

Although a person may participate as a protagonist in a sociodrama, the enactment would relate to just one of the protagonist's roles, one which represents a role shared with others in the group and/or of concern to all the group. Other particularities of the individual are not to be considered. Thus, sociodrama could be described as *group-centered.*

One of the principles of directing sociodramas is that in general they should not be allowed to turn into psychodramas. A great deal of learning and benefit can emerge just by sticking to the topic and exploring the full depth of experiences inherent in the role situation itself. The numbers of issues, the many levels of awareness, the different types of often conflicting sub-roles, all need to be brought into consciousness. For example, a group of nurses in training might use sociodrama to explore the challenge of dealing with certain kinds of patients. When one of the nurses (as the protagonist) becomes involved in a scene, the emotional issues of the problem will be expressed. However, the director should bring out those facets of the relationship that would likely be present in many or most nurse-patient interactions; those feelings unique to the protagonist would not be emphasized. In other words, it would be inappropriate in a sociodrama for a director to deal with the personal aspects of the nurse who is the protagonist, for this might imply to the others in the group that the difficulties in the interaction were due to deficiencies unique to that nurse (Sternberg & Garcia, 1989.)

Psychodrama, in contrast, addresses the particularities of a single person who is at the nexus of many roles, and more, specific role relationships—not only with a spouse and child, for example, but with this specific spouse with unique qualities, and a particular child with certain abilities and problems. So psychodrama, in this case, has a very *individualized* focus; it is *protagonist-centered.* The drama may shift among the many facets of the protagonist's life—

his past, present, and future. Usually psychodrama moves toward relatively deep emotional issues (Kellerman, 1987; Kipper, 1988).

It is possible to use sociodrama as a warm-up for a psychodrama, but it is unethical to do so without the clear consent of the group and the people involved to such a personal exploration. In most situations, therefore, where sociodrama is the expected process, one should not intrude on people's privacy by subtly manipulating group members to disclose elements of their private lives.

However, depending on the composition of the group and its goals, and with the cautions mentioned above, it is possible to interweave several modalities. A psychodrama may arise out of or lead into a sociodrama; a role training exercise might be used as a warming-up or integrating process, complementing psycho- or sociodrama.

PSYCHODRAMA AND DRAMA THERAPY

In the last two decades the field of drama therapy has emerged as one of the recognized creative arts therapies, and there has been a gradual process of cross-fertilization between it and psychodrama. The two fields differ in the following ways: Psychodramatists generally begin as psychotherapists and then take specialized training in the use of Moreno's contributions. Many use psychodramatic methods in conjunction with other approaches, and some apply psychodrama also in nontherapeutic contexts, such as education and consulting to businesses. Drama therapists generally are trained first in the theater and then receive specialized training in drama therapy and psychotherapy. Psychodramatists emphasize protagonists playing scenes involving their own lives, while drama therapists give more emphasis to the taking of roles other than their own (Jennings & Minde, 1993). For example, drama therapists might have group members create improvisations (usually purely imaginary, but sometimes based on characters and/or plot themes in myths or recognized plays), and their spontaneity exercises are often adapted theatre games, because there is healing in the act of self-expression itself. Also, the act of playing and pretending often leads, albeit obliquely, to self-revelation. Drama therapists are also somewhat more group centered and work towards the general cultivation of spontaneity and group interaction rather than the focusing of one of the group members' problems. Finally, while psychodramatists avoid any rehearsal, some drama therapists recognize the value of having clients prepare for a performance which expresses aspects of their own personal experience.

I see value in both approaches. Some patients in fact need "role distance," the protection provided by not playing their real selves, but rather some other character. Then they can reflect on how they engaged in that presentation. Some psychodramatists, therefore, use these more skit-like drama therapy approaches for certain groups. Also, while earlier drama therapists used more scripts, psychodrama relied on improvisation; however, drama therapy in the last few decades has also moved far more toward almost completely unscripted work. (Interestingly, Moreno, in the early years of his New York City open session, sometimes had protagonists go offstage and plan with an auxiliary a small skit to express their situations; soon, however, the process evolved into entirely spontaneous productions.)

More recently, drama therapy has integrated actual psychodrama as part of its own general range of methods (Emunah, 1994), while psychodrama in turn has been integrating more drama therapy exercises as warm-ups and is recognizing the value of sometimes using ritual to close or intensify aspects of a more classically Morenian enactment (Blatner, 1994). Furthermore, the theoretical foundations of drama therapy as developed by a number of authors (many of whom are noted in the Bibliography) also are relevant to the understanding of the psychological, historical, and sociocultural basis for psychodrama.

ACTION TECHNIQUES

In addition to its classical rendering, psychodrama's major contribution has been (and may yet be) its component methods. Their importance, in fact, is emphasized by the title of this book. Role reversal, doubling, multiple parts of self, and many other techniques may be modified and applied in individual, couples, conjoint family, and group therapies, and integrated with other schools of thought.

A number of psychodramatic methods have become so incorporated into other approaches to therapy that many professionals aren't aware of their origins. Striking examples include the use of "sculpture" in family therapy, and Fritz Perls' employment of the "auxiliary chair" technique into his method of Gestalt therapy. The value of knowing the origins is not merely a matter of giving Moreno credit, but rather of leading practitioners to the conclusion that there is value in learning all the associated techniques and principles in this rich complex of innovations.

Equally important, while classical psychodrama requires both more training and a number of associated conditions and cautions, counselors and therapists working with individuals and families can readily apply its component methods. And because these techniques can powerfully catalyze the process of psychotherapy, making it more efficient, it becomes an even more valuable tool in light of the present reality of cost restraints.

The idea of using specific action techniques—sometimes called *experiential techniques* or *structured experiences*—has also become incorporated into a variety of other fields, as discussed in the chapter on applications. In the encounter groups and the "human potential movement" of the late 1960s through the mid-1970s, psychodramatic methods were integrated with imagery techniques, bodywork techniques derived from Alexander Lowen's post-Reichian method of bioenergetic analysis, and "sensory awakening" methods developed by Charlotte Selver and Charles Brooks. Other expressions associated with these methods included "growth games," and "nonverbal exercises." The human potential movement evolved into a wide range of more focused programs for personal growth, but the use of structured experiences continues.

Moreno's early work with improvisational theatre was largely forgotten, but "improv" began again in the United States in the late 1950s and what Fox (1994) called the tradition of the "nonscripted theatre" drew from many sources to become the kind of cultural force that Moreno would have enjoyed.

SUMMARY

This chapter introduced some of the basic elements and features of psychodrama, its terminology and relations to other fields of endeavor. While classical psychodrama is a complex approach, many of its methods can be integrated with other types of psychotherapy and thereby add to the efficacy of treatment.

REFERENCES / RECOMMENDED READINGS

Blatner, A. (1988). Principles of psychodramatic techniques. In *Foundations of psychodrama* (pp. 151–157). New York: Springer.

Blatner, A. (1994). Foreward. In R. Emunah, *Acting for real: Drama therapy process, technique and performance.* New York: Brunner/Mazel.

Corsini, R. J. (1966). *Role playing in psychotherapy.* Chicago: Aldine. Has annotated bibliography.

Emunah, R. (1994). *Acting for real. Drama therapy process and technique.* New York: Brunner/Mazel.

Enneis, J. M. (1952). Establishing a psychodrama program. *Group Psychotherapy, 5*(3), 111–119.

Fox, Jonathan. (1994) *Acts of service: Spontaneity, commitment, tradition in the non-scripted theatre.* New Paltz, NY: Tusitala.

Jennings, S. & Minde, A. (1993). *Art therapy and dramatherapy: Masks of the soul.* London: Jessica Kingsley.

Kellerman, P. F. (1987). A proposed definition of psychodrama. *Journal of Group Psychotherapy, Psychodrama & Sociometry, 40*(2), 76–80.

Kipper, D. A. (1986). *Psychotherapy through clinical role playing.* New York: Brunner/Mazel.

Kipper, D. A. (1988). On the definition of psychodrama: Another view. *Journal of Group Psychotherapy, Psychodrama & Sociometry, 40*(4), 164–168.

Moreno, J. L. (1946). Psychodrama and group psychotherapy. *Sociometry, 9*(2–3), 249–253.

Moreno, J. L. (1971). Psychodrama. In H. I. Kaplan & B. J. Sadock (Eds.), *Comprehensive group psychotherapy* (pp. 460–500). Baltimore: Williams & Wilkins.

Schramski, T. G. (1979). A systematic model of psychodrama. *Group Psychotherapy, Psychodrama & Sociometry, 32,* 20–30.

Sternberg, P., & Garcia, A. (1989). *Sociodrama: Who's in your shoes?* Westport, CT: Praeger.

2

The Auxiliary

Moreno used the term *auxiliary ego*, to refer to any person other than the director who participates in a psychodramatic enactment in order to help the protagonist explore his problem. More frequently in the last 20 years, this term has been shortened to *auxiliary*. Some practitioners have avoided Moreno's terminology, using "assistants" or "helpers." Auxiliaries not only play a variety of roles in psychodramatic, sociodramatic, and role-playing situations, but they also can take part in an action technique in ongoing psychotherapy groups (Zinger, 1975).

TYPES OF AUXILIARY ROLES

There are six types of roles that may be performed by an auxiliary:

1. *The role of a significant other person.* The auxiliary becomes someone in one of the protagonist's social networks, for example, a wife, son, employer, friend, or therapist. When this person is the main character in the enactment playing opposite the protagonist, he or she is occasionally called *the antagonist.*

2. *The double.* As the double, the auxiliary takes the role of the protagonist's alter ego. In this role, the auxiliary helps the protagonist to express inner feelings more clearly. The technique of using an auxiliary in the role of double is extremely important in psychodrama and will be discussed more fully in the next chapter.

3. *Generalized supporting character.* The dramatic situation may call for a police officer, teacher, client—but not a specific person known to the protagonist. These supporting character roles may seem to be somewhat clichéd, but they serve to support the protagonist's experience.

4. *A fantasied figure.* Examples of fantasied roles include God, a judge, a tempter, an idealized parent the protagonist never knew, or the "Prince Charming" who will rescue the protagonist.

5. *An inanimate object to which the protagonist relates.* The object could be his bed, doorway, house, the desk that mocks its owner (the protagonist) for his lack of self-discipline: "Hey! What about all this work you've piled on me? You're always saying you'll get to me, but you never do!" The psyche has an innate tendency to personify, attribute feelings and intentions to things, animals, natural phenomena, and spirits. For example, a woman exploring her relationship with her daughter-in-law might interact with an auxiliary playing the part of her daughters-in-law's living room. "It" becomes embarrassed when the mother-in-law pays a visit, and says in an aside to the audience: "Oh-oh, here she comes . . . she's going to want to change everything!" Then, to the mother-in-law: "You think I can't possibly look good unless you have a hand in fixing me up?"

6. *The role of an abstract concept or a collective stereotype.* Auxiliaries may play, for example, "society," "contemporary youth," "they," "the church," "justice," and so forth.

FUNCTIONS OF THE AUXILIARY

The basic idea of the auxiliary role is that it challenges the protagonist with something responsive and alive, which brings a kind of immediate role demand to the process. *Role demand* is a term that describes the way certain behaviors, such as a baby's crying, a sibling's grabbing one's toy, or a mother's worried criticism, tend to generate complementary roles, such as a comforting parent, a competitive child, or a submissive or rebellious adolescent.

As a related principle, the auxiliary's speaking in the here-and-now and her manner of encountering "in role" tends to pull the protagonist into the interaction as if it were actually happening there for the first time. Thus the auxiliary functions to involve the protagonist more deeply in the psychodramatic enactment, which in turn tends to bring out his basic conflicts and suppressed feelings more rapidly and completely.

Zerka Moreno (1978) notes five functions of the auxiliary, each one taking the protagonist to a deeper level of insight:

1. *Representation.* The first is as a concrete representation of some other—perhaps a person, figure in a dream, or part of the body. The auxiliary must warm up to the role assigned. The art lies in picking up the hints and statements from the protagonist's responses in the ongoing interview between the director and protagonist as well as from cues which occur as the scene unfolds. For example, an auxiliary characterized as critical must be able to behave in a "calling-on-the-carpet" manner; a mother who is said to be infantilizing should be able to mix worry and control. The performance of this role must be similar in essence to the behavior of the person being represented, but need not be exact. Indeed, a small amount of unexpected behavior on the part of the auxiliary often increases the protagonist's spontaneous involvement in coping with that challenge.

2. *Co-investigation.* Auxiliaries also participate in their second function as co-investigators, so their behavior serves to evoke spontaneous reactions from the protagonist. They must probe to find out if the scene is reasonably true to the protagonist's experience. If not, the director can help warm the auxiliary up a little more, the way a director coaches an actor. It's important that the auxiliary approximates the protagonist's perception of the way the role needs to be

played, expressing the essential qualities in the problematic interaction. If the auxiliary doesn't generate a sufficient match, the protagonist is liable to fall out of role. (If that happens, the director has the protagonist reverse roles with the auxiliary and *show* how the other role should be played.) If the role behavior continues to be incongruent with the protagonist's sense of the appropriate behavior, it interferes with the flow of spontaneity.

As part of the co-investigation, the auxiliary may try some unexpected behaviors, either spontaneously, based on intuition, or in response to a director's suggestion. The protagonist's spontaneous reaction may in turn lead to an "action insight."

3. *Depth.* The third function is that of presenting the other in some greater depth so that the protagonist must become aware of the fullness of feeling, the mixture of motives, or other new dimensions which might not have been previously considered. For example, if the director senses the secrecy of a theme, the auxiliary may be coached to whisper, which draws the protagonist into a greater degree of speaking confidentially. On the other hand, if the auxiliary escalates into screaming and cursing, this may bring out a symmetric response, a similar expressiveness on the protagonist's part. On the other hand, the auxiliary's role behavior might stimulate the protagonist to take a "complementary" role: if the auxiliary acts judgmental, the protagonist responds with defensiveness, rebelliousness, or gives an explanation; if the auxiliary acts helpless, the protagonist becomes protective; or dominant behavior might evoke a complementary submissive reaction.

4. *Therapeutic.* When it is appropriate and with the guidance of the director, the auxiliary can implement a fourth function, which is to behave in a reparative or otherwise therapeutic fashion. Admittedly, there's an interpretative component implicit in this, and its application is an intrinsic part of the art and teamwork of psychodrama.

5. *Bridge to reality.* Finally, a fifth function is that of serving as a bridge for a protagonist who is out of touch with reality by creating a role that partakes of the protagonist's world-view and yet also introducing graded degrees of consensual reality. In the appendix to my *Foundations of Psychodrama* I include an old story about the way a sage, acting in this fifth function, helps cure a delusional prince, exercising a kind of mental *aikido*.

There are occasions when it's probably best that the protagonist plays all the parts in the enactment. The drama with no auxiliaries is called *autodrama* or *monodrama*. The protagonist may shift places using one or two empty chairs, and have an encounter between different parts of himself, or with his projection of someone with whom he has a conflict. Fritz Perls used monodrama as a core technique in Gestalt therapy.

Some of the indications for the directors choosing to use monodrama instead of using auxiliaries include: (a) when the protagonist is in individual therapy, (b) when the director wants the protagonist to find out that the "answers" to his questions are to be found within himself, or (c) when the protagonist could play both roles in an encounter much more easily than could any auxiliary.

THE SELECTION OF THE AUXILIARY

The role of the auxiliary is usually played either by one of the group members or by a trained staff member or cotherapist. Such a trained auxiliary is most often found in situations where there is an ongoing program of psychodrama. The person may be a psychodrama director-in-training, a nurse on an inpatient ward, a cotherapist, or simply another staff member who is experienced in the use of psychodramatic methods.

The main advantage of using a professional auxiliary to play key roles is that she is experienced in warming herself up to the roles involved. An auxiliary who can play a variety of roles and easily express feelings (i.e., one who has a high degree of spontaneity) can galvanize a psychodramatic enactment. Furthermore, a great deal of spontaneity is especially necessary in roles that involve the exhibition of grossly crude, childish, cruel, arrogant, spiteful, seductive, or humiliating behavior.

On the other hand, even when there are trained auxiliaries present, there are times when it is best to allow different group members to be auxiliaries and play the various parts. For example, in a psychodrama in which a girl is exploring her competitive feelings toward other women, the auxiliary who is to be the man over whom the girls fight may be played by one of the shy men in the group. While his role as auxiliary serves a function in the girl's exploration of her problem, it may also benefit him. Even in warm-up techniques, group members may be picked to play parts that would normally oppose their habitual style: The constricted, nice-guy type might benefit by acting in the role of a villain; the shy, plain girl may discover some sexy aspects of herself by playing a seductress; a "stuffed shirt" may loosen up by playing a role which gives him permission to be silly, that is, a child, a monster, or an animal.

Another factor to be considered in the selection of auxiliaries is the degree to which a group member identifies with the protagonist's situation, or with the position of one of the other parts in the enactment. If an auxiliary has a conflict in her own life that is similar to that of the protagonist, the value the psychodrama has for the protagonist can either be increased or decreased. To some extent, the "carry-over" from the auxiliary's own situation can validly be applied to the protagonist's life, but beyond a certain point it can become a disconcerting pressure that only confuses the protagonist. Unless the director is alert to the auxiliary's behavior and applies firm control, the auxiliary can impose artificial issues upon the protagonist's drama. The director may occasionally check with the protagonist by asking: "Is this the way your [wife, mother, etc.] acts?"

TECHNIQUES IN THE SELECTION OF THE AUXILIARY

Most often the director asks the protagonist to choose the auxiliaries for specific roles. (Later the protagonist can be asked the basis for those "intuitive" choices.) In the next most common option the director asks the group for volunteers to play the designated roles. If the auxiliary is to play a supportive, "doubling" role, as will be discussed in the next chapter, the director might inquire, "Has anyone here been in Joe's situation and able to double for him?"

The role of *trained auxiliary* is another kind of technique. Some roles are best played by another person who is experienced in role taking. This might be someone who assists as a cotherapist, a staff member in a psychotherapy program, or an advanced student "apprentice." Trained auxiliaries can be especially helpful for portraying the more difficult, angrier, aggressive, or otherwise negative roles that might make most group members feel too vulnerable or stigmatized. Roles that require a great deal of flexibility and ingenuity are often filled best by a trained auxiliary.

The director may suggest certain group members for specific auxiliary roles, either because she thinks that person (a) might be especially effective in that role; (b) might benefit from playing the role; (c) is familiar with some aspect of the role; or (d) is the only person in the group who could either play or identify with a very narrowly defined role.

Sometimes the group process is such that the allocation of roles in an enactment may best be the decision of the group, or at least the group members may be queried as to which of their number should take which role. This is particularly effective in sociodramas or when working with sociometry and transferences in order to assess subtle projection patterns and bring out tendencies to assume roles within the group.

SHARING "IN ROLE"

After an enactment the auxiliary is often asked not only to "share" her own feelings regarding the protagonist's situation, but is also invited to comment on her own experiences in-role as an auxiliary. As an example, in an enactment a woman was playing a scene between her perfectionistic father and herself (as an eight-year-old child). The man chosen to be the auxiliary had to yell at the protagonist-as-child. Afterwards, during the sharing, this man, then in his forties and a rather mild-mannered person, said he was also raised by a harsh, judgmental father. On being asked how he felt playing the role, he replied that he found it difficult. It brought back many memories, but he wished he could feel more often the power associated with giving himself permission to express aggression openly.

Another technique is for the director to ask the group members after an enactment to discuss roles in which they would be most or least comfortable. The group could also discuss which roles would be most helpful for each to play in the future. These discussions further help the group members to develop receptivity toward playing the auxiliary role in later enactments.

OTHER AUXILIARY ROLES

The auxiliary chair. An empty chair can be used in a warm-up (see Chapter 4, p. 53) and can also represent the significant other in an enactment. If the protagonist feels angry, he may beat the chair with cushions or kick the chair—actions he would not be permitted to perform with a live auxiliary. The chair can also be a barrier to get around, representing either an emotional or physical block. Lastly, two empty chairs are often used as props for the protagonist to move to and from. For example, the director says: "Joe, in this chair, the nice, obedient part of you speaks to your mother (played by an auxiliary); in that chair, the rebellious, sullen part of you can also talk to your mother in a way you have never expressed yourself" (see Figure 2.1).

The silent auxiliary. There are times when it is sufficient to keep an auxiliary on stage even if she is to be silent, for she can provide support simply by being present. In general, though, an auxiliary who is not being utilized should be released from the role. It is unfair to expect the person to stand around, sometimes in an uncomfortable position, while a more focused sub-scene is explored.

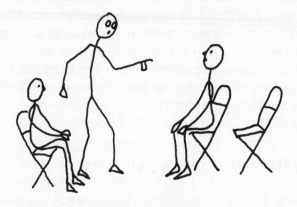

Figure 2.1

THE AUDIENCE AS AUXILIARY

Members of the audience can be asked to give comments, either in
the discussion period or during a break in the enactment. Sometimes
specific roles will be assigned: someone to observe the process;
someone to identify with the protagonist and/or one of the auxiliary's roles; someone to try to think of alternate solutions. Several
group members may chant or repeat some fixed statement in the
background as a *chorus*, such as the contents of a hallucination, obses-
sion, delusion, judgmental attitude, secret wish, and so on.

The audience may be used as objects of the protagonist's statements: The protagonist makes a statement reflecting an internalized attitude, the director may have that attitude "played out"
until it becomes hollow. For example, the protagonist says, "I am
an adult," but continues to act childishly. Using a technique from
Gestalt therapy, the director says, "Go around to each person in the
group and tell him or her that."

The *behind-the-back* technique is indicated if the director and protagonist agree to get some feedback while not yet being directly
confronted. The audience is instructed to imagine that the protagonist is not present, symbolized by his turning his back. With this
dramatic device, he nevertheless gets to overhear what others say
about him. This may be part of a family enactment or as a tech-

nique to foster disclosure within an interactive group process. It must be managed with tact and discretion, though (Corsini, 1973).

Audience members can double for each other and speak out on issues where they might otherwise be silent. A trained auxiliary might start this, and the others follow. For example, the audience is getting bored, but says nothing. An audience double exaggerates the group's slouching, nonverbal behavior and shouts, "Boy, is this boring!" or "He's manipulating the heck out of us!"

GUIDELINES FOR THE AUXILIARY

The many techniques whereby the director can involve auxiliaries are known as warming-up the auxiliary. Much of what is said about warming-up in Chapter 4 applies here. These techniques also apply to the warming-up of the double (see Chapter 3).

At the outset of the enactment, the protagonist can *role reverse* (i.e., change parts) and demonstrate the behavior that the auxiliary is to portray. The protagonist may state the opening lines spoken by both parties. The director can then ask the protagonist in the role of the other person to show not only the other's words, but also the other person's mood, posture, tone of voice, and nonverbal behavior.

From the moment the auxiliary is selected, he or she should be encouraged to move right into the role, acting in the here-and-now. For example, if a group member is picked to be the protagonist's mother, she may begin talking even as she moves onto the stage: "Look at you! You're so thin! Doesn't your wife feed you?"

The auxiliary should play her hunches, take risks, and follow the cues of the director and the protagonist. If the protagonist corrects her, the auxiliary should change set quickly, for example:

PROTAGONIST: No, my mother is different, she only talks about herself.

AUXILIARY: (changing set) Oh, Bill, why haven't you written me?! You know how lonely I am....

PROTAGONIST: (nods his head, and answers) But Mom...

As the scene changes or parts are reversed, the auxiliary is instructed to repeat the last spoken line in her role, for example:

PROTAGONIST:	(as mother) Why haven't you written?
AUXILIARY:	(as protagonist) Well . . .
Director:	(interrupting, to let protagonist answer for himself) Change parts. (They change places on the stage.)
Auxiliary:	(as mother, repeats last line) Why haven't you written?
PROTAGONIST:	Mom, I wrote you last month!
AUXILIARY:	(Carrying on) Last month is too long, [and so forth]

Other guidelines for directing and performing the auxiliary role are:

- The director should consider briefing the auxiliary as to her role, or have the protagonist brief the auxiliary to the side while the director keeps the attention of the group.

- Even if one of the people in the protagonist's situation smokes a good deal, and in spite of smoking being a popular (but declining) theatrical "piece of business," smoking should be prohibited on stage in order to free the participants' hands for dramatic gesture or action, as well as in consideration of the sensitivities of the group members. (Most psychodrama groups nowadays are nonsmoking, and if they involve extended sessions, breaks are arranged for those who smoke to step outside.)

- The auxiliary can be asked to bring up her own chair or prop, thus mobilizing her activity.

- The auxiliary can be helped by yet another auxiliary who doubles for her; this technique thus warms up the auxiliary. (This works best when the situation is sociodramatic. In more protagonist-centered enactments the auxiliary's double is really a projection of a projection and may distract the protagonist; it's better simply to reassign the auxiliary.)

- The auxiliary should be instructed to follow the director's directions, which may be spoken out loud—not whispered—to her.

- If the protagonist tends to drop out of role, the auxiliary should address him as if he were still in role: "How dare you turn your back on your mother!" The auxiliary may even grab the protagonist's arm.

- The protagonist should be consulted occasionally to see if the auxiliary is playing the scene with reasonable accuracy. If the auxiliary cannot satisfy the protagonist's sense of how the role is to be played, the director should feel free to dismiss the auxiliary and ask someone else to assume the role.

- A scene can be staged that precedes the main scene in time or logical sequence. For example, the "employer" plays a brief scene in which he receives information from another auxiliary, the "foreman," about the protagonist "employee's" difficulties in work; following this, the confrontation between protagonist and employer can be staged.

In summary, the auxiliary's function is to play a variety of roles in the protagonist's enactment. The auxiliary's behavior and confrontation provoke the protagonist into a deeper involvement in the here-and-now of the drama. The effective use of the auxiliary can heighten the power of any action approach.

REFERENCES / RECOMMENDED READINGS

Brodie, R. (1992). Training the auxiliary ego. *Australian & New Zealand Psychodrama Association Journal, 1,* 37–49.

Corsini, R. J. (1973). The behind-the-back encounter. In L.R. Wolberg & E.K. Schwartz, *Group therapy, 1973: An overview.* New York: Intercontinental Medical Book Co. (pp 55–70).

Moreno, Z. T. (1958). Reluctant audience technique. *Group Psychotherapy, 11(1),* 278–282.

Moreno, Z. T. (1978). The function of the auxiliary ego in psychodrama with special reference to psychotic patients. *Group Psychotherapy, Psychodrama & Sociometry, 31,* 163–166.

Seabourne, B. (1985). The role of the auxiliary. In *Practical aspects of psychodrama.* St. Louis, MO: Author. (first written as training papers around 1961).

Toeman, Z. (1946). The auxiliary ego, double, and mirror techniques. *Sociometry, 9,* 178–183.

Zinger, N. (1975). A working paper for group auxiliary egos. *Group Psychotherapy & Psychodrama, 28,* 152–156.

3

The Double

The double technique consists of the use of an auxiliary in the specialized role of playing the part of the inner self of the protagonist. The double—also occasionally called the *alter ego*— is perhaps the most important technique in psychodrama because it helps protagonists clarify and express a deeper level of emotion and preconscious ideation. This technique is also fairly readily integrated with more conventional types of individual, family or group psychotherapy.

FUNCTIONS

The double can provide a number of services, its functions being similar to those described for the auxiliary in the previous chapter. More specifically, this technique can be used for the following purposes:

1. *Stimulating interaction.* A double facilitates the portrayal of the protagonist's psychological experience to its fullest range.

2. *Providing support.* The double can encourage the protagonist, helping him to take more risks and enter the interaction more completely.

3. *Giving effective suggestions and interpretations.* If the auxiliary playing the double role has built a bridge of rapport through his behavior, the protagonist is relatively open to

considering statements made by the double as if part of his own self were speaking. Of course, it is imperative that the director establish the norm in which the protagonist is free to disagree with, modify, or expand on the double's statement.

The empathy function of doubling can be used in many settings. For example, in individual or family therapy, the therapist may use a modified double technique in order to draw the client out further (Hudgins & Kiesler, 1984, 1987; Leveton, 1991). I use a form of doubling that I call *active empathy* in these more conventional therapeutic contexts. I introduce the technique by saying something like the following: "Now I want to understand you, so let me talk as if I were in your situation. You correct me until I get it right." Then I make inferences about what might not be explicitly expressed, but perhaps felt or thought subconsciously. These are informed by my (the therapist) having a broad experience regarding what others have gone through under similar circumstances.

After speaking for 10 to 45 seconds in role, I pause and ask, "How accurate am I?" I make it known that I want to be coached, corrected, even to the appreciation of small nuances. During this process the client figuratively shifts into the role of the director or playwright and the therapist is momentarily like actors in the early phase of rehearsal, just learning to "feel into" the character they are to play. In this way, the process of making "interpretations" is greatly softened. Instead of the therapist as authority presuming to know what a client feels, the role shifts to a fellow human seeking to understand empathically, and being open to feedback until that understanding is felt to be accurate by the client.

Active empathy in this way operationalizes the goal described by Heinz Kohut as being a core technique in his "self psychology" school of psychoanalysis (Kohut, 1971); and it further extends the major principle of therapy described by Carl Rogers thirty years earlier, that of giving empathic feedback (Rogers, 1959). Also, doubling uses what Rogers called the "self-system," the wording clients might use to describe themselves—in contrast to the jargon typically used by therapists.

THE TECHNIQUE OF THE DOUBLE

As a group or family technique, the double is selected in the same way as the other auxiliary (see Chapter 2). (For purposes of illustration, the double will be imagined as a woman and feminine pronouns will be used.) The director introduces the double to the protagonist as follows:

> Consider this person your double, your invisible self, your alter ego with whom you may talk at times, but who exists only within yourself. She may say things that you may be feeling—things you would be hesitant to express. If her statements represent your true feelings, repeat that statement in your interaction. If what the double says is not an expression of your feelings, say no. This will negate what she says. You can then correct her and she will then try again to better reflect your thoughts and emotions. If your double can't help you effectively in this way, you're free to dismiss her and we'll get someone else. (See, for example, dialogue in Chapter 5, p. 71.)

The director may use either of two minor variations of the technique. In the first variation only the protagonist may respond to what the double says, and if the double's statement is to be answered by the other people in the drama, the protagonist must repeat it. The protagonist, thus, must take responsibility for what transpires. Use of this method is indicated for relatively passive protagonists. In the second alternative, what the double says is spoken so that all may hear and it may be considered an open expression of the protagonist's feelings, unless specifically contradicted by the protagonist. This variant has the advantage of speeding up the interaction.

As with the role of the auxiliary, there is no requirement that the person chosen to play the double resemble the actual person she portrays. "There is no age, sex, status, or race in psychodrama," says Moreno. (It is true that protagonists often pick people who resemble the real person for auxiliary parts, but this is not necessary.) Under any circumstances, if the auxiliary behaves even somewhat true to role, the protagonist fully accepts her in role even as mother, wife, or double.

If there is role reversal in the enactment, the double should take on whatever role the protagonist is involved in. Throughout the enactment the double should continue to speak in the first person: "I think," "I feel," and never (to the protagonist) "you think."

KINDS OF DOUBLING

In helping to express emotions, the double can emphasize or amplify statements made by the protagonist. If the double stresses that the protagonist is feeling something strongly but is not expressing those affects, the double may speak out and ventilate the anger, love, or whatever is experienced.

A good example of this occurred during a multiple-family therapy group at a community mental health center where a daughter lashed out at her father, accusing him of being unfair and stating that she hated him. He trembled, but with his characteristic efforts at self-control, responded, "Why do you hate me?" The double stood behind him and shouted, "Damn it all! You're humiliating me! I'm trying to be controlled, but, oh, that hurt! I want you to love me!" At this, the father wept and agreed with the double, and the interaction proceeded at a more intense pace. Other ways of doubling are as follows:

Dramatizing the feelings. An extension of the first approach of doubling is the principle of maximizing the emotional content of an attitude. Thus if the protagonist says, "I like you," the double can say, "I need you"; "I'm irritated" becomes, "I hate you." Obviously, this approach should be used only when it seems that the maximizing expression is either accurate or would be productive in clarifying the protagonist's feelings.

Verbalizing nonverbal communications. Here the double begins to add more "content" to the self-system of the protagonist. If the protagonist smiles ingratiatingly, the double responds, "Why must I smile when I speak to him?" A tense jaw or clenched fist may be verbalized as, "This is getting me angry" (Taylor, 1983).

Physicalizing words and gestures. The double extends herself to hug, cling, shove, or push the other auxiliaries in the interaction. She may strike a pillow, cringe in a crouching position, or stand on a chair to speak. This is dramatization in the nonverbal sphere.

Support. The double reinforces the protagonist's right to his feelings: "Dammit! Why should I live up to your expectations?" or, "I don't buy that load of crap!"; "It's okay if I *feel* like this!"

Questioning the self. The double questions the protagonist's attitude; again, this must be used with discretion: "Maybe I'm kidding myself," or, "Is that how I really feel?"

Contradicting the feelings. The double contradicts the protagonist, but only if she wants to evoke a reinforced statement or if she believes the protagonist's self-system includes a stance opposite to his statement: "Y'know, I don't really feel this way at all!"; "I *don't* hate you, I need you!"; or, "I hate you *and I* love you!"

Defending against the feelings. The double actively verbalizes the paradigms of the protagonist's habitual defense mechanisms of denial ("This can't be happening!"), isolation ("I don't feel a thing"), projection ("I would never feel toward you the way you feel toward me"), displacement ("Dammit! Someone's got to take the blame!!"), and so forth.

Self-observation. The double notes the protagonist's general situation by introducing some comment on the protagonist's behavior: "I seem to be getting more tense"; "Oh-oh, I'm explaining again." Related to this is the noting of emotions in the here-and-now: "I'm talking about the past, but I'm feeling embarrassed now." The double can also act as a counselor: "Say, I'm reacting as if he's judging me!"

Interpretation. The double must be very sensitive in his introduction of materials that are outside the protagonist's awareness.

Commenting on what is *not* being said is one form: "I'm not saying anything about Dad, just talking to Mom!" Referring to past incidents or other issues is another form of interpretation: "I used to feel this way as a kid!"

Interpretation of carry-over to other relationships. An important variable to be remembered is that at times the protagonist is responding to those in his enactment on two levels: not only in terms of who the other person as auxiliary is portraying (father, employer, etc.), but also in terms of who the auxiliary is in real life. For example, if the auxiliary role of father is being played by the person who is also the protagonist's therapist in other settings, the statements of the protagonist may reflect not only feelings toward the father, but also feelings toward the therapist. (This is a kind of reverse transference.) For example, in one session, the protagonist was expressing a series of demands to his "father." The double then added: "—and I'm not only saying this to you as my father, but also as my *therapist!*" This led to the protagonist's agreement and a further shift of scene toward a reevaluation of the therapist-patient relationship. This kind of doubling can be applied to the generalization of other feelings, irrespective of who plays the other auxiliary roles: for example, "I'm frightened of you...I'm frightened of everybody!" or "I've felt this way with all women!"

Satire. The use of humor in psychotherapy and in doubling may be one of the most delicate arts, but at times can be very effective: "Yeah, I *want* it! I want love *and* guarantees *and* obedience!" or, "Of course I don't resent it! I like being put down!" The use of satire, opposition, and provocation in doubling can add power to an enactment if used with sensitivity and the proper timing. Without the "art," the use of shock only leads to dissonance. The stubborn double who believes that she is making an interpretation when she repeats or amplifies her comments in the face of repeated denials by the protagonist is only making a fool of herself or hurting the protagonist.

Divided double. Here the double is assigned to play a specific role or part of the protagonist's psyche, usually made explicit by the director. The double may be the obedient or the defiant part; the self-blaming or the externalizing, self-justifying part. This frees the protagonist to clarify his feelings about the other, complementary attitudes. In this technique the director may have more than one double for different parts of the protagonist. Thus two or three doubles may be on stage.

Multiple doubles. The director may allow several people to express their feelings to the protagonist as doubles. Whereas the auxiliary as a divided double plays one "complex" or *part* of the protagonist's psyche, as a multiple double, each auxiliary doubles for the protagonist as a whole person. This technique is even more effective in sociodrama, or if the protagonist is enacting an issue that involves others deeply. Again, it must be emphasized that it is still the protagonist's feelings that must be clarified.

The group or collective double is an extension of the multiple double: This simply throws the interaction open to the audience and has them shout their double statements (always in the first person tense) from the floor. Sachnoff (1991) describes a variation in which group members spontaneously enter the scene, take the double position, say a few things, allow themselves to be agreed with or corrected, and then leave.

The auxiliary's double. In sociodramas, both parties in an interaction may have a double. In general, in protagonist-centered psychodramas, a double for an auxiliary can confuse the protagonist, because as Zerka Moreno points out, this is an extra extension of the interpretative process of the auxiliary (personal communication, 1994). If the auxiliary isn't playing the role accurately (according to the perception of the protagonist) then this should be corrected or a different person assigned to that auxiliary role. However, in more sociodramatic interactions, the challenge is to bring out the possible feelings of all parties, and then the stage may hold the protagonist, his double, his "wife" (played by an auxiliary), the wife's double (played by a third auxiliary), and possibly other roles and their doubles (see Figure 3.1). This technique helps those playing the other roles in the enactment to express their feelings more effectively.

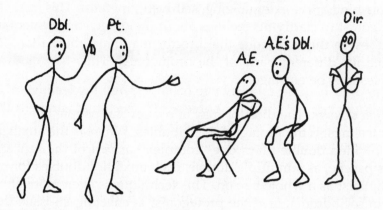

Figure 3.1

Soliloquy. The double can be with the protagonist even when there is no specific interpersonal interaction, that is, when enacting a soliloquy. Examples would be "on the way home" scenes; "getting ready for bed," or simply walking around the stage with one's double, "talking to oneself out loud."

Doubling for audience. A double may be assigned to help the audience express its feelings, positive or negative, toward the events on the stage or any of the participants in the enactment, including the director. For example, in a drama that had become "bogged down" in overintellectualized verbosity, the audience double stood behind some group members and stated, "I'm getting bored. I want to help Mary reach out." This approach may catalyze a reaction, which, in turn, may further the action in the drama.

Doubling in the warm-up. From the outset, the double can be used to help the protagonist move toward readiness for action on the stage. For example, the director is talking to a potential protagonist, and the trained auxiliary moves behind that "protagonist" and begins to double: "Say, this is embarrassing, having the director put me on the spot. I thought I would just observe."

Leveton (1992) has an especially good chapter on the double technique which complements this chapter.

SOME SUGGESTIONS FOR DOUBLING

The tasks of helping another person to express his feelings may seem imposing, but there are some approaches that can help the potential double in her role. It is not true that an extensive historical background must be understood before one person can make inferences about another's feelings. A great deal of information is easily available from some very obvious cues. The double cannot hope to be absolutely accurate, but will find that he or she is empathizing "correctly" in over half the statements made if talk focuses on three areas of the protagonist's life: his nonverbal communications, his use of words, and the general roles and role transitions in which the protagonist finds himself. I will describe how the double can draw inferences from these dimensions in this section, and then suggest some exercises that can be used to practice the skill of doubling.

The first group of cues for the double comes from the protagonist's nonverbal communications. By imitating the protagonist's posture, expression, gesture, and voice tone, the double experiences the same kinds of body sensations as the subject. These sensations act as somasthetic cues that provide the double with a wealth of intuitive information about how the subject feels. For example, if a double were to imitate a protagonist who is slumped in his chair, the sensation of the distribution of weight in that posture might suggest to the double the quality of the feeling of the subject (e.g., it might help the double to discern whether the protagonist is sulking, or if he is really depressed). I would suggest that the reader try out the following: unobtrusively imitate others, and to a surprising extent you find yourself "feeling" as they do (Krainen, 1972).

The best physical position for the double is behind, slightly to the side of, and facing the protagonist at about a 30° angle. From this vantage point she can observe and imitate her subject without being distractingly obvious. The proximity of this position may facilitate a sense of symbolic identification. Rapport may be occasionally heightened by the double's placing one hand on the protagonist's shoulder.

A second source of information for the double may be derived from the way the protagonist uses words. As long as the double is in the process of trying to understand his subject, he or she should try to get a feeling for the protagonist's "self-system." What kinds of words, what connotations, what levels of abstractions does the protagonist use? (Some knowledge of semantics is often very helpful in this regard.) In the early stages of doubling, the double should try to paraphrase what the protagonist is most consciously trying to express. Only later, after rapport has been established, may the double go on to amplify, express, dramatize, and in other ways extend the doubling to the many functions noted earlier in this chapter. In the beginning, however, the double wants simply to understand, and thus needs to listen almost uncritically. Any caricaturization of the protagonist by the double in the early phases will disrupt the relationship.

Also based on the protagonist's use of words the double can find clues as to how his subject is feeling from the discrepancy between voice tone and content. If the protagonist speaks in an emotion-filled voice about trivial issues, the double may be led toward thinking about what that emotion means. On the other hand, if the protagonist is speaking in a flat, affectless tone about rather dramatic problems, the double may attend to (and later, comment on) the defense mechanism of isolation of emotion.

The third major technique for the double's building an empathic awareness of the protagonist is to comment on the obvious characteristics of the most apparent of the protagonist's roles, such as: (a) physical features, (b) stage in life, and (c) the challenges, advantages, and disadvantages of any present or imminent life roles. It is not necessary for the double to feel she must have the "whole story" in order to make inferences about these roles, since the relationship permits mutual interactions and an error can easily be corrected. Nevertheless, the double will find that a surprisingly high proportion of her or his inferences will be accurate. Each accurate response of the double develops rapport with the protagonist while an inaccurate response is not alienating unless it is extreme or humiliating.

For example, an auxiliary may make a number of statements in the double role that might be part of the situation of anyone who has a physical characteristic that is different from most of the people in his social situation: a different or minority ethnic, racial, or religious affiliation; being tall or short, overweight or thin; having any disfiguring scars or unusual features; and so on. What does a man feel when his hairline begins to recede? What special issues concern someone who is short? The double can similarly make any comments that would reflect feelings shared by most people at the following stages in life: new parenthood, a promotion, approaching retirement, the revelation of a serious illness, and so forth.

Related to the issue of role transition are the groups of feelings that accompany most life roles in the sexual, family, vocational, social, and financial areas. What could any double say about the following situations: The man who reaches his fiftieth birthday and whose income and status have not met his expectations, the woman in her thirties who finds that her husband has recently been unfaithful, or the young man who feels himself falling into a vocational rut?

The double can thus utilize the inferences that any person can make about a situation or quality, if she will give herself permission to take the risk of playing her hunches out loud.

EXERCISES FOR BUILDING THE CAPACITY FOR DOUBLING

Here are some of the exercises that may be used for building empathic skills; they also are excellent warm-up techniques.

Quality exchange.
The group breaks into pairs. All participants are instructed to list on a piece of paper four qualities that they like about themselves and four qualities that they dislike. After the lists are made, the group members are instructed to exchange lists with their partners. All of the pairs conduct the exercise simultaneously as they

sit around the room. One member of each pair starts off by reading the partner's list. After reading each item, such as, "I am overweight," the person reading the list goes on to describe how it might feel if this were their own personal quality. Drawing on any actual experiences, the person speaks for about a minute, exploring the inferences that can be made regarding the item on the list—advantages, disadvantages, implications.

The partner whose list is being read is to listen but make no reply until after both have finished the exercise. When one finishes reading and commenting on the partner's list, the other does likewise. The exercise should take about 20 minutes. Only after both partners have read each other's lists should they give feedback and engage in a discussion. It is unimportant whether or not the participants are correct; what is essential is the willingness to make intuitive inferences based on the qualities noted on the lists.

Secret pooling.
This is a similar exercise for a group. Each group member writes a "secret" on a piece of paper. The secret should be about something which the person would feel quite uncomfortable revealing to the group. The papers are all folded in the same fashion and mixed thoroughly with those of the others in the group to ensure anonymity. When the papers are redistributed members check quickly to make sure they didn't pick their own secrets. Then, in turn, each person reads out the secret as if it were a personal secret. All participants speak in the first person and go on to explain (making inferences and taking risks of interpretation) how it feels to have that secret as part of one's own life history. Each person speaks for about a minute, talking about the feelings and attitudes that are associated with the contents of the secret.

It is often surprising and relieving to group members to find that others talk about their anonymously written secrets with empathy and kindness; the commonness of themes is also usually striking in this exercise. Through the discovery of shared feelings about emotional issues, the group moves toward greater group cohesion. This exercise, thus, serves many functions—developing empathic skills as well as serving as a warm-up for further group activities.

Directed fantasy double.
This is a more playful exercise. The director speaks to the group as follows: "Think of an object, animal, or character in a fairytale— and then become that thing. What is your future? Past?" The more you do this, the more you will be ready to empathically move into a variety of roles.

SUMMARY

The auxiliary and, in particular, the double are distinguishing characteristics of psychodramatic enactment that are contributions to the field of action approaches in psychotherapy and education. The opportunity for building the empathic skills of role reversal in the person who doubles is as important a function of the double role as the powerful stimulus it provides to the protagonist.

REFERENCES / RECOMMENDED READINGS

Ferreira, A. (1961). Empathy and the bridge function of the ego, *Journal of American Psychoanalytic Association, 9*(1), 91–105.

Goldstein, S. (1967). Effects of doubling on involvement in group psychotherapy. *Psychotherapy: Theory, Research & Practice, 4*(2), 57–60.

Hudgins, M. K., & Kiesler, D. J. (1984). *Instructional manual for doubling in individual psychotherapy.* Richmond: Virginia Commonwealth University.

Hudgins, M. K., & Kiesler, D. J. (1987). Individual experiential psychotherapy: An analogue validation of the intervention module of psychodramatic doubling. *Psychotherapy: Theory, Research & Practice, 24*(2), 245–255.

Kohut, H. (1971). The analysis of the self. *Monograph Series of the Psychoanalytic Study of the Child (No. 4).* New York: International Universities Press.

Krainen, J. M. (1972). Counter-playing: A group therapy technique. *American Journal of Psychiatry, 129*(5), 600–601.

Leveton, E. (1991). The use of doubling to counter resistance in family and individual treatment. *The Arts in Psychotherapy, 18,* 241–249.

Leveton, E. (1992). *A clinician's guide to psychodrama* (2nd ed.). New York: Springer.

Perrott, L. A. (1975). Doubling from an existential-phenomenological viewpoint. *Group Psychotherapy & Psychodrama, 28,* 66–69.

Rogers, C. R. (1959). The essence of psychotherapy: A client-centered view. *Annals of Psychotherapy, 1,* 51–57.

Sachnoff, E.A. (1991). Why and when to use "hit and run" doubling. *Journal of Group Psychotherapy, Psychodrama & Sociometry, 44*(1), 41–43.

Taylor, G. (1983). The effect of nonverbal doubling on the emotional response of the double. *Journal of Group Psychotherapy, Psychodrama, & Sociometry, 36*(2), 61–68.

Toeman, Ż. (1946). The auxiliary ego, double, and mirror techniques, *Sociometry, 9*, 178–183.

Toeman, Z. (1948). The double situation in psychodrama. *Sociatry, 1*(4), 436–448.

4

Warming-Up

To warm up to an activity is to become gradually more spontaneous and involved. In psychodrama spontaneity is a desirable state, the best way that creativity can be generated. The *warm-up* refers to the first phase of a psychodramatic enactment in which group members become more comfortable with each other and the task at hand. From this a protagonist and problem emerge leading to the second phase, the action.

To conduct an effective warm-up it is necessary to appreciate the importance and nature of the process of warming-up, because without an effective warm-up many a role play or psychodramatic enactment fails. I have been in group and family therapy sessions in which the therapists erroneously expect the clients' own anxiety to serve as the source of motivation. Often this backfires, especially with clients who have little tolerance for this nondirective or psychoanalytic technique—and nowadays this constitutes the majority of the population.

Aside from its practical value, warming up has a great psychological value (Kipper, 1967). Many people are delighted to be given some structure and time to gradually get their mind focused and active. I make this process explicit, and my clients and group members seem to enjoy being encouraged to use these principles and techniques in other settings too. It's nice to feel that one need not have all his thoughts neatly packaged and ready for the consultant's inspection, but that rather the process of exploration can proceed gently towards clarity and discovery.

The principles of warming-up thus apply not only to therapy or psychodrama but also to many areas of everyday life. Learning how to optimize vitality and spontaneity may well be one of the greatest challenges in our culture, and this skill requires a variety of techniques and an appreciation of the importance of spontaneity as a core value (Blatner, 1988). This chapter will focus primarily on the practical aspects of using warm-up techniques in psychodrama.

The most important issue in warming-up is the establishment of a context that fosters spontaneity. The necessary conditions for spontaneous behavior include (a) a sense of trust and safety; (b) a receptivity to intuitions, images, feeling, and other non-rational mental processes; (c) a bit of playfulness—so one doesn't feel overidentified with the success of every move in the process—and (d) a movement toward risk taking and exploration into novelty (Moreno, 1947). In addition, getting people moving, interacting, and improvising are important.

The first phase of any group activity involves the development of some consensus as to the purposes, methods, duration, dimensions of the group and division of responsibilities in the group. these issues first arise as the director warms herself up.

THE DIRECTOR'S WARM-UP

In order to warm up a group a director needs to apply the principles to herself. She may begin by introducing herself or getting to know the group members, striking up a conversation. To stand and walk about or sit and talk? It depends on the norms of the group and the organization. One shouldn't be too flamboyant in certain settings, and a bit of drama is quite effective (if not expected) in others.

If she begins in a sedate fashion, then after introducing herself and beginning to explain the process, she should gradually begin to model it by becoming physically active, standing up, walking about, moving chairs, talking with the group about a variety of topics, carrying on her introduction. Themes to be addressed include a general orientation to the task of the group and to obtaining some consensus on this, the time allocated to the group, and other norms regarding who will be included. Related issues that will probably be touched on are confidentiality, cost, people leaving the group, bathroom breaks, smoking, and new people entering the group.

In addition, the director begins to talk about (and model) some of the elements directly associated with psychodrama, such as physical movement or shifting a chair's position. She can model playfulness when demonstrating the taking of a role. Few things are more counterproductive to a group's warming-up than a director who continues to work from a sitting position. Movements and an improvisational introduction also increase the director's own spontaneity (see Figure 4.1).

Figure 4.1

Part of the group's warm-up is to begin trusting and liking the group leader, and this requires some self-disclosure on the leader/director's part. What people really need to know is how judgmental, shaming, authoritarian, mutual, flexible, playful, nondefensive, and in other ways comfortable the director will be—and by extension, this is what most of the group members are consciously or subconsciously wondering about each other, also. So, during her own warm-up, the director discloses some of her own style. If she can communicate a sense of authenticity and warmth, her warming up begins to allow the group to know and trust her (Sacks, 1967). Her behavior further models for the group the norms of self-disclosure, spontaneity, acceptance of humor, toleration of some distance (i.e., the acceptability of some reserve on the part of the group members and a respect for some unwillingness to engage in significant self-disclosure at first), and the acceptability of action and forceful expression.

Spontaneity can only flower in a context of safety. It's difficult to improvise if one is feeling vulnerable. So a vital element in the warming up process is building a sense of connectedness and trusting between the group and the director, and among the group members. Moreno had a special word for this quality of interpersonal preference, *tele*, which suggest also elements of reciprocity, and real dynamics—as opposed to transference—which are part of any group process (Barbour, 1994; Blatner, 1994). (A phenomenon of negative tele, a sense of mutual repulsion, has also been noted, but spontaneity grows in a context of positive tele.) Sharing spontaneous feelings and actions tends to promote tele.

Of course, during this first phase the director is also mentally warming up to the task that lies ahead. She must be able to assess the many factors that could affect the group process: a skill that only comes with extensive experience and reading (see Chapter 10). The director must also become aware of her own resistances to the group, if any are present. A director most commonly experiences resistance to the group through her own lack of preparation or through the presence of artificial expectations she may have. Does the director feel she must "put on a show"? Does she have stereotyped attitudes toward some of the group members? Does she wish she could avoid dealing with the group's stereotypes of herself?

The director may cope with these mixed feelings and expectations of herself using several techniques, all of which facilitate her own warming-up. She may discuss her plans and apprehensions in advance with a co-worker. As part of her introduction to the group, she may review her own tolerance for the nonoccurence of a "dramatic happening," thus clarifying her own position at the outset. Or she may allow her own negative tele to be first on the agenda for the group discussion or psychodrama (Z. Moreno, 1958). Of course, if a director feels a great deal of overinvolvement, she should decline to direct, and if another potential director is available, that person should be allowed to take over the leadership role.

GROUP COHESION

In the next phase, following the basic self-introduction and her own warm-up, the director helps to develop group cohesion—another term for a growing degree of positive tele among the group members. The first step in building a sense of group identity and trust is to get the group members to know each other. The director may choose to employ a variety of introductory exercises. She can modify these exercises to meet the purposes of the group task.

In one activity, for example, the director asks each member to find a partner to get to know. Then, in a few minutes she asks each of the group members to introduce the partner to the group.

Themes to be elicited may include background, expectations of the forthcoming group experience, or interesting aspects of the other person's personality. Partners may be chosen as people one knows, strangers, someone who seems very different from oneself, someone with whom one has felt some conflict, or one's spouse.

A series of two-person (dyadic) structured experiences may be useful in order to have each group member not only meet but experience something different with each partner. Nonverbal exercises can also be included in these dyads: "talking" with hands or backs, trust walks, and so forth. (In the *trust walk* or *blind walk*, one partner takes the blindfolded other on a little tour, emphasizing the awareness of trust issues.)

The use of action exercises early in the group's development may blend into the use of other structured experiences that are designed not only as introductions, but also as steps in building trust, self-disclosure, and playfulness. They are also useful as an introduction to a variety of modalities, such as guided imagination and nonverbal communication.

GROUP TASK AND WARM-UP TECHNIQUES

The use of action exercises or structured experiences not only works toward the task of building group cohesion, but also serves to sensitize group members to those dimensions of their personalities with which they have the greatest conflict—their "blind spots." I find that about one fifth of any group is unaffected by any given exercise. Another fifth is quite affected—the technique really arouses an awareness of some conflict area—and the rest of the group is mildly affected. After several exercises, most of the group members become more aware of their own problems.

At this point, the director moves into developing a theme or finding a protagonist. If the group is warming up slowly, or the director would like to start at some distance, the discussion of some topic of general interest may come next. Some further techniques include:

The undirected warm-up. In groups that already know each other, the director may simply wait in the background while the group warms itself up, discussing and joking about a variety of topics. Often a common theme emerges after several minutes, which the director may capitalize on by turning it into an enactment.

The directed warm-up. If the group knows its own task, the director simply starts with a discussion, or uses a concrete example with which to explore sociodramatically some of the issues. This has been called a *directed warm-up* by Yablonsky & Enneis (1956). The sociodrama allows group members to explore the different feelings, attitudes, and experiences of some common role. Sometimes fictional, religious (e.g. Biblical or mythic), or political roles are played. In such cases, the process may, for a while, look like drama therapy, but the themes raised may then lead to a more personal exploration by one of the group members. (However, if the group is designed to explore general philosophical or social—but not personal—issues, the director should ensure that a more personal focus does not occur!)

After the group has developed some cohesion, the director discusses the group theme at a distance. The warm-ups below are still somewhat removed from real life.

The melodrama. Based on a traditional late 19th Century American theatrical tradition, this set of dramatic clichés can be fun and a pleasant vehicle for loosening up. A group member could possibly be the director. The members could then "audition" for the various parts of heroine, hero, villain, heroine's mother, father, or others. The basic plot is that the mortgage is to be foreclosed unless the heroine gives herself to the villain. The sawmill or railroad tracks scenes follow, then the rescue. Improvisations and "hamming it up" are encouraged. Fairy tales and myths can also be enacted.

Situation tests. Situations that present a challenge can be presented to individuals or groups. Examples include the "lifeboat" (who will be chosen to die?), "stranded on a desert island" (how will the group organize itself?), "the stranger in the town restaurant", "the employment interview," and so on. A range of dramatic, fantasied, humorous, tragic, or frustrating situations, from slight to extreme, can be used.

The magic shop. This is an especially useful technique (Barbour, 1992; Leveton, 1992). The director has the group imagine a small shop on the stage. The shopkeeper may be played by a trained auxiliary, a member of the group, or even by the director. The group is told that on the shelves of this magic shop all types of wonderful qualities can be found. Anyone who wishes to buy may come into the shop. Eventually someone volunteers to become the customer-protagonist.

The customer's first requests are often quite vague: I want "love," "wisdom," "immortality," or "success." As the first task, the shopkeeper engages the customer in a discussion in order to clarify more specifically what's wanted. From whom does the customer want love? What conditions will be accepted? This conversation should remain within the metaphor of a shopkeeper simply trying to understand what is desired. The more general the desire, the more expensive or inexpensive it may be: "You want love from everybody? Well, that will cost quite a bit more," says the shopkeeper.

The negotiation of the price comprises the second task within the technique of the magic shop. Money cannot be offered. The shopkeeper explains that the only barter can be some quality or facet of the customer's life or personality that will be surrendered—something that someone else might wish to buy some day from the magic shop. The price offered often leads to some thought-provoking challenges:

CUSTOMER: I'll give up my selfishness for love!

SHOPKEEPER: Are you willing to give up *all* of your selfishness?

CUSTOMER: Well now...

The director may allow either the protagonist or the auxiliary-shopkeeper to consult with the audience for their advice. What would be a fair price for immortality?

Often a customer will claim an inability to think of something to offer as payment. (The statement, "I don't know," betrays a passive-dependent stance and should be redefined as, "I'm having difficulty thinking of something.") This situation not only demonstrates the protagonist's passive style, but also can be a starting point from which to explore the protagonist's lack of awareness of inner resources.

Once the tentative bargain has been struck, the protagonist is encouraged to try out the newly purchased qualities, or to show how it feels to get along without the quality that was just given up. In follow-up symbolic enactments, the protagonist may find that there is a greater need than previously realized for what was given up. On the other hand, what was purchased may not be what was expected. For example, the man who wanted an agreeable wife found that he was bored by the enactment of his ideal mate. The woman who would give up "being controlling" felt too vulnerable when she had to enact a situation blindfolded.

In summary, the magic shop is an excellent technique not only for warming-up a group, but also for the purposes of clarifying goals and examining the consequences of one's choices.

It may be modified for different settings, such as in working with substance abusers (Rustin & Olsson, 1993).

Guided fantasy. There is a wide variety of exercises in which the director has the group members imagine a variety of general themes, the details of which are filled in by each individual's unique imagery. Picturing trips through one's own body, journeys through forests, mountains, houses, or into the sea are all common themes. This technique has also been called the *directed daydream* method, and has become a major approach within the general group of imagery-oriented therapies. The group can utilize these methods individually, while working in dyads, or they can share a fantasy together as a group (Leuner, 1969).

Another major group of warm-ups are those derived from the related fields of the creative arts therapies.

Creative dramatics. Theatre games and exercises from the mime can be adapted as warm-ups for psychodramatic enactments. Activities derived from improvisational dramatics are widely utilized in school settings and can easily lead to explorations of more meaningful issues (Spolin, 1963). Drama therapy techniques are especially useful in this regard (Emunah, 1994).

My wife and I have created a variation on creative dramatics by adapting psychodrama as a form of recreation which we call *The Art of Play* (Blatner & Blatner, 1988). This activity is used just to allow people to experience the richness of playing a role from one's own imagination. Also, in training workshops I often use a technique we've called "the talk-show-host game" in order to develop the skill of role taking (Blatner & Blatner, 1991).

Dance/Movement. Exercises from dance and movement therapy which lead to spontaneity and involvement in expressiveness can easily be part of any warm-up. Related to the field of dance are the activities derived from body movement, sensory awakening, bioenergetics, and rhythmical group rituals. Simple voiced intonations—chants, grunts, repetitive noises—can all be added to emphasize breathing and expressive action. These warm-ups not only generate a great deal of readiness for action, but also establish a norm of physical involvement within the group.

Music. The group members can create and/or play simple instruments in an improvisatory style. The interplay can be heightened by a mixture of making music, voice sounds, and body movement. The introduction of simple musical instruments, elementary circle dance, and stretching activities is especially valuable in working with patients who have been passive or institutionalized for long periods (Chace, 1945).

Background music may also be an effective catalyst to group interaction. The lyrics of many contemporary songs can suggest common emotional themes for group discussion. A music therapist can provide recordings that reflect different moods in music with which to accompany and heighten the flow of action in many enactments (J. J. Moreno, 1980).

Artistic materials. Paints, clay, papier-mâché, pastels, crayons, finger paints, colored sand, and a wide variety of collage materials can all be adapted to a group setting. Starting with ideas derived from art therapy, the group can move from the creative media to enactments and then back to further involvement in artistic creation.

One example of the use of artistic materials is *shared drawings*. Working in dyads, group members take turns in creating a picture together. After about five to fifteen minutes, they share their experience and picture with the group. Applied to a couples group, a variant involves each pair drawing a picture of their relationship without using any words.

All of the approaches above can become warm-up techniques that emphasize spontaneity and a validation of the creative dimensions within the self. Each director will undoubtedly improvise a variety of modifications of any of them. James Sacks (1967), for example, combines elements of many different approaches in one of his warm-ups. The group members form a fairly tight circle, sitting on cushions or low seats, leaning forward. In turn, members state their names (or nicknames) and mention what they hope to achieve in the group session. Each person's entire statement is to be no greater than one sentence in length. Other directions follow: "Share with the group something they don't know about you." "Tell an old, old memory." "Name someone with whom you have unfinished business." At this point, the one-sentence rule may be lifted. The group members are then asked to dictate a letter to the person with whom they have unfinished business. This technique is likely to be useful in building group cohesion, encouraging self-disclosure, and developing themes and protagonists for future enactments.

There are literally hundreds of other structured experiences or warm-up techniques, and books or articles describing many of them are noted in a special section at the end of this chapter's references.

THE SELECTION OF A PROTAGONIST

There are many ways in which a protagonist may emerge out of the group process:

1. The protagonist may volunteer in that or an earlier session. The director may want to have the group vote on whom is to be dealt with if there are several volunteers, or she may arbitrarily choose in what order they will be protagonists. The director may simply wait quietly until someone does volunteer, but the director has to know where to use this approach or it may backfire. Some groups will simply not respond.

2. The protagonist may be preselected by the therapists.

3. The director may walk around and converse with different people in the group until she finds someone who is ready to be the protagonist. (See Figure 4.2)

Figure 4.2

4. She may give a short talk on some theme, tell a story that seems relevant to the group's interest, and see if that can remind the group of issues which they might wish to explore further. This may encourage a protagonist to volunteer.

5. The protagonist may emerge out of the natural ongoing group process. This occurs when the group arrives and is catalyzed into some natural joking or discussion of a topic. This spontaneity should not be suppressed by an unspoken or explicit "Let's get down to business," which has the effect of a wet blanket on a fire. Many people find talking about their problems humiliating, and such a suggestion invariably quenches spontaneity in a group. Instead, the director should wait. She may even go along with the joking, trusting that she can gently turn it into a meaningful issue. Eventually both a theme and a protagonist emerge (Kumar & Treadwell, 1986).

6. *Action sociometry.* Using spectrograms, sociodramas, or other group-centered methods, a protagonist may emerge as one who is especially concerned about something triggered in the discussion. Moreno developed methods in the early 1930s whereby group members could systematically give themselves feedback regarding attitudes of the members towards each other and in relation to some specific theme. Paper-and-pencil tests could be given in which the results were correlated and presented to the group. Or group members can be asked to position themselves around the room. In new groups, group members can place their hands on the shoulders of those whom they've known before this group began; or to place themselves on an imagined map to show what part of the locale—region or even world—they come from (Seabourne, 1963).

If a group theme is present, either one that the group has expressly met to consider, or one arising in the course of the group process, often there will be some aspect of that theme which is at least potentially controversial. The group will want to know where people stand on this issue. A commonly used technique in such cases is that of the *spectrogram*, a type of action sociogram in which the group members place themselves at some point along an imaginary line which reflects their self-perceptions regarding some issue, from the "most" to the "least." This spectrum of responses gives the group an clearly observable demonstration of the distribution of feelings regarding the theme in question (Kole, 1967).

In addition, in order to stimulate a protagonist, or to help him become more involved in his life situation, the director can use more individual-centered warm-ups:

7. *The auxiliary, or "empty," chair* technique, is commonly used for warming-up as well as during the action phase of a psychodrama (Lippitt, 1958). The director puts forward an empty chair and says, "There is someone sitting in this chair—someone important to you. Visualize that person, what he or she is doing, wearing, possibly thinking about. . . . When it's clear to you, raise your hand." Then when most have indicated they have seen someone, the director may proceed to ask whom they see in the chair. The director may ask no one in particular and wait for volunteers, or address her question to a specific person. When someone responds, he is either asked to be that person (and sit in the chair) or is asked what he has to say to whomever he sees in the chair. This can lead to a brief interchange, which may lead to a further enactment.

A variation of this was shown me by Pam and Rory Remer: Members of the group walked around in a circle and addressed "themselves" in the empty chair, one at a time, giving themselves advice about their lives. In this way, the technique is a kind of soliloquy formed as a quasi-dialogue. Further variations establish the figure in the chair as oneself when younger, or require the person talking to the self to imagine that he or she is significantly wiser, older, and more mature.

During an enactment, the auxiliary chair can also be used when the protagonist has difficulty relating to a real person. The chair in this sense becomes the major instrument in monodrama. (See Figure 2.1, p. 24.)

8. *"Family sculpture"* is another type of action sociogram. The director helps the protagonist present his relevant social network as if they were a group of sculptures in a diorama, or a three-dimensional painting (see Figure 4.3). This technique has been incorporated into family therapy, but it should be noted that it was taken from psychodrama (Constantine, 1978). The sculpture tech-

Figure 4.3

nique can be applied to other nonfamily social networks, too, such as a person's co-workers at the office, the politics of a church group, one's school classroom (Leveton, 1992: 74; Horley & Strickland, 1984).

The action sociogram, or "sculpture" begins with the protagonist placing someone in the group (as an auxiliary) to represent himself, and then one by one other significant figures in his perceived social network are chosen and, with facilitation by an ongoing dialogue with the director, placed in positions that symbolically represent their perceived distance, attitude, and quality of relationship with the protagonist. Finally, the protagonist gives each figure in the scene a characteristic sentence or phrase to speak, which symbolically brings them to life. He then steps back and observes, or enters the scene and begins to relate to his family or central group.

Another variant of the sculpture type of action sociogram is the use of physical objects—a group of coins of various denominations; a chess set; or a set of hand puppets (preferably of animals)—to represent the protagonist's relevant social network. The protagonist is instructed to identify the chess piece (Schwab, 1978) or hand puppet of his choice with one of the people in his social network. It is often interesting for example, to watch a protagonist pick the mouse hand puppet or the pawn for the father, the bear puppet or bishop for the brother, and so forth. Which figure, where it is placed, and what it does can then serve as clues for understanding the protagonist's experience of his or her family relationships.

9. *The Social Network Diagram.* One of the most useful warm-ups I've found is that of simply having everyone draw a diagram of their own social network, that is, the five to fifteen most significant people in their lives. (Moreno called this complex of the individual and his or her relevant social network "the social atom," attempting to indicate the organic essence of his sociological vision but I find that term too idiosyncratic.) Placing themselves at the center of a wheel-like figure, and indicating with the lines drawn from the central symbol to the symbols of the various characters what kinds of feelings are sensed in the relationship, participants quickly capture much of great relevance (Buchanan, 1984; Taylor, 1984). (See Figure 4.4.)

The lines indicate the feelings of the subject toward the others up to the midpoint mark. The feelings the subject believes the others to have are shown from their symbol back to the midpoint. The woman in Figure 4.4 has ambivalent feelings toward her father and her father has positive feelings toward her. She and her fiancee's ex-wife both have negative feelings towards one another. Of particular note is the deceased grandfather to whom she has positive feelings which she believes would be reciprocated.

The number of people included in a social network diagram should be those who are active in a person's psychological life. It's important to note that pets and deceased persons be recognized when they play significant roles. This diagram represents a person's "object relations," those whom one needs, cares about, loves, and hates, enough to be worthy of consideration if one were in therapy.

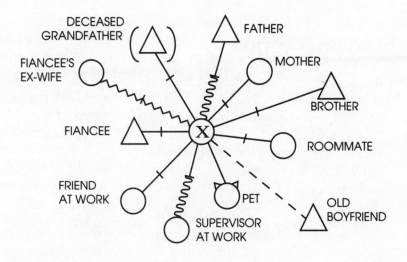

The subject, X, in this case a woman, is placed in the center of the diagram. Various relationships are indicated using the following symbols:

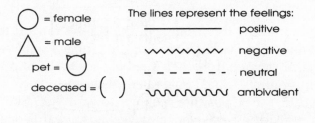

Figure 4.4 The Social Network Diagram

After diagramming, I have group members pair off and share with a partner the meaning of their drawing. In addition to reminding people of the web of social relations and roles which constitute so much of their experience, this technique also helps to promote a therapeutic alliance and a beginning diagnosis in individual therapy.

MOVING INTO ACTION

After the protagonist has emerged from the group, the last phase
of the warm-up remains. The basic issue is discussed with the protagonist. "Yes, that issue troubles me," is the essence of the contract. "Let's work on it," says the director, and the protagonist is
led gently by the hand to the staging area.

Depending on his readiness, the protagonist may sit at the second level edge of the stage, and the director sits with him (Figure
4.5). Often the director and protagonist stand or walk around in
the staging area as they discuss the issue in order to arrive at a spe-

Figure 4.5

cific example: a place or a person. At this point the enactment moves to the third level of the stage, if one is being used.

The director takes an appropriate cue that points to an enactment and suggests it. If a name of someone who seems important to the protagonist is mentioned, an interaction with that person might be the "first scene." If a time of life is mentioned, the director moves toward a specific memory or image.

During the warm-up, the protagonist is helped to engage in increasing activity. When a protagonist is warmed up to an unusually high pitch he will almost direct the drama by himself.

If, during the warm-up, the protagonist shows increasing anxiety manifested by resistance, the director must shift the enactment into a less emotionally loaded sphere of exploration while still continuing the action. This is similar to the process of desensitization by imagery and relaxation in the treatment of phobic patients: If the client indicates that he is picturing a scene that makes him too tense, the therapist allows him to return to a less frightening image with which he can relax, but the therapy continues. Similarly, if the protagonist "freezes," the director may ask him to soliloquize, or to use one of the following warm-up devices:

- *Hand puppets.* A puppet show can often be an effective warm-up, while giving the protagonist some distance (Kors, 1964). The use of masks may have a similar function (Leveton, 1992; Melson & Thurman, 1982).

- *Blackout.* The entire theater is blacked out, although all actions continue as if there would be full daylight. This is done so that the protagonist may go through a painful experience unobserved, and so the protagonist can retain the experience of solitude.

- *Turn your back.* A protagonist is occasionally embarrassed to present a particular episode while facing the group. He is then permitted to turn his back to the group and to act as if he were alone, in his own home, or wherever the episode takes place. Once the protagonist has reached a sufficient degree of involvement, he is then ready to carry on facing the audience.

- *Portrayal of a dream.* This offers an excellent first enactment for a protagonist's exploration of his problem. It is often used in Gestalt therapy, and is discussed further in the next chapter.

- *Hypnodrama.* The protagonist is hypnotized and then helped to enact his situation in a hypnotic state (Enneis, 1950; Moreno, 1950).

- *Subgrouping.* The group breaks into dyads and small groups which do various structured exercises together. Kroll, Mikhailova and Serdiouk (1992) found it necessary to use this and other modifications in order to deal with the special circumstances of people in Russia, and serves as a model inviting the spontaneity of other directors internationally to adapt these approaches to their own cultures.

After a sufficient warm-up, the protagonist is usually ready to enter the second phase of the psychodrama—the action—which will be discussed in the next chapter.

SUMMARY

The warming-up process is the first and an essential part of any enactment and is based on the fundamental need for any person to gradually develop increasing involvement and spontaneity through goal-directed physical action. In reference to group process, the warm-up phase applies to the components of (a) the director's warm-up, (b) building group cohesion, (c) developing a group theme, (d) finding a protagonist, and (e) moving the protagonist onto the stage.

REFERENCES / RECOMMENDED READINGS

Barbour, A. (1992). Purpose and strategy behind the magic shop. *Journal of Group Psychotherapy, Psychodrama & Sociometry, 45*(3), 91–101.

Barbour, A. (1994). A reexamination of the tele effect. *Journal of Group Psychotherapy, Psychodrama & Sociometry, 47*(3), 114–125.

Blatner, A. (1988). Spontaneity. In *Foundations of psychodrama* (pp. 63–71). New York: Springer.

Blatner, A. & Blatner, A. (1988). *The Art of Play: An adult's guide to reclaiming imagination and spontaneity.* New York: Human Sciences Press.

Blatner, A. & Blatner, A. (1991). Imaginative interviews: A psychodramatic warm-up for developing role-playing skills. *Journal of Group Psychotherapy, Psychodrama & Sociometry, 44*(3), 115–120.

Blatner, A. (1994). Tele: The dynamics of interpersonal preference. In P. Holmes, M. Karp, & M. Watson (eds.), *Psychodrama since Moreno.* London: Tavistock/Routledge.

Buchanan, D. R. (1984). Moreno's social atom: A diagnostic and treatment tool for exploring interpersonal relationships. *The Arts in Psychotherapy, 11,* 155–164.

Chace M., (1945). Rhythm and movement as used in St. Elizabeth's Hospital. *Sociometry, 8,* 481–483.

Constantine, L. L. (April, 1978). Family sculpture and relationship mapping techniques. *Journal of Marriage & Family Counseling, 4,* 13–23.

Corynetz, P. (1945). The warming-up process of an audience. *Sociometry, 8*(3–4), 218–225.

Emunah, R. (1994). *Acting for real: Drama therapy, process, technique, and performance.* New York: Brunner/Mazel.

Enneis, J. M. (1950). The hypnodramatic technique. *Group Psychotherapy, 3*(1), 11–40.

Enneis, J. M. (1951). The dynamics of group and action processes in therapy. *Group Psychotherapy, 4*(1), 17–21.

Horley, J. & Strickland, L. H. (1984). A note on Jacob Moreno's contributions to the development of social network analysis. *Journal of Community Psychology, 12*(3), 291–293.

Kipper, D. A. (1967). Spontaneity and the warming-up process in a new light. *Group Psychotherapy, 20*(1), 62–73.

Kole, D. (1967). The spectrogram in psychodrama. *Group Psychotherapy, 20*(1–2), 53–61.

Kors, P. C. (1964). Unstructured puppet shows as group procedures in therapy with children. *Psychiatric Quarterly Supplement, 38*(1), 56–75.

Kroll, L. M., Mikhailova, E. L., & Serdiouk, E. A. (1992). Pre-warm-up in Russian psychodrama groups: A cultural approach. *Journal of Group Psychotherapy, Psychodrama & Sociometry, 45*(2), 51–62.

Kumar, V. K. & Treadwell, T. W. (1986). Identifying a protagonist: Techniques and factors. *Journal of Group Psychotherapy, Psychodrama & Sociometry, 38*(4), 155–164.

Leuner, H. C. (1969). Guided affective imagery. *American Journal of Psychotherapy, 23*(1), 4–22.

Leveton, E. (1992). *A clinician's guide to psychodrama* (2nd ed.). New York: Springer.

Lippitt, R. (1958). Auxiliary chair technique. *Group Psychotherapy, 11*(1–2), 8–23.

Martin, R. B. (1991). The assessment of involvement in role playing. *Journal of Clinical Psychology, 47*, 587–596.

Melson, S. J. & Thurman, W. (1982). The making of masks in psychotherapy. *Psychiatric Annals, 12*(12), 36–39.

Moreno, J. J. (1980). Musical psychodrama: A new direction in music therapy. *Journal of Music Therapy, 17*(1), 34–42.

Moreno, J. L. (1947). *The theatre of spontaneity.* Beacon, NY: Beacon House.

Moreno, J. L. (1950). Hypnodrama and psychodrama. *Group Psychotherapy, 3*(1), 1–10.

Moreno, Z. T. (1958). The "reluctant therapist" and the "reluctant audience" technique in psychodrama. *Group Psychotherapy, 11*, 278–282.

Moreno, Z. T. (1959). A survey of psychodramatic techniques. *ACTA Psychotherapeutica, 7*, 197–206.

Pankratz, L., & Buchan, G. (1965). Exploring psychodrama techniques with defective delinquents. *Group Psychotherapy, 18*(3), 136–141.

Rustin, T. A., & Olsson, P. A. (1993). Sobriety shop: A variation on magic shop for addiction treatment patients. *Journal of Group Psychotherapy, Psychodrama & Sociometry, 46*(1), 12–23.

Sacks, J. M. (1967). Psychodrama, the warm-up. *Group Psychotherapy, 20*(4), 118–121.

Schwab, R. (1978). Use of a chess set: An application of psychodramatic and sociometric techniques. *Group Psychotherapy, Psychodrama & Sociometry, 31*, 41–45.

Seabourne, B. (1963). The action sociogram. *Group Psychotherapy 16*(3), 145–155.

Spolin, V. (1963). *Improvisations for the theater.* Evanston, IL: Northwestern University Press.

Taylor, J. A. (1984). The diagnostic use of the social atom. *Journal of Group Psychotherapy, Psychodrama & Sociometry, 37*(2), 67–84.

Warner, G. D. (1970). The didactic auxiliary chair. *Group Psychotherapy, 23*(1–2), 31–34.

Weiner, H. A., & Sacks, J. M. (1969). Warm-up and sum-up. *Group Psychotherapy, 22*(1–2), 85–102.

Yablonsky, L., & Enneis, J. M. (1956). Psychodrama, theory and practice, In F. Fromm-Reichman & J . L. Moreno (Eds.) *Progress in psychotherapy, Vol. 1.* New York: Grune and Stratton.

Miscellaneous Warm-Up Techniques, Structured Experiences:

Bond, T. (1986). *Games for social and life skills.* Cheltenham, England: Stanley Thornes.

Brandes, D., & Phillips, H. (1978). *Gamesters' handbook: 140 games for teachers and *group leaders*. Cheltenham, England: Stanley Thornes.

Brandes, D. (1982). *Gamesters' handbook two*. London: Hutchinson.

Caesar H., Florence B., Carroll R.D., et al. (1983). *Communicate! A workbook for interpersonal development*, (3rd ed.). Dubuque, IA: Kendall-Hunt.

Dayton, T. (1990). *Drama games: Techniques for self-development*. Deerfield Beach, FL: Health Communications, Inc.

Dynes, R. (1990). *Creative games in groupwork*. Bicester, England: Winslow.

Jennings, S. (1986). *Creative drama in group work*. London: Winslow Press.

Kranz, P. (1991). A demonstration of warm-up techniques with young children. *Journal of Group Psychotherapy, Psychodrama & Sociometry, 43*(4), 162–166.

Malamud, D. I. & Machover, S. (1965). *Toward self-understanding: Group techniques in self-confrontation*. Springfield, IL: Charles C. Thomas.

Morris, K. T., & Cinnamon, K. N. (1974). *A handbook of verbal group exercises*. San Diego: Applied Skills Press.

Morris, K. T., & Cinnamon, K. N. (1975). *A handbood of non-verbal group exercises*. San Diego: Applied Skills Press.

Otto, H. A. (1970). *Group methods to actualize human potential: A handbook*. Beverly Hills: Holistic Press.

Pfeiffer, J. W., & Jones, J. E. (1969–71). *Structured experience for human relations training* (Vols. 1–3). Iowa City: University Associates.

Pfeiffer, J. W. (1989). *The encyclopedia of group activities*. San Diego: University Associates.

Robbins, M. (1973). Psychodramatic children's warm-ups for adults. *Group Psychotherapy & Psychodrama, 26*(1–2), 67–71.

Russell, J. (1975). Personal growth through structured group exercises. In R. M. Suinn & R. G. Weigel (Eds.), *The innovative psychological therapies: Critical and creative contributions* (pp. 126–135). New York: Harper & Row.

Streitfeld, H. S., and Lewis, H. R. (1971). *Growth games*. New York: Harcourt, Brace, Jovanovich.

Stevens, J. A. (1971). *Awareness: Exploring, experimenting, experiencing*. Lafayette, CA: Real People Press.

Thayer, L. (Ed.). (1976, 1981). *Fifty strategies for experiential learning*. (Books I, II). San Diego: University Associates.

Weathers, L., Bedell, J. R., Marlowe, H., Gordon, R. E., Adams, J., Reed, V., Palmer, J., & Gordon, K. K. (1981). Using psychotherapeutic games to train patients' skills. In R. E. Gordon & K. K. Gordon, *Systems of treatment for the mentally ill* (pp. 109–124). New York: Grune and Stratton, 1981.

Zweben, J. E., & Hammann, K. (1970). Prescribed games: A theoretical perspective on the use of group techniques. *Psychotherapy: Theory, Research & Practice, 7*(1), 22–27.

5

The Action

Following the warm-up of the group and the selection of the protagonist, the psychodramatic process enters its second phase, the *action*, which involves the exploration of the protagonist's problem. The logic of the progress of scenes in a classical psychodrama has been illustrated in a diagram (Figure 5.1) developed by Goldman and Morrison (1984). This "psychodramatic spiral" shows the shifting of location and time of scenes used in exploring a typical problem.

While every psychodramatic enactment is unique, in general the action will start with an enactment of some aspect of the present situation, in an attempt to help the protagonist also express the underlying feelings and thoughts that accompany his behavior. Then other scenes are played, either in different relationships or, more often, in the past, which also reveal common concerns or patterns. Then the action moves into scenes that may have given rise to the basic attitudes and reactions that seem to be problematical for the protagonist.

In portraying core conflicts, protagonists often reexperience the original emotions of grief, fear, anger, longing, shame, guilt, or confusion. Expression of these feelings involve a process of catharsis (Blatner, 1985a). The challenge is then to help the protagonist find ways of constructively re-owning feelings which may have been repressed. Scenes involving expression of more vulnerable feelings need to be followed by scenes bringing forth feelings of effectiveness and hope. This two-stage process explains Moreno's dictum, "every catharsis of abreaction should be followed by a

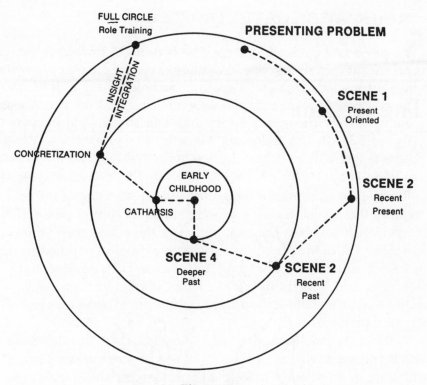

Figure 5.1

catharsis of integration," in which the protagonist reclaims some of the vitality and power associated with previously disowned aspects of self.

These phases of the process are illustrated diagrammatically in Figure 5.1 as the protagonist is helped to "spiral in" towards an elucidation of the "core" issues and then "spiral out" while applying those insights in expanding or training more appropriate role behaviors. The integration process, discussed in the next chapter, can involve a number of scenes which help consolidate gains through behavioral rehearsal. Or, further elements of "unfinished business" may be brought to the surface for psychodramatic exploration. Since each protagonist's situation has its own individual elements, there are no hard and fast rules about the sequence of scenes.

PRESENTATION OF THE PROBLEM

When the protagonist is selected, he is brought toward the stage and encouraged to describe his situation. As the director discusses the protagonist's problem, a specific example is sought. If the protagonist begins to narrate the situation, the director encourages him to portray the scene, rather than talk about what happened (Figure 5.2). In the following vignette, the protagonist, whose name is Joe, will be helped to psychodramatically explore a personal situation in his life. Joe begins to tell the director and group about it:

Figure 5.2

Joe: Well, I had this fight with my boss.

Director: Show us, don't tell us. (The director gets up and invites Joe into the stage area.) Where does the scene happen?

Joe: It was in the office.

Director: It *is* in the office—it's happening now! Let's see the office. Where is the boss's chair? ..desk? ..Are you sitting or standing? (Figure 5.3)

The director (who in the stick figure illustrations wears glasses) continues to speak as if the situation were occurring in the here-and-now, which brings a greater degree of immediacy to the process. The director both models speaking in the present tense

Figure 5.3

and reminds the protagonist to do so. This redirection may have to be repeated several times, because protagonists often lapse into narrating the situation as if it were in the past or in the subjunctive sense, that is, how it "might" be, or, "maybe would be." These are subtle linguistic distancing maneuvers, very common in our culture, but they interfere with people's experiencing clarity in their action, thinking, and deciding. With encouragement, protagonists often become warmed-up and involved, suspending much (but not all) of the awareness that they are is "just pretending.".

The director has the protagonist move around the stage, visualizing the scene in its particulars. As the protagonist describes the scene, the director asks him to amplify the descriptions, to physically point out the furniture, "feel" the textures of the materials, note the colors, the temperature, the weather—all concrete sensations that immerse him even more deeply in the enactment. In other words, the sensory immersion techniques of the great acting teacher and director Konstantin Stanislavski also have some relevance to the process of helping a protagonist warm up to a scene (Lippe, 1992). The setting of the stage is for the protagonist's benefit as much as for the audience's. It may be as brief or prolonged as the director feels is necessary in order to maximize the protagonist's continuing warm-up.

The physical involvement of setting up the props, moving the chairs or tables into place, or putting on a piece of fabric as a shawl or gown can further the warming-up process. And as the enactment progresses, the director should attempt to maintain an optimal level of actual movement in order to avoid becoming bogged down in a wordy interaction (one of the most common pitfalls of directing). Later in the psychodrama, the director continues to use a variety of scene changes, role reversals, standing on chairs, pushing, climbing over furniture, and many other techniques in order to keep up the pace of action.

BRINGING IN THE AUXILIARY

As the scene is set, the auxiliaries are chosen and encouraged to move immediately into their roles. Joe is asked to pick someone in the group (call him Bill) to be the auxiliary (Figure 5.4).

Figure 5.4

Bill comes on stage and the director immediately warms him up to his role:

DIRECTOR: Mr. Jones, you asked Joe to come in today. He can't hear you right now. As if you were just thinking out loud to yourself, giving a soliloquy, let's hear what you have to say regarding why you want to see him.

AUXILIARY: (Bill, as Mr. Jones) Well, Joe hasn't been performing very well at his job. (Figure 5.5).

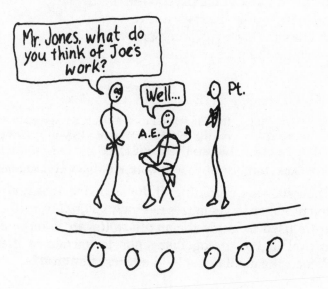

Figure 5.5

DIRECTOR: (glancing at Joe) Is that right?

JOE: No, that's not it. My work is fine.

DIRECTOR: Change parts—that is, reverse roles. Joe, be Mr. Jones and begin the encounter.

JOE: (as Mr. Jones) Look, Joe, this is the third time this week you've come in late.

DIRECTOR: Change parts and start again. Mr. Jones? (Aside to Bill as auxiliary, warming him up). Repeat the last line.

AUXILIARY: (Mr. Jones) Look Joe, this is the third time this week you've come in late.

Figure 5.6

JOE: But, Sir, when I took this job, we agreed that because of my
            having to take care of my kids my work time would be
            adjusted! (Figure 5.6).

AUXILIARY: Well, your co-workers are noticing and complaining.

The issues are unfolding. If the auxiliary does not play his part
as the protagonist visualizes its essential quality, further role reversals are used to guide the auxiliary toward a more accurate role
portrayal. If the protagonist tends to narrate to the director or
audience, the auxiliary should address him in-role:

AUXILIARY: You're talking as if I'm not even here! What's the big idea
            of being so late this morning?!

If the protagonist becomes lost in intellectualization or confused
as to his feelings, there are some other techniques that may be
used:

• *Accentuate the non-verbal communications.* Have the protagonist enact the scene without using actual words, but rather
  with exaggerated vocal tone, inflection, rhythm, and accom-
  panying facial expressions and physical gestures. This technique of using sounds without words ("blah-blah" or more
  complex pronunciations of nonsense syllables) is also called
  "gibberish." Through the action, the underlying emotion is
  expressed more clearly.

- *Soliloquy.* The protagonist is instructed to walk up and down and talk to himself out loud, in order to clarify his feelings. He can then reenter the interaction with the auxiliary in role.

- *Double.* If the protagonist has difficulty expressing his emotions clearly, a double may be brought in, an auxiliary who, as described in Chapter 3, will portray Joe's inner feelings (Figure 5.7):

Figure 5.7

DIRECTOR:	Mark, will you come in here. (Gives instructions for doubling, then carries on with the scene.)
JOE:	(continuing) Well, Sir, I think that wasn't our agreement.
MR. JONES:	Look, Joe, we have to run a business here.
DOUBLE:	Look, you bastard, here's how I really feel: #@%$!! (Figure 5.8)
JOE:	(nodding) Yeah! You can't push me around like this!
MR. JONES:	Now hold on there!
DOUBLE:	It's about time someone was frank with you! When you make an agreement—
JOE:	Yeah, you have to stand by what you say!

Figure 5.8

From this point, the interaction can be continued, or replayed, or the scene shifted and a related interaction portrayed. If Joe has problems with authority, many other encounters with authority figures can be explored, always moving to more central emotional issues.

MOVING FROM PERIPHERAL TO CENTRAL

In general, people cannot tease out the essential elements in a complex welter of emotions. Layers of self-justifications and self-reproach, explanations and excuses to others, difficulty in differentiating between the actual circumstances and one's beliefs or emotional reactions to events, and similar dynamics make it impossible to develop a clear insight into the basic issues involved. Yet there is an act hunger to express and explore personally meaningful experience. Thus, it's all right to begin with some superficial event, even one which the director may feel is peripheral to more "core" conflicts.

Some therapists may see presentations of such peripheral issues as avoidance, a kind of resistance, but in fact even these enactments can serve as sources of ideas fostering the warming-up process. Furthermore, it is an act of respect and wisdom to consider that the protagonist's unconscious may be trying to symbolically help rather than hinder. In other words, good directors go along with their protagonists rather than fight them.

For example, if the protagonist has difficulty in dealing with an emotionally loaded conflict with his mother, he may be helped to enact a similar situation with a saleslady. Another technique is to have the protagonist play the role of his own brother or sister, and to enact with his mother from that position. Marguerite Parrish (1953) wrote about the following two useful techniques:

The substitute role technique is frequently used and is helpful when working with protagonists who tend to be suspicious and resist portraying themselves on the stage. This technique was successfully used with a middle-aged woman diagnosed as having involutional melancholia with some paranoid traits. She was unable to enact her own situations and so was asked to play the role of her mother, who operated a boarding house. In this role she was at ease and seemed to enjoy going on the stage. During the third session the protagonist brought up the fact that one of her roomers was promiscuous. This story was also her own story. As a young girl her illegitimate pregnancy was followed by an abortion, and as she approached middle life she worried about this incident and felt sure her family would find out and would no longer love her. Psychodrama gave this women an opportunity to freely express her feelings about the incident, and the discussion of the audience helped her to see that she had the love of her family and would not necessarily lose it because of the past event.

In the *symbolic distance* technique the protagonist enacts a role very different from his own role and is gradually led to portray his own role. This technique is particularly valuable when working with children. A young boy and girl from broken and inadequate homes were treated in this way. Individual therapy had been helpful and outward behavior improved, but the children were afraid to leave the security of the hospital, for they felt sure they could not-get along in a home situation. Because the problems of these children were so alike, they were cast as brother and sister and were treated together. Following the portrayals, the group dis- cussed why the children acted differently in the various situations. From these scenes the children finally came to realize that they could get along in some types of family homes and expressed will- ingness to accept a family care situation.

If the protagonist tends to speak in terms of abstractions, con- cepts can be made concrete by symbolizing them as figures with their own personalities: "They," "society," "other people," "the establishment," and "young people" all can be portrayed by an auxiliary. "This woman is the Establishment. Talk to her now." The protagonist is directed to confront the auxiliary and eventually role-reverse with her, all of which brings the protagonist's conflicts into sharper focus.

FOCUSING ON THE NONVERBAL

One of the most useful approaches in clarifying the protagonist's problem is the emphasis on explicitly portraying the nonverbal communication involved, e.g.:

JOE: (protagonist) But Sir, you *said* you would.

DIRECTOR: Joe, step out of the scene. Mark (another group member), replay that interaction, acting the exact way Joe behaves (*mirror* technique).

The director asks Mark to shift out of the role of double and to take the role of the mirror. (Note: Any person participating in the enactment, except the director and protagonist, is designated by the general term *auxiliary*.) Figure 5.9 illustrates the scene that ensues:

MARK: (Auxiliary ego, whining dramatically) But Sir, you *said* you would!

JOE: Wow! Do I whine like that?

DIRECTOR: (to group) Is Mark's presentation fair? (Group agrees.) Well, Joe, with whom did you "whine" as a child?

JOE: To my father, when he . . .

Auxiliary Ego (A.E.) as Pt. →

Explain Whine

A.E. as Boss

Dir

Pt.

Mirror Technique

Figure 5.9

Often what is said in an interaction (the content) is less important than how it is said (the process). The dramatization of the expression, posture, tone of voice, angle of the body, and gesture all help bring out the factors that may have been the major determinants of the other person's reaction.

Body postures and other elements of nonverbal behavior communicate not only to other people, but also serve to cue or reinforce personal attitudinal systems. Thus, the stance and other correlations of whining behavior tend to reinforce a disempowered feeling and associated beliefs, while a provocative habit of posture or expression may promote a non-self-reflective attitude of self-righteousness.

Role reversal, observations from the audience, and the amplification of gesture, as well as the mirror technique, help the protagonist and group become more aware of the nature and importance of the nonverbal communication being portrayed in the interaction.

EXPLORING UNEXPRESSED EMOTIONS

Whether in psychotherapy or in a class on social problems, one of the challenges of consciousness raising is helping people become more self-aware. In this sense, psychodrama is a way of operationalizing Socrates' dictum, "Know thyself." That people are complex and self-deceptive is the major finding of dynamic psychology, whatever the particulars of the various schools of thought. How then to reduce this self-deception, to increase the awareness of the whole range of attitudes and ideas which may be influencing the people in a problematic situation? A further challenge is to more finely discriminate the issues involving the specific underlying assumptions and beliefs which may operate unconsciously in most people's life.

Psychodrama utilizes the integration of imagination and action with more traditional, verbal forms of self-reflection. In psychodrama, the realm of imagination is recognized as being a powerful dimension. By shifting from a passively visualized fantasy to a dimension in which events are concretized in enactment, this approach opens a new context for reexperiencing and reworking the meaning and emotional impact of experience.

Moreno believed that the realm in which imagination can be made manifest, phenomenological reality, deserves to be recognized as a definite category of existence. He named this ontological dimension *surplus reality* (Moreno, 1965). The value of this concept is that it validates as a dimension of being worthy of being taken seriously and explored those experiences of events that not only have occurred in the past, and may occur in the future, but also events that never occur—even events that could never happen!—such as an encounter with an unborn child, speaking with a relative who has died, replaying a scene so that one experiences mastery instead of humiliation, or having a dialogue with one's patron saint or guardian angel. Surplus reality scenes allow the whole range of the vehicle of drama to be fully utilized in the service of people discovering the deeper aspects of their own thoughts and feelings.

In the action of psychodrama, then, scenes are constructed which bring forth the protagonist's hopes, fears, expectations,

Figure 5.10

unexpressed resentments, projections, internalizations, and judgmental attitudes. Furthermore, the protagonist is helped to ventilate these feelings and symbolically live through them. In the case of the example being used in this chapter, Joe's muted conversation with the boss is converted into an emotional confrontation with the help of the expressive double.

As the scenes are changed to deal with other authority conflicts, a variety of techniques can be used to intensify the expression of feelings. Height may be used to exaggerate a dominance-submission gradient. For example, in a scene between Joe and his father, the auxiliary playing the father may be directed to stand on a chair, and even further, Joe could kneel or curl up on the floor to reflect the feeling of "You're so big and I'm so small." On the other hand, in another scene, the disadvantage can be shifted by having Joe deal with his feared father by standing on the chair, compensating for the earlier sense of imbalance in status or personal power (Figure 5.10). Using the gradient of height is often helpful as an aid in assertion training.

Manipulating other physical elements in the scene, such as adding some patronizing head patting, prodding, or even physical pushing, can sometimes be a catalyst to a catharsis, but such activities must be applied with caution and experience. Protagonists shouldn't be overloaded, but a degree of confrontation may evoke a decision for self-empowerment and counter-confrontation.

Directors should avoid overemphasizing only the negative, angry feelings which, in many cases, are mixed with a desire for a more positive and caring relationship. This desire may evoke even more vulnerability (and thus be repressed) than the anger. And for some people, anger comes too easily; the psychodramatist's challenge lies in helping them to learn to modulate the anger.

MOVING WITH THE RESISTANCES

One major challenge of psychotherapy or psychodrama is of helping the protagonist find a way to examine those inner feelings that threaten his sense of mastery or self-esteem. He may employ a wide range of resistances in order to avoid facing unpleasant experiences. I find that if the director works with the resistances, she can often find a way to gradually explore the deeper conflicts. Moreno puts it this way: "We don't tear down the protagonist's walls; rather, we simply try some of the handles on the many doors, and see which one opens."

When resistances become apparent, there are several steps to be taken. First, ground the protagonist in the purpose of the activity and the safety of the group and its process. Second, validate the hesitancy, help it find an explicit voice. Use doubling to further give words to this tension. For example, Joe stands transfixed as he begins to think about his father.

DOUBLE: This is very hard for me. I'm not sure I want to talk about this.

JOE: Yes, I feel very tense. (The director then has the opportunity to support Joe in his fear.)

DIRECTOR: Being honest with someone so close is difficult. Here, in psychodrama, we can face the challenge. It involves taking a risk, but it won't be overwhelming.

If the resistance is being acted out through a subconscious habit of becoming more elusive, make that avoidance more explicit, exaggerate the avoidance maneuver. For example, a resistance expressed in the tendency to explain may be portrayed openly by the director's asking the protagonist to talk to the group, to "explain" his position for one minute.

Reframing elusive phrases can remind protagonists of their own power. For example, the statement "I can't *seem* to" may be agreed with, but subtly redefined by the double or the director as, "I *won't*." "I don't know" can be reshaped as "I don't want to think about that." "Why do I have to do this?" can be restated as, "I don't like doing this." "It's no use" may be supported, but qualified with a statement of the temporary nature of the present resistance. *"Right now* I see no way out."

The point of going with the resistances is that through the explicit portrayal of the defenses, the protagonist becomes more fully aware that he is *choosing* to use a defense, that is, the portrayal increases his awareness of his own responsibility for his behavior and sense of mastery over his habitual behavior patterns. The more a protagonist can allow himself, with the support of the director, to say no, the sooner he begins to feel free to say yes when he is ready.

With a protagonist who is becoming overly anxious while dealing with a problem, it is often appropriate to allow him to move away from the core conflict, to obtain some distance. The move from peripheral issues toward central issues described earlier can be temporarily reversed.

A major block in many protagonists is use of the defense mechanism of isolation of affect—they are not even aware that they are feeling any emotion. The first step in dealing with this resistance is to help the protagonist become aware of the experience of emotion within himself. Only when he is moved toward an attempt to identify the quality of the feeling can he go on to explore the meaning of his emotions. In dealing with sensitizing a protagonist to his own feelings, the director focuses on (a) the protagonist's nonverbal communications and (b) his *imagery*. These two "avenues to the unconscious" bypass the most common forms of resistance: intellectualization, vagueness, explanation, rationalization, abstraction, and circumstantiality.

The protagonist's nonverbal communication is dramatized by treating the parts of the protagonist as if they were active beings in themselves. Areas of tension in the body, tightness of the voice, gripping of the hands all can be enacted as a little encounter between different parts of the self, for example:

JOE: (to his "father") Daddy, why don't you—

DIRECTOR: Joe, what is your voice doing?

JOE: It's choked.

DIRECTOR: Now become the part that's strangling the throat!

JOE: (as throat) I'm being squeezed and strangled!

DIRECTOR: Now become the part that's strangling the throat!

JOE: (as strangler, rasping) Shut up, you S.O.B., or you'll get us all into trouble! (twists his hands in a wringing motion).

This approach, like dream work, is used in Gestalt therapy and psychosynthesis. Working with dreams can be an important approach for healing (Leutz, 1986; Nolte, Weistart, & Wyatt, 1977). This method, too, utilizes the power of metaphor generated by the protagonist's unconscious symbolizing ability.

The use of the imagery is another avenue to the identification of deeper feelings. The different figures in a nightmare, hallucination, or a guided fantasy can interact using psychodramatic methods, and this can often clarify the nature of the protagonist's internal complexes, that is, the conglomerations of attitudes, images, and emotions.

Dealing with a protagonist's resistances is the core of psychotherapy or psychodrama. The art of the director is tested nowhere more than in this task. This section of the chapter has only indicated some of the avenues of approach to a challenge that demands an individual response in each situation.

PRESENTING THE BASIC ATTITUDES

An important step in the psychodramatic exploration of a problem is the explicit portrayal of the protagonist's attitudes and basic assumptions about himself, others, and the nature of human relationships. These attitudes are often phrased in terms of internalized sentences, that start with "should" and "ought." Encouraging the protagonist to make these statements explicit is necessary because they represent the values of his superego.

> JOE: (soliloquizing on stage with his double) How could I hate my father? You're not supposed to hate your father!
>
> JOE'S DOUBLE: Right! I shouldn't hate him no matter what!
>
> JOE: And anyway, I *love* him! How could I hate him?
>
> DOUBLE: I can't love and hate at the same time!
>
> JOE: Well, maybe I can.

Not only the protagonist's feelings are to be expressed, but also the attitudes that forbid the feelings from being accepted as part of his self-system. Some of these common attitudes include:

Men aren't supposed to cry.

I should be able to handle this myself.

Being emotional is a sign of weakness.

If I start crying I may never stop.

If I express my anger I'm afraid I might lose control or kill someone.

If I try to love someone, that person should be happy.

If I'm not happy, it's because they don't really love me.

People should be able to resolve their conflicts.

I should have known this by now.

If I haven't lived up to my expectations, I must be a failure.

There are hundreds of such "internal commands." Many of what I've called the "lies we live by," the clichés, popular overgeneralizations, and general attitudes are described and critiqued in many self-help books (Gillett, 1992). These core beliefs were part of what Adler referred to as "private logic" (Manaster & Corsini, 1982). They were made more explicit in the pioneering work of Albert Ellis (1962) and the increasingly popular cognitive therapy

approach. Knowing about them is as important for a psychodramatist as for a physician to know about the different kinds
of infectious micro-organisms.

Another way to portray the different attitudes and complexes is
to split the protagonist into different "selves." For example, one
part might be the judging, rule-pronouncing complex, while the
other part is the rebellious, or passive-aggressive, sulking self. This
analysis is similar to Fritz Perls' (1969) concept of *top-dog* versus
underdog, or Eric Berne's terminology of *parent, adult,* and *child*
(Naar, 1977).

EXPLORING THE CORE CONFLICTS

The problem originally presented is often not at the root of the protagonist's emotional concerns. Basic attitudes have been established in earlier life, and it is the relationships of that period that
are the next to be enacted. Sometimes what is indicated is not a
movement from the present to the past, but from a relatively
superficial to a more personal conflict, such as a sexual problem
with a spouse or a struggle between different needs within the protagonist himself.

As these core relationships are portrayed, it may seem obvious
to the director or the group that the protagonist is distorting the
feelings of the other persons in his life. The director should be in
no hurry to correct these distortions. First, the protagonist must
present the situation as he experiences it: This is *his* truth. He must
experience being listened to. Only then does he become more
receptive to exploring the possibility that the situation might have
other points of view.

In our example of Joe, the director may explore scenes in which
Joe wanted to be accepted by a father who had unrealistically high
expectations of him. Joe's fantasies can be portrayed in scenes in
which he is abandoned, rejected, or judged as inadequate by his
father. Exaggerating the physical relationships may help in clarifying the protagonist's experience of significant events (Figure 5.11).

Joe role-reverses and portrays his own conception of his father's
behavior. Indeed, Joe's portrayal of the father's judgment may be

Figure 5.11

so harsh as to seem unrealistic to the audience, as if Joe is carica-
turizing what a "bad father" does. This is probably because he is
projecting onto his father the anger and guilt he feels within himself toward the weaknesses that only he himself secretly knows
and condemns. Thus, through role reversal the protagonist is
helped to portray the distortions of his interpersonal perceptions
by acting out what he believes others think (i.e., his own projections). This kind of approach can thus be an effective form of diagnosis of the protagonist's psychodynamics.

ACT HUNGER

Directors should not be impatient to have their protagonists "be
realistic," because this demand denies them the experience of having their psychological truth validated. One of the implications of
the major development of "self-psychology" in psychoanalysis in
the 1980s was the recognition of people's need for empathic reso-
nance. It's as if the "inner child" cannot listen until it first feels
really listened to, and it can't have that experience unless it's

allowed to fully express itself. People need to hear themselves think and feel, and this is aided by having other people around who validate this process.

One of Moreno's more perceptive insights is that people need even more than mere self-expression. They need—at least symbolically—to experience doing things that fulfill their needs, not just to talk about them. People who work with children know this, and we should not presume that this need is lost in the process of normal development. Moreno used the term *act hunger* to describe the drive toward a fulfillment of the desires and impulses at the core of the self. The director should help the protagonist achieve a symbolic fulfillment of his act hunger, because it, too is a fundamental part of the protagonist's psychological truth.

In the example of the enactment we have been using, the protagonist, Joe, first presents his father in the most caricatured form. It is not time to explore who the father "really" was through role reversal—that time may come later. First, Joe needs to overcome his denial of his own vulnerability and discover his associated rage, and this can only happen through a scene in which he finally confronts his father; he may gain some insight into the rage he has held toward his father by the director's helping him to portray his anger in *act fulfillment*. As the protagonist portrays the anger, themes of need and frustration, which are the bases of the anger, should be interwoven.

It is important that the director be aware of the psychotherapeutic maxim, "Don't ventilate the hostility without the protagonist's also experiencing his dependency." That is to say, deal with the protagonist's need for something that is frustrated by the significant other. The catharsis of rage is usually a catharsis of longing (Blatner, 1985a).

For example, as Joe confronts his rigid, demanding father, whose unshakable coldness is dramatized and exaggerated by an auxiliary ego, Joe escalates his efforts to "get across to the old man," without any success. Finally, he is ready for violence; the director throws him a pillow and says, "There's your father — what do you feel like doing to him?" Joe begins to beat the pillow, curse at the father, and, with the help of the double and director, express his pent up frustrations (see Figure 5.12).

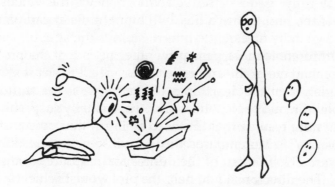

Figure 5.12

JOE: You never cared about me! All you saw was what you
       wanted! (He continues to strike the pillow, and is begin-
       ning to cry.) You bastard! I wish you were dead! (Beats the
       pillow furiously and cries.)

At this point, after a full expression, the director can move in
several directions. He may bring onto the stage an auxiliary to be
the "good father" who can "see Joe for what he really is." The
"reformed" auxiliary may hold Joe and talk to him (Sacks, 1970).

Another very powerful technique is the *death scene*. It can be
applied either to the death of the protagonist himself or as a vehicle to review the feelings in relationship to a significant other person (Siroka & Schloss, 1968). In the first form, the protagonist is
instructed to visualize his own death (the director may dim the
lights). The director might warm up to the situation by asking him
how he died, what it felt like, who is around him, and other related questions. The questions and final statements to others and
(through role reversal) of others toward the "dead" protagonist
help clarify some of the emotional issues (Rowan, 1973). (This
method is useful for emphasizing the role of the choosing, respon-
sible self—the adult ego state, in transactional analysis terms.)
Finally, the death scene can move toward a "rebirth scene."

The death scene may be interwoven with judgment scenes,
judgment of others, or of the self (Sacks, 1965). The encounter with
St. Peter is often a useful technique. (St. Peter is the archetypal fig-

ure guarding the gates of heaven who reviews the values and meaning of the protagonist's life with him.) St. Peter can play the role of the friendly and gentle interrogator. If the situation seems more appropriate for a judgment by other people of the protagonist's life, members of the audience can be called in as jurors.

One variation of the death scene I like to use is the shift in St. Peter's role from judge to philosopher. This usually surprises people, for they are expecting St. Peter to be impressed by status and "righteousness" issues, and upset by pecadilloes. Instead, St. Peter simply asks: "How was it?" He does not respond to answers reflecting the protagonist's status, that is, what the protagonist "proved." Rather, he asks about the protagonist's values and enjoyments: "Did you do what you had to do? Did you do it in your own way? Did you 'create' along the lines of your natural strengths, inclinations; or did you fulfill your life in a role that was alien to your soul, because you were trying to live up to someone else's expectations?" Sometimes I follow this scene by giving the protagonist an opportunity to enact the role he would choose if he could be reborn in any kind of life he wanted.

A second major format of the death scene is more commonly used, and involves the death of the significant other person. With a protagonist who seems involved in continuously struggling to change the other person, to "make him see," the director may stop and say, "He's dead now." or, "You have just received a telegram notifying you of his death. You rush back and stand at his bedside." Another variation is for the director to say to the protagonist, "You have five minutes to talk to him before he dies. Now is the time to make your goodbyes, ask your final questions, express your honest resentments and appreciations." For example:

JOE: (to "dying father") Y'know, Dad, I resented your judgment of me as a child.

DIRECTOR: Reverse roles. (Joe moves over to the empty chair, becoming the father)

JOE: (as father) Well, son, I wanted so much for you, but you've done okay. (Change parts)

JOE: Dad, how do you feel about me now? (Change parts)

FATHER: Joe, I'm kinda proud of you, I really am.

> JOE: Dad, I love you, you know that?
>
> AUXILIARY: (as father) I know, son (Joe weeps.)

Often the son makes his peace with his father in an atonement (at-one-ment). "Saying goodbye" is an important method also for reinforcing the protagonist's sense of identity (Blatner, 1985b; Kaminsky, 1981): "I'm going on. I don't need your support any longer. I can say goodbye. It hurts, but I can let go."

An important principle of healing is that the protagonist, with the help of surplus reality, is enabled to create the desired experience. In the spirit of what the psychoanalyst Franz Alexander called "an emotionally re-educative experience," imaginary scenes function to bring into consciousness the person's needs that have been repressed. The technique of *the reformed auxiliary* (Sacks, 1970) symbolically gratifies that need with the validation of the director and the group. An example of this is a scene in which the auxiliary, having played a rejecting or withholding role in a previous enactment, now is directed to play a more nurturing, positive role (Greenberg-Edelstein, 1986).

Another powerful technique that can sometimes follow a death-and-rebirth scene is the "crib scene." This method is also useful in allowing the protagonist to experience his own dependency needs. The technique is often applied to the entire group, including the protagonist. Doris Twitchell Allen (1966) describes it as follows:

> "Today we can be babies—just young infants in a crib. And we can lie on the floor like babies. Pretend that you are a baby." The director has the group lie on the floor, as if they were babies in a crib. Then the director, in the role of the nurturing mother, walks around from one to the other, patting them and covering them with an imaginary blanket:
> "So the baby goes to sleep, warm and quiet. So the baby gets heavy, and goes to sleep. And the mother comes and loves the baby. Takes care of the baby. Covers the baby and keeps it warm. Feeds the baby and gives it milk. Pats the baby. Watches over the baby and loves the baby. While the baby sleeps and sleeps." (This is usually repeated several times during a 5–20-minute sleep.)
> The sleep period is followed by the waking-up period:

"So the baby begins to wake up. Begins to move a little,
stretches a little. Opens its eyes. Begins to sit up. Feels
good, feels alert, feels happy and content, sits up, gets
up, gets back in the chairs."

This is repeated as often as necessary for the group to
wake up, and finally ending with:

"Now as you sit back in your chairs you are adults again,
acting like adults. But for a while you were a baby and
the mother came and loved the baby and took care of the
baby." (pp.24–25)

Often, in the discussion that follows, a number of group members have been profoundly touched by the opportunity to experience regression within a context of unconditional nurturance.
Other reactions also make for a vigorous sharing.

Of course, the above-mentioned techniques can be applied in a
multiplicity of situations, all depending on the sensitivity of the
director.

Act hunger involves more than the expressions of anger and
dependency: The protagonist can gain important insights through
fulfilling the desire to boast, perform, demand attention, express
tenderness, dance, soar, hug, wrestle playfully, fall effortlessly, and
so forth. Scenes of act completion can involve death and rebirth,
risking and trusting.

Act completion validates the protagonist's emotional experiences, thus reinforcing an integration of the previously rejected
and suppressed dimensions of the personality. As some protagonists remark after a catharsis, "It's OK for me to cry—it doesn't
prove I'm weak," or "Wow, I didn't know I had all that anger in
me—I thought if I would start to let it out I'd never stop, but I
guess I have more self-control than I thought." Thus, the protagonist can accept the anger, dependence, and other negatively valued
emotions as part of himself and can redefine himself as one who,
as a vital living being, contains many different feelings (Blatner,
1985a; Kellerman, 1984).

Act completion further validates the sense of active choosing as
part of the self. There are many people who experience life as happening to them. They take a passive attitude and feel themselves
to be rather lifeless and empty inside. The catharsis that so often

accompanies the psychodramatic process represents an active taking into the conscious self all the different mixed feelings that had heretofore been rejected and suppressed. Along with the feelings of anger and yearning, there is a sense of "determination to go on," which becomes integrated into the progatonist's self-concept and in turn adds a great deal of vitality to the sense of self.

It should further be noted that the excesses of emotion expressed within a psychodramatic enactment are not likely to lead to a complete loss of control. The presence of the director and group and the expectation of staying within limits act as influences to sustain a small amount of "observing ego" and "controlling ego" in the protagonist's personality. It is rare that a protagonist may begin to extend his destructiveness and stop "pulling his punches"; and even then an experienced director can quickly regain control.

SURPLUS REALITY AND ROLE REVERSAL

Following the portrayal of many of the protagonist's fantasies, attitudes, and the fulfillment of act hunger, the protagonist has usually achieved a measure of insight into the nature of his own feelings. To this is now added an exploration of some of the other emotional dimensions of the situation.

For example, the adolescent who has explored some of his own conflicts about taking responsibility (and his externalizations of this conflict onto authority figures) may then portray his future. This is another application of the previously mentioned principle of surplus reality, using the ideas of an alternative or possible existence in which other events occur. In the *future projection* technique, the adolescent can enact his life five years in the future (Yablonsky, 1954). The protagonist may discover that, as George Bernard Shaw once said, "There is only one thing worse than not getting what you want—and that is getting what you want!" Through future projection the protagonist can approach a more realistic viewpoint, and begin to portray scenes in which he can achieve some successes based on his own work.

Figure 5.13

Another major form of utilizing surplus reality is to invite the protagonist to put himself in the place of the others in his life (role reversal). Through reversing roles (or changing parts) with the important figures in his psychodrama, the protagonist can develop some important practical and emotional insights into the others' situations (Figure 5.13). Thus, role reversal becomes a major technique for building the capacity for empathy with others (Kellermann, 1994).

For example, in the psychodrama of Joe, the director may have the protagonist explore some of the others' feelings after his catharsis:

DIRECTOR: Now, be your father.

JOE: (as father) All right, I *admit* I did want you to be a football player, 'cause *I* never had the chance.

DIRECTOR: Change parts.

JOE: (less whining) Well, Dad, that was your dream. I have my own interests——I'm not going to make excuses for myself anymore.

Later, the director may have Joe experience his employer's situation, and in the reversed role position Joe considers the possibility that Mr. Jones is susceptible to pressures from his other subor-

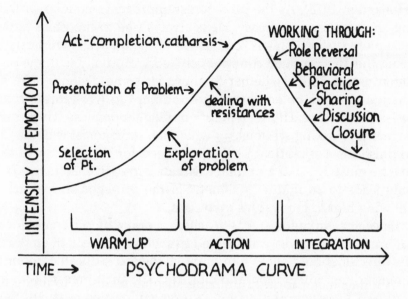

Figure 5.14

dinates, Joe's co-workers:

> JOE: (as Boss) Look, Joe, I really don't like being in this posi-
> tion—

Then Joe can be helped to creatively find some approaches that might support his boss and yet help his own position, a way of self-assertion that might include making tactful constructive suggestions.

In addition to the use of role reversal and surplus reality, the process of integration involves behavioral practice, role training, sharing, discussion, and supportive closure. These dimensions and techniques will be discussed in the next chapter.

THE FLOW OF INTENSITY

Progress through the warm up, the action, and the closure can further be viewed in perspective by following a curve of intensity of involvement and feeling over the time in the session (Fig. 5.14)

(Hollander, 1978). As the protagonist approaches an apex of feeling, the resistances increase. He is always free to choose or refuse to explore further. This is established at the outset. As resistances grow, the director must continuously work mutually with the protagonist and decide whether to allow for some distance, take an alternative route on another day, or attempt to work through the resistances and reach the point of emotional openness. There may be many "working sessions" in which the protagonist is not ready to finish his exploration. There is no need for the director to feel that he must produce a dramatic catharsis in each enactment. This only leads to an undue "pushing" of the protagonist, instead of allowing him to grow at his own pace.

Once the protagonist has reached a point of act completion, catharsis, or otherwise has seemed to achieve his peak of emotion, the director should allow him to move toward reduced emotional intensity (i.e., integration and closure). The protagonist becomes confused by attempting to follow one exploration with another. Usually he has enough energy to deal with only one dimension of his life experience in any one session.

SUMMARY

During the action phase the protagonist is helped toward the gradual portrayal and exploration of the many dimensions of his life. The director generally attends to the protagonist's progress according to the following sequence:

1. Address first peripheral and then central issues.

2. Portray the spectrum of the protagonist's inner realities (for which reason psychodrama is called "the theater of truth").

3. Explicitly present internal attitudes and feelings, and their integration in "action insight."

4. Fulfill act hunger in act completion.

5. Allow a catharsis if it seems natural.

6. Begin exploration of the worlds of the significant others in the protagonist's social network through role reversal.

7. Then begin to develop the integration of whatever insights have been gained, which will be discussed in the next chapter.

REFERENCES / RECOMMENDED READINGS

Allen, D. T. (1966). Psychodrama in the crib. *Group Psychotherapy, 19*(1–2), 23–28.

Blatner, A. (1985a). The dynamics of catharsis. *Journal of Group Psychotherapy, Psychodrama & Sociometry, 37*(4), 157–166.

Blatner, A. (1985b). The principles of grief work. In *Creating your living: Applications of psychodramatic methods in everyday life* (pp. 61–72). San Marcos, TX: Author.

Ellis, A. (1962). *Reason and emotion in psychotherapy.* New York: Lyle Stuart.

Gillett, R. (1992). *Change your mind, change your world: A practical guide.* New York: Fireside.

Goldman, E. E., and Morrison, D. S. (1984). *Psychodrama: Experience and process.* Phoenix, AZ: Eldemar.

Greenberg-Edelstein, R. (1986). *The nurturance phenomenon.* Norwalk, CT: Appleton-Century-Crofts.

Hollander, C. (1978). A *process for psychodrama training: The Hollander psychodrama curve.* Denver, CO: Snow Lion Press.

Kaminsky, R. C. (1981). Saying good-by, an example of using a 'good-by' technique and concomitant psychodrama in the resolving of family grief. *Journal of Group Psychotherapy, Psychodrama, & Sociometry, 34,* 100–111.

Kellerman, P. F. (1984). The place of catharsis in psychodrama. *Journal of Group Psychotherapy, Psychodrama & Sociometry, 37*(1), 1–13.

Kellermann, P.F. (1994). Role reversal in psychodrama. In P. Holmes, M. Karp, & M. Watson (Eds.), *Psychodrama since Moreno: Innovations in theory and practice.* London: Routledge.

Leutz, G. A. (1986.) The psychodramatic treatment of dreams. *Group Analysis. 19,* 139–146.

Lippe, W. A. (1992). Stanislavski's affective memory as a therapeutic tool. *Journal of Group Psychotherapy, Psychodrama & Sociometry, 45*(3), 102–111.

Manaster, G. J., & Corsini, R. J. (1982). *Individual psychology: Theory and practice.* Itasca, IL: F. E. Peacock.

Moreno, J. L. (1965). Therapeutic vehicles and the concept of surplus reality. *Group Psychotherapy, 18,* 211–216.

Naar, R. (1977). A psychodramatic intervention within a TA framework in individuals and group psychotherapy. *Group Psychotherapy, Psychodrama & Sociometry, 30,* 127–134.

Nolte, J., Weistart, J., & Wyatt, J. (1977). The psychodramatic production of dreams. *Group Psychotherapy, Psychodrama & Sociometry, 30,* 37–48.

Parrish, M. (1953). Psychodrama, description of application and reviews of technique. *Group Psychotherapy, 6*(1–2), 74–77.

Perls, F. (1969). *Gestalt therapy verbatim.* Lafayette, CA: Real People Press.

Rowan, P. J., Jr. (1973). Psychodramatic treatment of death fantasies in adolescent girls. *Handbook of International Sociometry, 7,* 94–98.

Sacks, J. M. (1965). The judgment technique in psychodrama. *Group Psychotherapy, 18*(1–2), 69–72.

Sacks, J. M. (1970). The reformed auxiliary ego technique: A psychodramatic rekindling of hope. *Group Psychotherapy, 23,* 118– 126.

Schulman, B. (1960). A psychodramatically oriented action technique in group psychotherapy. *Group Psychotherapy, 13*(1–2), 34–38.

Siroka, R. & Schloss, G. (1968). The death scene in psychodrama. *Group Psychotherapy, 21*(4), 202–205.

Yablonsky, L. (1954). The future-projection technique. *Group Psychotherapy, 7*(3–4), 303–305.

6

Integration: Behavioral Practice, Sharing, and Closing

Following the warm-up and action portions, the third and last phase of psychodramatic enactment is the time for integration. (In previous editions, this phase was called *working-through*, relating it to a psychoanalytic term which refers to similar dynamics.) It is not enough to become aware of one's previously disowned feelings, misunderstandings or denied attitudes which emerge with the catharsis of abreaction; one must further discover some hope that there are ways for effectively dealing with life's challenges. The restoration of morale implicit in this task is called the *catharsis of integration*. Integration includes (a) developing some sense of mastery over the problem, (b) receiving group support and (c) preparing to re-engage the realistic challenges of the outside world.

For some enactments, the major task is discovering and practicing an effective behavioral response to problematic situations such as asking for a raise, ensuring a more pleasant relationship with parents during a forthcoming holiday visit, or renegotiating a relationship with a demanding friend.

In more therapeutically oriented psychodramas the goal is to help the protagonist achieve some insight regarding the nonrational feelings which affect his decisions. The kinds of deeper explorations described in the previous chapter, including ventilation, association, and catharsis, are often essential in this kind of work. However, in settings which are not congenial to personal self-disclosure, such as at school or work, psychodramatic meth-

ods modified to role playing can be most helpful, with goals limited to better understanding of the issues and thinking about more
practical alternatives. Such forms of role training or sociodramatic
role playing don't require the protagonist's exposing the particulars of personal life. Indeed, directors in many settings need to
actively work to help the protagonists from allowing the spontaneity of the moment to render them vulnerable to shame or
blame. But, returning to therapy, forms of *behavioral practice* often
have a place in the course of comprehensive treatment.

It is only partly true that once insight has been achieved then
creative energies are released sufficient to resolve problems. Shifts
in identity do offer new impetus to trying things a new way, but
there's still a considerable challenge in then exploring and consol-
idating those new strategies. So directors need to include in the
organization of their work, as suggested by the structure of the
psychodramatic spiral, opportunities to implement what has been
learned.

BEHAVIORAL PRACTICE

The function of behavioral practice is to experiment with a variety
of new behaviors. A "fail-safe" context, feedback regarding the
effectiveness of the trial behaviors, and opportunities for repeated
attempts until some degree of satisfaction is achieved are three
essential conditions to the protagonist's working through of his
problem. The behavioral practice may or may not be associated
with a deeper level of emotional exploration (Flowers & Booraem,
1980).

The first step in behavioral practice sets up an enactment in the
same way as described in the warm-up and the first part of the
chapter on action. Once the protagonist and auxiliaries are
involved in the scene and the situation is presented, the director's
job is to help the protagonist get constructive feedback about his
performance.

Instead of immediately turning to the audience for criticism and
suggestions, which may be experienced as reproach by a protagonist who already feels "on the spot" in risking some exposure of

his inadequacy, it's best for the director to imply that the protagonist is capable of creativity given a little chance to explore with some new "tools."

The first tool is the technique of *replay*. This is nothing more than the opportunity to try again, the essential component of practice and rehearsal in almost any skill. Furthermore, after enacting the problem, the spontaneity of the process often generates new ideas. The protagonist may well have some idea about what wasn't working well and how it might be played better. The director simply says, "Okay, try it again." Sometimes the opportunity to rehearse is sufficient—and it's not something most people get a chance to do often enough in life.

If the protagonist is uncertain how a behavioral response is less than optimal, before getting outside feedback, let him try the technique of *role reversal*. The protagonist plays the scene in the role of the other person while the auxiliary shifts places and enacts the scene in the same way the protagonist had performed the role. Of course, this allows the protagonist to experience what it's like to be "on the receiving end" of his previous approach. If he's gotten some new ideas from this, he's allowed to go back to phase one and try again.

If role reversal doesn't illuminate the problem, and the protagonist still feels unclear regarding what isn't working well in the interaction, the director tries the *mirror* technique. The director removes the protagonist from the scene and another auxiliary comes in and plays his part. It's as if he's able to watch a video playback of the situation without needing all the actual technology and its constraints. From this outside, slightly more objective, viewpoint (standing with the director, or sometimes sent off to some more distant position in the room), the protagonist may get clues about nonverbal style, context, or some other variable which had been previously overlooked.

It's important to instruct the auxiliary who is playing the protagonist's role in the scene not to overact or caricaturize the protagonist. The director must work to create an atmosphere of respect for the realistic nature of the challenge, and support for the courage to take part in the self-critical process of finding a better way of dealing with it. This is the scientific process, I sometimes say, and in other ways keep a patter going that maintains a balance of slight playfulness and sustained respect for the protagonist.

I also use group feedback to ensure that the auxiliary who is mirroring the protagonist's behavior is fairly accurate. Sometimes the auxiliary will not have picked up the essential element in why an interaction isn't successful, or, on the other hand, may exaggerate it. So the director should ask, "Has the auxiliary played it correctly?" If the group feels that the auxiliary is inaccurate, he or she is either given another chance to replay the scene and correct the behavior, or someone else can reenact the scene. When the protagonist indicates that he has some idea of how else he might behave, sometimes involving only a rather subtle change in nonverbal style, again he replays the scene.

Is there uncertainty about the range of possible behavioral responses? Try the technique of *the worst way to do it*. This should be introduced in a somewhat playful way. I often use the metaphor of computer program menus: There are many different alternatives, and sometimes just seeing everything on the menu can be a source of ideas. So the scene is played in a way that would be totally ridiculous or sure to backfire. Still, what sometimes happens is that a certain role component gets energized which might not have been operational previously. On occasion the protagonist simply acts twice as assertive, expecting catastrophe, and the group replies, "Now you're getting close!"

A variation of this is the technique of *not me*. The protagonist is instructed to play the scene in a fashion entirely different from his own typical style. Of course, we're subliminally suggesting an activity of role expansion, akin to George Kelly's (1955) "personal construct therapy." The protagonist may then decide himself or be coached to play the scene in a manner that is silly, brutally frank, very cautious and indirect, or confrontational. Experimenting with these artificial manners gives the protagonist freedom to take a risk (because he was told to act that way) and to perhaps find that there are aspects of his new behavior that he might wish to integrate into his own style. For example, in a group setting, two of the participants in a nonverbal exercise interacted in a very constricted fashion. After some discussion, the two people were asked to repeat the exercise in a way in which they would never behave in their everyday lives. They proceeded to interact in a silly, awkward, rough-and-tumble manner. Afterwards, they reported feeling foolish, but admitted that they enjoyed themselves tremendously. To their surprise, the group reinforced their risk taking by responding that they were delighted with the two persons' spontaneity.

In some situations, direct *coaching* is sometimes indicated. After developing a sense of trust and alliance with her protagonist, the director then can act as a theatrical director, suggesting specific behaviors—a slightly raised voice, a more direct eye contact, less of a smile, or some change in the phrasing of a sentence. Musical conductors during rehearsal often coach the players in an orchestra this way, also.

This technique also has the benefit of introducing the group to the power of nonverbal communications, and becomes an educational process for everyone. For example, the director might coach the protagonist, "Try asserting yourself while you stand with your pelvis tilted forward and your jaw thrust out"; or, "Answer your mother with the palms of your hands facing downwards instead of turned upwards in a pleading gesture." Attending to nonverbal behavior is important not only because it significantly alters the quality of the interpersonal communications, but shifts in posture or expression also serve as internal cues which reinforce emotional and cognitive attitudes (Walters, 1984).

If the protagonist still feels stumped, then we use the technique of *modeling*, having someone else show how he or she would handle the situation. Another person takes on what had been the protagonist's role in the scene while the protagonist and director stand to the side and observe. Sometimes I have several group members show their own variations. This practice neutralizes the idea that there is only one "correct" way to play the scene and invites the protagonist to pick and choose elements from several of the approaches demonstrated. Again, the emphasis is on supporting the creativity of the protagonist.

The other value of this technique is that instead of group members offering suggestions verbally—which might feel to the protagonist like uninformed advice mixed with a tone of reproach, they prove their good will by taking on the stress of enactment, entering the scene and struggling with the problem itself. The idea is to maintain an optimal degree of group cohesion, sharing the problem rather than implying that one person is foolish for not knowing "the answer."

When the protagonist is again allowed to replay the scene with some new understandings and variations, the director should also emphasize the need for individualizing the response. One person's style may be impossible for another person to emulate because of differences in temperament. Talking about helping the protagonist finding a style that feels right for his own temperament is another way of offering support and respect.

It should be emphasized again that in psychodramatic enactments in which the protagonist's self-understanding is the major task, it is best to deal with issues of working through and behavioral practice only after the protagonist has first fully ventilated and has explored the meaning of his emotions. Moreno notes: "Enactment comes first, retraining comes later. We must give [the protagonist] the satisfaction of act completion first, before considering retraining for behavioral changes."

APPLICATIONS OF BEHAVIORAL PRACTICE

Psychodramatic methods are often applied in many contexts, and one of the most common of these is the general area of skills training. Ironically, these active techniques have been incorporated into a behavioral psychology framework and, judging by most of the literature, few professionals know that these methods arose from psychodrama! (Aside from the virtues of knowing the history of one's profession, greater knowledge should lead to integration of more of the other techniques and principles of psychodrama.)

In psychodrama as well as in many other areas of psychotherapy, one of the more common themes has been that of *assertion training*. For many people, inhibition of assertiveness serves in a feedback process to reinforce victimization. Learning how to feel more empowered is not generally taught in school, and assertion training since the late 1960s has become a major area of behavior therapy in clinical psychology: How should one stand up to a dominating friend or resist peer pressures? How can one say "no" to a persistent salesman? How does one ask for a date? What is the best way to speak up at a meeting? (Powell, 1985). These methods can be used to help shy, constricted people become more forceful, which in turn develops their self-esteem.

Another common theme is a variation of assertion training: *affect modulation*. Many people don't know how to negotiate or present their needs without escalating to an excess of emotionality. Some enjoy the illusion of power that comes with this, while others feel they've "lost control" and become guilt-ridden. Disappointment, rejection, sentimentality, and other emotions can be habitually overdone, and more modulated alternatives can be practiced. In psychodrama, this behavioristic approach can be integrated with attitudinal shifts, and cognitive therapy or rational-emotive therapy techniques may be helpful aspects of this process. In this way, psychodramatic methods can help those who are histrionic or overly dramatic personalities to be less dramatic and instead develop more matter-of-fact and appropriate styles of relating.

A variation of this is the use of psychodramatic scenes as intermediate techniques in *desensitizing* people to fears. Between very imaginative relaxation processes, such as Wolpe's (1958) technique of "reciprocal inhibition," and actual in vivo exposure—going on that airplane or out into the mall—, one can also use role playing techniques. Simply rehearsing an inevitable confrontation is most helpful in reducing anxiety regarding situations such as "coming out" to parents regarding one's homosexuality, telling a parent that one is pregnant, asking a certain person for a date, or saying "no" to a manipulative child or friend.

One of the earliest applications of psychodrama was in the focused form called *role training*. This approach, now often called *skills training*, has been applied especially in helping chronically institutionalized psychiatric patients prepare for leaving the hospital by practicing situations of seeking employment, returning home, and even simple tasks such as opening a bank account or going on an airplane. Parents-to-be can practice simulated bathing of the baby; a teenager who has recently had a colostomy can prepare for embarrassing questions from schoolmates; parents can

explore different approaches to the management of behavior problems in their children (Sprafkin, Gershaw, & Goldstein, 1993).

A variant of applied behavioral practice is *spontaneity training*,
helping people to become more spontaneous and to rediscover
their capacity for playfulness and imaginativeness. Sometimes I
will help a protagonist integrate the previously disowned "inner
child" by fostering a context in which he can give himself permission to be playful, perhaps using some techniques derived from a
synthesis of creative drama and sociodrama (Blatner & Blatner,
1988).

Behavioral experimentation is also facilitated by taking a role of
a fictional or mythical figure. This technique can sometimes provide enough role distance so that certain behaviors which might
not be part of one's everyday role repertoire—such as the triumph
and swagger of the hero, the wickedness of the caricaturized villain, the innocence of a newborn baby, or the seductiveness of a
temptress—may be tried.

Finally, behavioral practice can be used outside of therapy, not
just for helping fairly unskilled people develop some degree of
competence, but even for *professional skills training*, for helping
those who are well educated to develop more highly refined interpersonal skills. Medical or mental health professionals can be
helped to acquire skills in interviewing, history taking, counseling,
or giving support through the method of role playing: What
should one say to a dying patient? How does one ask about sexual issues in interviewing? What is the best response to an irritated
or dissatisfied customer? Some references regarding this are noted
at the end of Chapter 8.

Thus behavioral practice in its many forms can serve as an
invaluable aid in working through a problem. Trial behaviors are
explored in a fail-safe context, and support and reinforcements are
given to more appropriate responses.

SHARING

Once the protagonist has finished his enactment, he is in the
process of becoming gradually more reflective, less warmed- up,

and is ready to receive some feedback. In the enactment, his physical involvement and spontaneity have rendered him very vulnerable to the judgments of the others in the group—much more vulnerable than if he had used only his verbal defenses in a narrative form. Instead of permitting a potentially humiliating "analysis," the director uses the psychodramatic technique of *sharing*. In sharing, the director seeks feedback that puts a premium on support and on the self-disclosure of the group members (Barbour, 1972, 1977; Pitzele, 1980).

The director and the protagonist sit down together to begin the interaction with the group. I often leave an empty chair next to the protagonist so that if someone in the group wants to come forward to share on a more personal, one-to-one level in front of the group, it is possible to do so. The spontaneous feelings of closeness or the intuitive sense of the protagonist's needs determine how close people are to sit and whether body touching is appropriate.

Psychodramas that have produced a catharsis or a portrayal of a very moving situation sometimes close with hugging and shared crying among the group members and the protagonist. Other enactments in which the protagonist has made a "breakthrough" using the media of playfulness may close with triumphal activity. The primary guidelines for the director are based on the genuine feelings of the people involved, rather than the applications of any superficial technique.

I discourage the ritualistic practice of applause after a psychodramatic enactment: I think it cheapens the whole process. (This is to be differentiated from an allowable spontaneous burst of joyous applause when something happens during an enactment that evokes the group's enthusiasm.) Once the protagonist is seated, the director explains sharing to the group:

> "Now is the time for sharing. The protagonist [use his name, e.g., "Joe"] has shared with you a very personal part of his life; he has left himself vulnerable to your comments. Rather than give an 'analysis,' it would be more appropriate for us to respond authentically and subjectively. How has Joe's drama touched each of you? What have you experienced that relates to Joe's situation?"

Figure 6.1

At this point, several people usually express past or present conflicts in their own lives and share the mixed feelings that they too have felt (Figure 6.1). The auxiliaries may also be invited to share the reactions they experienced in role as the protagonist's father, employer, spouse, or other auxiliary part as well as their own real life feelings.

Some group members tend to express opinions rather than sharing personal associations, for example, "I felt you were being really passive with your father and that this is probably due to your relationship with your mother." (Just because a sentence begins with "I feel" doesn't mean it is indeed a genuine feeling—it may nevertheless be a disguised opinion, a pseudo-interpretation.) The director should abruptly intervene and reiterate the instructions about sharing: "This is not the time to talk about Joe's problem. How has his story touched *your* life?" If others try to talk about their own feelings, but because of defensive habit, continue to say, "You feel..." or "You want..." the director may gently remind them to take responsibility for their own statements: "You mean, 'I feel'" Usually group members will respond quickly and proceed talking about their own experiences in the first person.

If no one in the group initiates the sharing, it could be due to several causes: (a) the group is not warmed-up enough, (b) group cohesion is still weak and members are afraid to disclose themselves, (c) the protagonist's enactment was too abstract or the situation too foreign to the group, (d) the protagonist's position was very different from group norms or values, or (e) the group is angry with the protagonist or director. Each situation must be dealt with creatively by the director.

At least a minute of waiting for sharing to begin may be appropriate. In some more reticent cultures, it often takes a while before someone "breaks the ice." When I worked with a Japanese group, there seemed to be a rather awkward moment before the sharing began, but once it started, sharing was extensive and moving— and I learned that, perhaps because of the acculturation towards social sensitivity, this phase for them was particularly important and a good deal of time needed to be allocated to allow it to flow most spontaneously to its own conclusion.

One approach to resistance in the group's sharing is for the director to simply repeat that the protagonist has given each of them a "gift," and that it would be unfair for the group not to share in return. In another approach, the director says, "Look around at the group... look at their eyes ...they are telling you their feelings." Or, she can ask the protagonist, "Who do you think is touched by your story?"

Sometimes the group may have a need to share not only with the protagonist, but also with the role played by one of the auxiliary egos—such as the protagonist's father: "I really understood what you had to go through, Mr. Smith, because I, too, have a son like Joe (the protagonist), and I felt the same way..." The director asks the group to share with the significant other person in the protagonist's life after the group shares with the protagonist. This technique can keep the end of the session in action and may allow for a more complete closure.

Most of the time, sharing proceeds smoothly. Often the sharing by one of the other group members may lead directly into another psychodrama. For example, a member might share, weeping, "My mother never understood me either; and I rejected her ...and now she's dead!" The group member who shared now becomes the protagonist and is helped to enter his own enactment (he is already warmed up!). Indeed, a long session may have several psychodramas, each triggered by the other.

It is very important to both group members and the protagonist that at least 15 minutes or more be allotted for sharing. Not only does this provide mutual support, but misunderstandings that may have arisen during the session can then be clarified through the opportunity for questions and feedback.I made a mistake early in my work in connection with this issue. In a role-playing session with nursery school teachers, the problem arose as to how to set up a conference with the resistant mother of an aggressive child. Several teachers in turn took the role of the one who was trying to coax, cajole, or firmly instruct the "mother" (played by one of the group members) to make an appointment. Finally, one of the teachers, Mary, risked being "too hard" and set down an ultimatum: "Either you come in by a specified date or your child must leave the school." The teacher playing the mother became furious, and vigorously tongue-lashed Mary for this "unreasonable" position. The group broke into a burst of spontaneous applause. After the role playing was over, there was no time left for sharing.

In the next session, a week later, Mary reported having experienced anxiety during the interval: She felt the group rejected her because of her stand. She felt that the group's applause at the angry response of the other teacher (as mother) was evidence of rejection. The group was surprised, and vociferously reassured Mary that the applause was not against her; indeed, they felt her stance was most effective. The applause was for the other teacher's burst of spontaneous, "angry" emotion! The group did not agree with the "mother," but they were delighted with the other teacher's open expression of affect—so hungry were they for some active, emotional interchange. Although Mary was pleased to receive this reassurance, she had still undergone a week of unnecessary worry. As director, I should have paced myself so that the sharing and feedback occurred right after the enactment.

Thus, the sharing period provides an opportunity for all of the participants in a psychodrama to ventilate their feelings. The group members need this as much as the protagonist does. The catharsis in the drama may then spread, be reexperienced, and subside as the group realizes its common bond of human feelings.

CLOSING-

At the end of a group session, the director may wish to finish with a variety of approaches. The length of the session, the degree of cohesion and self-disclosure achieved, and the task of the group are all variables to be considered. Often a period of discussion may follow the sharing, which could lead to a further winding down of the level of tension. Some of the components of closing to be considered include the following:

- *"Reentry."* How will the group members adapt what they have learned to their everyday lives? This is especially important after long or otherwise intensive sessions.

- *Summarizing.* In more task-oriented groups, where personal involvement has been limited, a summary of what has gone on and discussion of implications and plans may be in order.

- *Planning the next session.* In ongoing therapy groups, future agendas may be discussed. Perhaps one of the group specifically volunteers to be a protagonist, or a certain theme is agreed upon.

- *Support.* If one protagonist has become particularly vulnerable due to his participation and risk taking in an enactment or confrontation, and the director feels he may need some additional support, she may wish to use a specific ego-building technique. (For example, all of the members in the group tell the protagonist something they like about him.)

- *Unfinished business.* There may yet be a sense of unspoken feelings between group members (including the director). One technique is called *resentments and appreciations:* "Before we close, we can ventilate any unfinished business. It's not always necessary to work these things out, but it's important that the unspoken feelings be expressed openly before we end." The group is drawn into a circle. "You may want to share directly the resentments and/or appreciations you feel for each other. Now is the time to do so." Then the group members speak up as they feel the need: "Nancy, I resent the

way you judged me"; "Bill, I appreciate your support, and
resent your pity"; and so forth. Ideally, this should be
reserved for ongoing groups in which there will be opportunities to follow up on the issues raised using this technique.

- *Closing rituals.* There are a variety of closing techniques such
  as simply holding hands in a circle, or leading the group in
  a guided fantasy. (Weiner & Sacks, 1969).

- *Separation.* The degree of intimacy in groups that have had
  much emotional exchange is often such a new experience to
  the group members that they resist breaking the group cohesion. Ritualizing the separation experience can often be useful. For examaple, a group may form a close circle and each
  person looks at the others and says "goodbye" to every other
  person in the group. (It is not necessary to do this one at a
  time; all can do it simultaneously.) Further techniques are
  discussed by Treadwell, Stein & Kumar (1990).

SUMMARY

This chapter has discussed the activities of the third and last phase
of the psychodramatic enactment, integration. The working
through of the problem using behavioral practice may either be a
way of following up an insight gained in the preceding enactment
or may itself dominate the session. Following the integrative
enactment, the director moves into the sharing phase, and finally
closes, using a variety of techniques.

REFERENCES / RECOMMENDED READINGS

Barbour, A. (1972). The self disclosure aspect of the psychodrama sharing session.
    Group Psychotherapy and Psychodrama, 25, 132– 138.

Barbour, A. (1977). Variations on psychodramatic sharing. *Group Psychotherapy,
    Psychodrama & Sociometry, 30,* 122–126.

Blatner, A., & Blatner, A. (1988). *The art of play: An adult's guide to reclaiming imag-
    ination and spontaneity.* New York: Human Sciences Press.

Feinberg, H. (1959). The ego building technique. *Group Psychotherapy 12*(3–4), 230–235.

Flowers, J. V. & Booraem, C. D. (1980). Simulation and role playing methods. In F. H. Kanfer & A. P. Goldstein, *Helping people change: A textbook of methods* (2nd ed.). Elmsford, NY: Pergamon.

Goldfield, M. (1968). Use of TV videotape to enhance the value of psychodrama. *American Journal of Psychiatry, 125*(5), 690–692.

Kellerman, P. F. (1988). Closure in psychodrama. *Journal of Group Psychotherapy, Psychodrama & Sociometry, 41*(1), 21–29.

Kelly, G. A. (1955). *Psychology of personal constructs.* New York: Norton.

Pitzele, M. S. (1980). Moreno's chorus: The audience in psychodrama. *Group Psychotherapy, Psychodrama & Sociometry, 33*, 139–141.

Powell, M. F. (1985). A program of life-skills training through interdisciplinary group processes. *Journal of Group Psychotherapy, Psychodrama & Sociometry, 38*(1), 23–34.

Sprafkin, R. P., Gershaw, N. J., & Goldstein, A. P. (1993). *Social skills for mental health: A structured learning approach.* Boston: Allyn & Bacon.

Speros, T. (1972). The final empty chair. *Group Psychotherapy, 25*(1–2), 32–33.

Sturm, I. E. (1965). The behavioristic aspects of psychodrama. *Group Psychotherapy, 18*(1–2), 50–64.

Treadwell, T. W., Stein, S., & Kumar V. K. (1990). A survey of psychodramatic action and closure techniques. *Journal of Group Psychotherapy, Psychodrama & Sociometry, 43*(3), 102–115.

Walters, R. P. (1984). Nonverbal communication in group counseling. In G. M. Gazda (Ed.), *Group counseling: A developmental approach* (pp 203–233). Boston: Allyn & Bacon.

Weiner, H. & Sacks, J. M. (1969). Warm-up and sum-up. *Group Psychotherapy, 22*(1–2), 85–102.

Wolpe, J. (1958). *Psychotherapy by reciprocal inhibition.* Stanford, CA: Stanford University Press.

7

Principles and Pitfalls

Psychodrama is a powerful methodology, and it can be misused. In other chapters I have likened it to surgery or the use of electric power tools in carpentry, and one of the implications of the latter metaphor is that knowledge of the craft must be greater than merely knowing how to use the tools. Even the best tools cannot substitute for basic good judgment. Judgment must be applied not only to the achievement of the task, but also to the safety of all concerned, which requires also a recognition that if used carelessly, the tools themselves can be dangerous.

Moreno (1957) was aware of the ethical aspects of leading psychodrama and promulgated one of the first codes of ethics for group therapists. Psychodramatists, whether they engage in therapy or work in a non-clinical context, must become increasingly alert to the problems of clarity, boundaries, and ethics in their professional roles. Our culture has begun to critique a wider range of authority roles, and even the role of physician and healer has been shown to be capable of corruption under the guise of benign intention. Distortions of the helping relationship arise both from clients who may unrealistically idealize their helpers and from helpers who may deceive themselves about the nature of their own expertise.

This is why the use of psychodramatic methods, particularly "classical" psychodrama, requires a fair amount of training. Yet on the whole, the process can be made fairly safe if two general categories of principles are maintained: (a) the humility of the director; and (b) the promotion of mutuality with the protagonist and the group. But it is not enough to merely affirm ideals; in the spirit of Moreno's commitment to methodology, these two general principles may be operationalized through the use of a number of specific techniques.

110

HUMILITY

An operational definition of humility is keeping in mind the possibility—nay, the inevitability—of being wrong some of the time. So instead of being defensive, the psychodramatist remains vigilant against her own errors.

One barrier to this healthy attitude—an attitude held by the most successful executives—is a director or therapist's expectation of knowing everything important about the protagonist or client. In fact, this is virtually impossible. It reflects a mechanistic model, more appropriate for dealing with simple systems. But humans are highly complex, operating at many levels, and shifting in their minds among many different frames of reference. Thus, working with people requires a "systems-oriented" model in which the actions of the helper are guided by the reactions of the individual receiving help in an ongoing fashion.

Thus the director must become comfortable with a state of ambiguity, and be quite open and willing to accept suggestions. For example, in the course of directing a drama the director might turn to the group and ask, "Does this seem to be the right direction?" or "Might I be missing something here?" An evident comfort in asking for help creates a model of confidence in a method while relinquishing any arrogant attachment to a particular hypothesis. The psychodramatic method is based, after all, on experimenting with ways to facilitate the natural act hunger of the protagonist. The director then abandons the illusion of being right, and instead affirms with humility what Dreikurs called "the courage to be imperfect" (Terner & Pew, 1978).

The director can afford to be humble while serving a methodology which relies not so much on the cleverness of the director but rather on the creativity of the protagonist. In allowing all parts of this system to communicate among themselves, wisdom tends to follow. The variety of dramatic devices, possible scenes, and alternative techniques is rich enough to offer some kind of help to even the most blocked protagonist.

As mentioned in the section on dealing with resistances in the chapter on action (Chapter 5), the director need not become overly forceful in attempting to generate a breakthrough. Do not be deceived by the suffix "drama" in the name of this method: Psychodrama can be gentle, subtle, and seemingly nondramatic, in the sense of lacking in histrionics. While there are clients and situations which certainly benefit from a profound emotional catharsis, in other situations the appropriate enactments may call for toning down emotionality and encouragement of a more matter-of-fact manner.

MUTUALITY

The principle of mutuality is an implementation of the more basic principle of humility and refers to the idea that the director must be guided by feedback from the protagonist. When the director makes a suggestion that the protagonist feels is unhelpful, the protagonist must be free to express his feeling, and must know that the director will openly listen to the objection and be willing to change. The idea that the therapist knows what's best for the client must be challenged, because work within highly complex systems requires an ongoing interactive process—and the human mind is indeed highly complex. Because each individual has a unique set of abilities, temperament, past experiences and goals, help must be *individualized.* Furthermore, these variables change, sometimes moment to moment. The director must explicitly build into the psychodramatic and group process ways not only to work with the problem, but also ways to work with the helper. Because there are so many variables of individuality, helpers can never know exactly how to be most effective; the person being helped must learn first of all to give ongoing feedback to the helper regarding timing, the type of help, even the choice of words.

The first technique, then, of mutuality is role training the protagonist to correct not only the role playing of auxiliaries, but also to correct the coaching of the director! With clients who are overly deferential, I sometimes make this a playful process, caricaturing an erroneous behavior of a rather innocuous sort, and having the protagonist practice correcting me in front of the group. In turn, I reinforce this assertive behavior by responding appreciatively. (People are not merely afraid of the group leader, they are also protective of and afraid *for* the group leader, lest the leader be "hurt" by the group's challenges.) The protagonist and the group then see that the director won't become defensive, manipulative, or belligerent, but rather is comfortable with a clear, courteous, yet firm feedback process.

As the psychodrama continues, the director can periodically pause and ask group members to assess the process, while maintaining a balance between humility and confidence. An excessively deferential or hesitant manner can be as off-putting as an arrogant attitude.

A third technique is to make explicit the issue of therapist-client power. For example, the director may comment on the group norms in her introductory remarks:

> "During this group session, each of you will be responsible for choosing your own directions. You may proceed at your own pace. You will benefit from these sessions in direct proportion to your own active participation and the extent to which you are willing to take some risks. My role is to help you clarify your goals and feelings. I can show you some methods which you may find helpful in redefining your experiences more creatively. More importantly, in this group I will attempt to develop an atmosphere in which you will feel ready to explore."

Group procedures are emotionally loaded, capable of shaming and frightening participants, whether they are in the context of psychotherapy, education, team building or personal growth. They have a potential for "second wounding" patients who have been hurt or traumatized, or who have felt overwhelmed or discounted in earlier experiences with groups or so-called helpers. The emergence of an increased awareness regarding the prevalence of the dynamics of abuse, addiction, and the capacity for allowing abuse to happen all require an increased level of meticulousness in keeping patients and groups empowered.

Many of these principles apply to anyone who moves into an authoritative or helping role, whether or not psychodramatic methods are being used. I find most therapeutic problems arise not from a misuse of a technique, but rather from forgetting (or not understanding) the deeper principles of group leadership.

A fourth and related technique for promoting a more conscious approach to the helping situation is for the director to explicitly comment on the issues of authority versus authoritarianism and the irrational elements attending this "power gradient." The audience can be invited to actively support each other in challenging the director regarding even the slightest breach of full respect and mutual interchange.

A fifth technique for a director to maintain an optimal degree of mutuality in the helping relationship is to pause at intervals and explain the rationale for how one is proceeding. Then the director reengages the protagonist and/or the group, reaffirming or adjusting the implicit contract regarding what shall be addressed and how the process will be pursued. (This emphasis on the "contract" was a major contribution of Eric Berne, the inventor of Transactional Analysis.) An objection to this technique is that it would break the flow or momentum of the action. Certain phases of the process do need to unfold spontaneously. But breaking out of the slightly entrancing process, becoming regrounded, and questioning the proceedings might, at other times, be both spontaneous and appropriate. The point is to optimize the empowerment of the clients by developing their capacity to reflect on the helping process as well as their own issues.

ACTION versus AWKWARDNESS

Although the director of a psychodramatic enactment should generally strive to keep the action going, she must nevertheless avoid the pitfall of trying too hard to attain what seems like technical virtuosity. Allowing for some awkwardness at times is preferable to attempts at cleverness. While a truly polished enactment can result from the use of scripts and rehearsals, there tends to be a corresponding loss of spontaneity, the vitality of which is essential to much of the effectiveness of psychodrama. Spontaneity can really flow with remarkable smoothness at times, but it can easily shift into moments of awkwardness (Z. Moreno, 1969, p. 236).

Awkward occasions serve to shift the protagonist into the meta-role of the co-investigator. I sometimes use those moments of becoming blocked to act as if I were a scientist in a laboratory: "Hmm, let's see what we have going on here." This shift in role can be used to clarify the contract, affirm the treatment alliance, get reassurance from the group, and reflect on what has transpired so far. Openness to breaks in the flow also model the director's comfort with the basic method rather than promote the illusion that a magic spell must be maintained.

One aspect of both humility and mutuality is a determination to demystify the process, and thereby reduce the mystique of the director. There is sufficient power and novelty in psychodrama itself that no further efforts are needed to increase the authority of the group leader. If anything efforts should be made at reducing the charisma of the director and returning the power to the protagonist and the group.

One can be humble with an aura of gentle confidence. Too much deference, as mentioned, is distracting. People begin to feel sorry for the director and by extension, they begin to question the value of the method itself. So the director need not be self-consciously hesitant with statements such as, "Why don't you..," "How would you feel about ..," or "Would you like to...." It is better to be gently positive. Once the freedom to say "no" has been clearly established, the director can speak with assurance: "Okay, be your father..," "Now, show us..." "In this next scene we'll..," or "Change parts."

Another ethical principle states that the leader remind protagonists and groups that the procedure is at all times voluntary because creativity requires spontaneity and spontaneity requires freedom. The freedom to say "yes" is predicated on the freedom to say "no." So if protagonists indicate that they feel "finished" in the course of an exploration, or if someone is reluctant to enter the protagonist role, this preference must be honored. Any coercive or manipulative behavior on the director's part, or even manipulations of the group that are permitted by the director will result in a loss of trust in the group (Sandron, 1973).

PATHOLOGICAL SPONTANEITY

The principle of spontaneity can also be misused. It must be differentiated from mere impulsivity (Blatner, 1988.) Group leaders often deal with countertransference reactions to a protagonist by getting angry at him, and then rationalize this behavior by calling it "being authentic," "modeling anger," "confrontation," or "feedback." Exhibiting any and all impulses is not the purpose of developing spontaneity. When grossly misused, this kind of expressiveness could be called *pathological spontaneity.*

The attacking behavior described above sometimes represents a form of acting-out of the director's own countertransference (i.e., the therapist's emotional reaction to her patient). Another form of countertransference behavior is the inappropriate use of undue physical contact, sexual advances, or sarcasm. The motivating forces for these types of behavior are manifold, and the director is cautioned to continuously assess her own behavior to prevent this most prevalent pitfall for all those in the helping role (Shaffer, 1995).

One of the most common sources of pathological spontaneity arises from the director's need to prove that she is professionally competent by obtaining "results." She thus becomes impatient with the reality that personal growth is a very gradual process, fraught with resistances, defenses, and flagging motivation. If the director feels personally threatened, whether consciously or unconsciously, by her protagonist's slow progress or reactions, she is likely to engage in a variety of maneuvers: subtly provoking guilt, generally barraging the protagonist with words in an effort to get a point across, and other confrontations. If the director is not aware of her counter transference reactions, she may fall into the major error of pushing and coercing her clients, or allowing other group members to act out her own needs (Kane, 1992). Coercion accounts for most of the worst abuses that occur in therapeutic groups and similar settings. A less obvious abuse occurs through a leader's passivity. It is not helpful for a group leader to indulge in excessively nondirective behavior. Important countertransference issues are apparent in this leadership stance also. Many of these reactions happen to even the most experienced therapists, but one must learn to watch out for them and not inflict them on the group.

REGARDING CONFRONTATION

Psychodrama draws on three sources of healing: The clients' own act hunger, the support of the group, and the novelty and creative insights offered by the use of the psychodramatic methods themselves. However, clients can become too impatient and even masochistic in order to achieve a fantasized breakthrough. A group can unconsciously collude in a desire for a quick and dramatic catharsis and push too hard. With the goal overshadowing the process, the methods can be applied insistently without a full respect for the natural flow of learning.

It is essential to trust the method, and to beware of feeling a need to "jump in" with clever interpretations and confrontations. Instead, warm-up techniques should be aimed at establishing a norm of mutual trust and respect. An approach that suggests a confrontational attitude only tends to increase the defensiveness of everyone in the group.

Not only should the director avoid confrontational attacks, but she should also limit the tendency of group members to subtly attack each other. The practice of giving feedback when it is not asked for is often a form of externalization or projection on the part of the person making the interpretation. The director may identify the source of such thinly veiled attacks by gently saying to the speaker, "You seem genuinely concerned about X's behavior. Would you care to explore what it is about his behavior that affects you so deeply?"

PROFESSIONAL CONSIDERATIONS

The director should be aware of the problems in leading different kinds of groups, so becoming well grounded in the principles of group psychotherapy is important. The principles of working with hospitalized psychiatric patients are quite different from those involved in leading a personal development group for relatively healthy clients. The following issues are only some of the challenges that should be carefully considered by any group leader:

Selection

The director should be aware of the problems inherent in including people who have certain types of problems in a group. These refer not so much to diagnostic categories so much as issues such as psychological-mindedness, voluntariness, ego strength, and access to socioeconomic resources. Voluntariness involves the degrees to which the prospective group member really wants to engage in the types of self-reflection that therapeutic or personal growth-oriented groups require. If people feel pressured to attend to satisfy family members or the criminal justice system, their role is undermined by a sense of having been coerced. Psychological mindedness refers to the degree to which people are able to reflect on the workings of their own mind. It involves the awareness of the possibility of self-deception and some degree of ability to be introspective regarding their own personal beliefs and habits of mind. The following categories may pose threats to a group or warrant exclusion on other grounds:

1. Those who are embroiled in a life crisis may dominate the group's attention unless they have someone else from whom they can receive counseling. It is not the purpose of a group session to take full responsibility for helping one of its members to make decisions about major life transitions, or to cope with losses. Of course, the group may serve as a useful adjunct in such cases.

2. Those who would likely become disruptive or unusually demanding should be carefully evaluated in the selection process, especially clients who are actively psychotic, depressed, histrionic, or intoxicated with alchohol or any drugs.

3. Those who are attending the group against the advice of their therapist risk becoming psychiatric casualties. Another category of persons who are particularly vulnera-

ble to the group process are the alienated and socially isolated who have no network of family or friends to which they return after the group.

4. Those who, against their better judgment, allow themselves to be overtly or covertly coerced into attending the group may undermine the process. For example, those coming as part of an institutional in-service training program, as a requirement of work or at the request of a supervisor or employer, as part of an educational curriculum in order to obtain required credits, or under pressure from family, friends, or other helping persons in the community may sabotage their own and the group's development in a number of ways.

5. Those expecting a level of participation or self-disclosure that is different from the plans or expectations of the group leader or group may find the experience frustrating. The director should see to it that the group is informed regarding the proposed group norms before they decide whether or not to attend. People coming to discuss a social issue need to know in advance if they will be expected to deal with personal issues in what may feel like an intrusive or intimate fashion. On the other hand, if people are coming for an intensive personal growth experience and the director is planning a more superficial exploration of assertion training strategies, this, too, should be made explicit.

Follow-Up

The director should be in a position to assure her group members access to further psychotherapy if needed. It is advisable for the director to have some (medical) psychiatric support—that is, colleagues who can provide medication, hospitalization, or other forms of crisis intervention. Although these forms of follow-up are rarely needed, arranging for this back-up reflects the director's professional awareness of the nature of the impact of group process.

A recent development has added an interesting challenge to this theme: Psychodramatists working in psychiatric hospital units where the average length of stay has been drastically shortened and the numbers of therapeutic staff reduced must be clear about ensuring adequate preparation and follow-up for their work. It may be necessary to modify the use of psychodrama to avoid over-loading patients (Kane, 1992). Negotiation must be made with the administration for enough time, for unit staff as cotherapists who can then communicate with the other therapists, and especially for the assurance of staff time to attend to patients who need to further "process" their experiences.

Working with Systems

The director may be asked to lead a group of co-workers or stu-dents within an organization such as a community agency, a busi-ness, or a school system. There are some pitfalls to consultation to systems. It is advisable for the director to be well-versed in princi-ples of consultation before undertaking the leadership of such a group. Some of the pitfalls include the following:

1. When dealing with co-workers, the director should beware of the personal vulnerability that can be engendered through the use of action techniques. For this reason, it is often better to limit the use of psychodramatic methods to problem-oriented rather than person-oriented approaches (i.e., using role playing or sociodrama rather than psy-chodrama). It is rare that a group of those who live, work, or study together is so cohesive and free of internal com-petitiveness that it can tolerate the extensive, symmetrical self-disclosure that is required in the use of psychodrama. However, many psychodramatic methods can be adapted to these group situations.

    It's important to address issues of confidentiality and assess which kinds of secrets can be shared in a given group. Co-workers and coprofessionals may have certain concerns that deserve thorough discussion. (There is much that needs to happen in group process which involves no enactment, just straight talk.)

2. The use of physical contact is an especially powerful modality and should be used with the greatest of caution. Among adolescents and other groups, the use of touching and hugging tends to take on a distinctly sexual and/or threatening significance. If there is to be wrestling, make sure the area is adequately cushioned or carpeted (Moreno, 1994).

3. The group will often subtly manipulate the director into staging a scene dealing with a co-worker (usually a supervisor) who is not present. "How do you deal with this person?" is the innocent topic of the role playing. Actually, the director is being asked to ally against this person as the group works out its externalizations, displacements, and avoidance of self-examination. The director should beware of this trap: The content of the session often backfires when it comes to the attention of the supervisor.

THE CLIENT-CENTERED SPIRIT OF PSYCHODRAMA

Much of what has been described in this chapter reflects an underlying philosophy that is essentially consistent with the spirit of Carl Rogers' (1951) *client-centered therapy.* It should be noted at the outset that the therapist need not be passive in order to engage mutually with her client. Rogers' nondirective approach relies on the therapist's avoidance of determining the content of the interaction. It is quite possible, however, for a therapist to be quite active and directive in helping her client to use a variety of methods to explore his problem. Thus, as in psychodrama, one can be directive in terms of process while still maintaining a true client-centered mutuality.

Rogers' most valuable contribution, in my opinion, has been his noting the essential conditions for an effective helping relationship, whatever the theoretical orientation of the helper. These conditions include: (a) the authenticity of the way therapists relate to their clients; (b) the establishment of empathic bonds between therapists and clients; and (c) the therapists' development of a capacity for *positive regard* for their clients. Rogers's ideas are applicable to educational or consultative as well as therapeutic contexts.

SUMMARY

When psychodramatic methods are used without the proper philosophical foundations, the director is in danger of falling into some common errors. These pitfalls can be avoided if the director applies certain basic principles that allow the protagonist to develop at his own pace, in a context of mutuality, and without aggressive confrontation from the group leader. In short, they follow the conditions of client-centered therapy. The director must also remain aware of such group process issues as problems of selection and follow-up, the tendency to idealize one approach, and the ability of the director to tolerate ambiguity.

REFERENCES / RECOMMENDED READINGS

Blank, L. (1971). Confrontation techniques—A two-sided coin. In L. Blank & C. Gottsegen (Eds.) *Confrontation: Encounters in self and interpersonal awareness.* New York: Macmillan.

Blatner, A. (1988). Spontaneity (pp. 63–71). In *Foundations of Psychodrama.* New York: Springer.

Fink, A. K. (1963). The democratic essence of psychodrama. *Group Psychotherapy, 16,* 156–160.

Gazda, G. M. (1975). Some tentative guidelines for ethical practice of group work practitioners. In G. M. Gazda (Ed.), *Basic approaches to group psychotherapy and group counseling* (2nd ed.) (pp. 55–65). Springfield, IL: Charles C Thomas.

Hurewitz, P. (1970). Ethical considerations in leading therapeutic and quasitherapeutic groups: Encounter and sensitivity groups. *Group Psychotherapy, 23*(1–2), 17–20.

Kane, R. (1992). The potential abuses, limitations, and negative effects of classical psychodramatic techniques in group counseling. *Journal of Group Psychotherapy, Psychodrama & Sociometry, 44*(4), 181–189.

Knepler, A. E. (1959). Role playing in education—Some problems in its use. *Group Psychotherapy, 12*(1), 32–41.

Moreno, J. L. (1957). Code of ethics of group psychotherapy. *Group Psychotherapy*, 10, 143–144.

Moreno, J. D. (1991). Group psychotherapy in bioethical perspective. *Journal of Group Psychotherapy, Psychodrama & Sociometry*, 44(2), 60–70.

Moreno, J. D. (1994). Psychodramatic moral philosophy and ethics. In P. Holmes, M. Karp, & M. Watson (Eds.), *Psychodrama since Moreno: Innovations in theory and practice*. London: Routledge.

Moreno, Z. T. (1969). Psychodramatic rules, techniques, and adjunctive methods. In J. L. Moreno & Z. T. Moreno, *Psychodrama, Vol. 3* (pp. 233–246).

Rogers, C. (1951). *Client-centered therapy*. Boston: Houghton Mifflin.

Sandron, L. (1973). Psychodrama with hostile group members. *Handbook of International Sociometry*, 7, 29–36.

Shaffer, Amy. (1995). When the screen is not blank: Transference to the psychodrama director in theory and clinical practice. *Journal of Group Psychotherapy, Psychodrama & Sociometry*, 48(1), 9–20.

Terner, J., & Pew, W. L. (1978). *The courage to be imperfect: The life and work of Rudolf Dreikurs* (especially pp. 288–9). New York: Hawthorne.

8

Applications of Psychodramatic Methods

Psychodramatic techniques may be effectively used in any field that requires some exploration of the psychological dimensions of a problem, such as education, psychotherapy, and industrial relations. Understanding and dealing with contemporary issues often requires a process of participatory, experiential learning integrated with verbal and cognitive analysis. This chapter will note some of the major categories of the contexts in which psychodramatic methods are currently being applied. Of course, each director must modify the methodology in order to meet the needs of her own style and ability, as well as the situation of the client and the realities of her helping role. (In addition, references pertaining to various areas of application are listed at the end of this chapter.)

THE MENTAL HEALTH PROFESSIONS

The most common area in which psychodramatic methods are applied is in the field of mental health. In hospitals, clinics, daycare centers, crisis units, alcohol and drug programs, therapeutic communities, and many other settings, many professionals have found a role for psychodramatic methods. Sometimes psychodrama itself is used as a distinct program. More often, methods and techniques derived from psychodrama are integrated into the processes of individual, group, and conjoint family therapy.

Group Therapy

Enactments of varying lengths may be interspersed with periods of discussion. Action methods (such as those mentioned in the chapter on warm-ups) can often be woven into the ongoing group process. Especially effective are the techniques of doubling, role reversal, and the interjection of an exercise of nonverbal communication. These function to circumvent some of the verbal impasses that occur so often in therapy groups.

For example, at one point in a group session, the members became involved in a series of abstract generalizations about philosophical issues. They seemed to have lost their sense of direction. The conversation was sparse and full of platitudes, and the members were no longer in touch with their own concerns and needs. The director threw a book of matches onto the floor in the middle of the group and told them that this was to be a symbol of something they all wanted, even though they might not be clear on just what that was. They were asked to physically deal with the matchbook, as if it were that valuable "something" they desired. One member picked it up, played with it, then gave it to another. A variety of responses followed: a sequence of giving, grabbing, tearing, holding, offering, and rejecting the book of matches. When the action was stopped a few minutes later, the group felt it had quite a bit to talk about: why one person used the matches one way, and how another person reacted in a different fashion. The group began to talk about their interactional styles, their associations to the symbol, and their feelings about the way they had dealt with it. (In a different group, a chair was introduced as the symbol; the increase in physical involvement needed to manipulate a chair led to a great deal of group interaction.)

Another group problem is the situation in which a member or a subgroup is dissatisfied or planning to leave the group. The *spectrogram* is a psychodramatic technique that can be used to clarify the issues and illustrate the feelings of the group: Those feeling one way place themselves toward one side of the room, those feeling a different way go to the other side, and those who are indifferent in the middle (Kole, 1967). This is followed by a discussion about any or all of the subgroups, and it helps to minimize the anxiety of members who feel that they are the only ones in the group who feel the way they do. In groups dealing with a member of a subgroup who wants to leave, the facilitator may use the *behind-your-back* technique. Using this technique, those who wish to leave may symbolically do so by turning their backs, and the rest of the group is instructed to discuss their leaving as if it had actually happened. (It should be noted that the behind-your-back technique can be a very powerful and potentially destructive method of confrontation unless used with skill and judgment.) As the group talks, those who have "left the group" may be tempted to reenter the group in order to correct misunderstandings and represent their case. They might also hear that there are others in the group who sympathize with them and defend them, and this too may induce them to return. In either case, the technique offers a shared experience that the group will then be able to discuss with an increased feeling of cohesion (Figure 8.1).

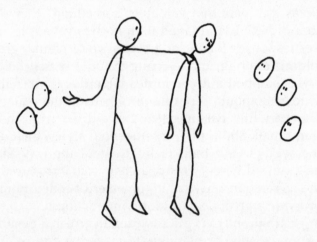

Figure 8.1

A third example is illustrated in a therapy group with adolescents. Bill, a young man, was explaining his tendency to joke and be superficial in his relationships with others. He said that he was aware that he was not letting himself become "close." Bill explained that he was afraid he would be deeply hurt if he were to be rejected after he had allowed himself to really care about another person. He said that he wouldn't be able to stand it. The therapist and Bill set up some scenes in which he would be rejected. Moving between the role of one who is rejected and an observer of the situation, he was helped to desensitize himself to this fear. In addition, the underlying beliefs and feelings of shame were brought out. In facing these issues, Bill learned that being rejected need not result in a catastrophic injury to one's self-esteem; indeed, although he was hurt, he was strong enough not to break down. This sense of inner strength was an enjoyable alternative to Bill's rationalized avoidance of closeness, and was reinforced by the group norm of not having to treat each other "with kid gloves."

In similar ways, this technique can be used to enact threats of loss of control over love, anger, grief, and other emotions, as well as other excuses for avoiding goal-directed behavior. The result of these enactments, in which the fear is faced, results in an increasing sense of self-control.

Family Therapy and Marital Counseling

Psychodramatic methods can escalate the interchange to a more authentic level of emotional encounter, which, in turn, facilitates a more productive exploration of the problems in the relationships among the participants (Blatner, 1994).

In some marital couple therapy meetings it becomes apparent that an "adversary system" has been established in the couple's relationship; that is, each partner seems to be trying to "win" by justifying personal actions and blaming the other's behavior. For example, Nancy and Doug seemed to be stuck in complaining about what they do not want the other to do or say. In such confrontations, I have utilized the technique of role reversal, directing each person to take the part of the spouse. Then, I address them using the spouse's name and ask them in-role to tell each other, not what they do not want, but rather what they do want. If it seems that the person caricaturizes the partner by demanding the obviously impossible, I point this out, and encourage a more realistic portrayal. This approach, I found, has frequently "broken" the mental set in which each partner views the other as uncaring, selfish, or withholding.

PSYCHODRAMATIC METHODS WITH CHILDREN AND ADOLESCENTS

Psychodramatic techniques are utilized to help young people explore the emotional conflicts in their lives at all age levels, and in all contexts—in the home, the child guidance clinic, residential treatment centers, speech and hearing clinics, nursery schools, recreation centers, summer camps, or the classroom. It is often used *in-situ* when a situation arises on the playground, in the front yard, or wherever the problem occurs (Figure 8.2).

In addition, psychodramatic methods, when modified for the setting, can be remarkably effective for children with relatively poor cognitive and verbal skills—such as the mentally retarded or preadolescent delinquents. Indeed, the use of role-playing techniques is a valuable approach to building verbal skills in these action-prone children. Furthermore, psychodramatic techniques can be integrated with other forms of activity, play, and storytelling therapies.

Figure 8.2

APPLICATIONS IN PRIMARY AND SECONDARY EDUCATION

Psychodramatic methods can be applied in many different school settings. Most of the time, the use of these methods should be limited to role-playing or sociodrama. This is because the more personal explorations that are involved in psychodrama may lead to too much self-disclosure for the protagonist in a context of peers. In the following contexts the teacher or counselor can make good use of psychodramatic methods:

1. *Discussion of class material.* Historical, literary, or contemporary social problems can all be addressed through role playing. Classes on the more complex personal relations involved in family life education programs may use role-playing materials to explore dating and marriage relationships, conflict resolution, and so on.

2. *Creative dramatics* is a field that is receiving widespread attention in many contemporary school settings, especially in Great Britain, Australia, and to some extent in Canada. However, the effectiveness of creative dramatics is in direct proportion to the degree to which the children are allowed to throw away their scripts and begin to improvise.

3. *Special situations.* Community crises relating to interracial strife, drug abuse programs, parent-student conflicts, or other issues of current attention can often become the focus of a sociodrama in a classroom or at an entire school assembly.

4. *Special education.* In special classes for children with learning disabilities, psychodramatic methods are used to help with the common problems of defeatism, behavior problems, and poor self-esteem. These special education classes include children who have specific learning disabilities, are severely emotionally disturbed or psychotic, or have behavior problems of hyperactivity.

A common theme of concern to children in special education is being different. This problem can be dealt with by including role playing as part of group discussions. Other children who can benefit from exploring the emotional aspects of their disease are those with asthma, diabetes, deafness, blindness, or other crippling handicaps.

5. *Learning about feelings.* Increasing attention is being given to the challenge of teaching children about their feelings, along with the development of coping skills in interpersonal relationships. Once called "affective education," more recent terms include the development of "emotional intelligence" or "emotional literacy" (Goleman, 1995). The use of psychodramatic methods in the schools can catalyze this education for human awareness and has many potential benefits, if the approach is modified appropriately to the task at hand (Blatner, 1995).

PROFESSIONAL TRAINING

An important area for the applications of psychodramatic methods is in the development of interpersonal skills and sensitivity for students in training for the helping professions. Teachers, nurses, pastors, policemen, medical students, and many other groups can best deal with some items in their training through experiential rather than didactic modes of education.

For example, the problem of death and bereavement in our culture was one of the items brought up in a postgraduate development program for a group of nursery school teachers. Using psychodrama, the experience of grieving was explored. One teacher in the group started by asking how to deal with a child's questions about death. This led to another one of the teacher's enacting the loss of a spouse, which catalyzed a dramatic and emotion-filled catharsis by many of the teachers as they shared their own experiences of mourning. The results were: (a) a heightening of each group member's ability to help others with bereavement by using the empathy that arises from contact with personal feelings; (b) an awareness of the importance of sharing the experience, talking about the feelings of grief rather than avoiding the issue, of the need for touching and physical contact; and (c) an increased tolerance and openness not only to the experience of grief in the group members themselves and others, but also tolerance for the defenses against the expression of grief. These experiences enabled the group members to relate to the children and each other with greater authenticity.

Certainly, the problem of learning to help others grieve demands an experiential form of training. Nurses, medical personnel, and others who must deal with this reality in their work could benefit from understanding the stressful situation through role playing.

Not only is the problem of bereavement an issue for experiential training, but learning to help others with any complex role transition is a challenge. The plight of the young mother, the father of his first newborn, the man who has suffered a small stroke, the prospect of compulsory retirement are all subjects that involve a wide range of status changes and the demand for shifts in role behavior and values. Those who are in training for positions in which they will be helping people with life crises such as these would benefit from participating in role-playing situations that are part of discussion seminars.

APPLICATIONS IN BUSINESS & INDUSTRY

Classical psychodrama would rarely be appropriate for most work situations, for the same reason that one should not use psychodrama in the classroom: A context with co-workers usually has more internal competition and distrust than people may wish to admit to themselves. Limited applications of psychodramatic methods, however, such as the use of role playing and action techniques, are widely used in industrial psychological consulting.

As in the fields of professional training, the major application of role playing in industry is to develop the skills of managers and the personnel and sales staff. In addition, sociodramatic skills are often useful in resolving informal management-labor conflicts or other difficulties in communication. Most important, however, are

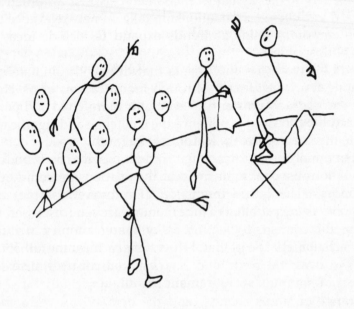

Figure 8.3

the challenges of developing a broader imagination as to the implications of industry's actions in contemporary society and the
building of psychological-interpersonal sophistication in management (Figure 8.3).

The potential director of role playing in an organization must
become aware of the fundamental principles of consultation, the
different needs of the clients, and the many competing agendas of
the group (see Chapter 7). Nevertheless, if the management consultant is well trained, knowledge of appropriate psychodramatic
methods can vastly extend the effectiveness of the work.

APPLICATIONS IN RELIGION

It is interesting to note that Moreno's ideas about creativity and
spontaneity were first reflected in his poetic and theological
works, which were written before he ever developed the psychodramatic method as a psychotherapeutic technique. Moreno's

writings about the dynamic encounter between a human being and God in a cocreative relationship take on new relevance today, as contemporary religious trends expand to include ideas from other philosophies.

Moreno's word for enactments that deal with ultimate values and concerns is *axiodrama*. Through modifications of psychodramatic methods, a minister can search for more vivid and personal ways to help others to experience the challenge and significance of prayer, meditation, death, ethics, and so forth.

Some possible enactments that could be used as an introduction to a religious psychodrama include: the relationship between Jesus and Judas, "The Grand Inquisitor" (Dostoyevsky's story within *The Brothers Karamazov)*, the judgment in heaven (discussed in the therapeutic context in Chapter 5), or the creation of a ritual for Christmas or Passover that is personally meaningful. Pitzele's (1995) work in "Biblio-drama" is an especially interesting example of this adaptation of sociodramatic techniques.

SUMMARY

Psychodramatic methods can be applied to achieve many kinds of goals and in a variety of contexts. This chapter has presented some of the major categories in which psychodramatic methods can be used, as well as providing references related to each area of application and several other topic areas in addition.

REFERENCES / RECOMMENDED READINGS

A. Inpatient Treatment

Anzieu, D. (1982). Psychodrama as technique of the psychoanalysis of institutions. In M. Pines & L. Rafaelsen (Eds.), *The individual and the group: Boundaries and interrelations: Vol. 1. Theory* (pp. 379–387). New York: Plenum.

Buchanan, D. R., & Dubbs-Siroka, J. (1980). Psychodramatic treatment for psychiatric patients. *National Association of Private Psychiatric Hospitals Journal,* 11(2), 27–31.

DiCori, F. (1977). Psychodrama in a hospital setting. In S. Arieti & G. Chrzanowski (Eds.), *New dimensions in psychiatry: A world view.* (Vol. 2, pp. 273–304). New York: Wiley.

Gonen, J. (1971). The use of psychodrama combined with videotape playback on an inpatient floor. *Psychiatry, 34*(2), 198–213.

Johnson, D. R. (1984). Representation of the internal world in catatonic schizophrenia. *Psychiatry, 47*, 299–314.

Jones, M. (1953). *The therapeutic community* (pp. 63–66). New York: Basic Books. Psychodrama was used as part of this pioneering experiment.

Ploeger, A. (1982). The therapeutic community and the psychodrama; Relations and countereffect in the therapeutic process. In M. Pines & L. Rafaelsen (Eds.), *The individual and the group* (pp. 193–197). New York: Plenum.

Polansky, N. A., & Harkins, E. B. (1969). Psychodrama as an element in hospital treatment. *Psychiatry, 32*(1), 74–87.

Rabiner, C. J., & Drucker, M. (1967). Use of psychodrama with hospitalized schizophrenic patients. *Diseases of the Nervous System, 22*, 34–38.

Sakles, C. (1968). The place of psychodrama in an inpatient psychiatric treatment program. *Group Psychotherapy, 21*(4), 235–240.

Schatzberg, A., Lobis, R., & Westfall, M. P. (1974). The use of psychodrama in the hospital setting. *American Journal of Psychotherapy, 28*(4), 553–565.

Starr, A., & Weisz, H. S. (1989). Psychodramatic techniques in the brief treatment of inpatient groups. *Individual Psychology: Journal of Adlerian Theory, Research & Practice, 45*(1–2), 143–147.

B. Alcoholism and Chemical Dependency

Blume, S. (1977). Psychodrama in the treatment of alcoholism. In N. Estes & E. Heinemann (Eds.), *Alcoholism, development, consequences and interventions.* St. Louis: Mosby.

Blume, S. (1978). Psychodrama and the treatment of alcoholism. In S. Zimberg, J. Wallace & S. Blume (Eds.), *Practical approaches to alcoholism psychotherapy* (pp. 77–97). New York: Plenum.

Blume, S. (1989). Treatment for the addictions in a psychiatric setting. *British Journal of Addiction, 84*(7), 727–729.

Duffy, T. K. (1990). Psychodrama in beginning recovery: An illustration of goals and methods. *Alcoholism Treatment Quarterly, 7*(2), 97–109.

Moffett, L., & Bruto, L. (1990). Therapeutic theatre with personality-disordered substance abusers: Characters in search of different characters. *The Arts in Psychotherapy, 17*, 339–348.

Weiner, H. (1965). Treating the alcoholic with psychodrama. *Group Psychotherapy, 18*(1–2), 27–29.

Weiner, H. (1967). Psychodramatic treatment for the alcoholic. In R. Fox (Ed.), *Alcoholism: Behavioral research, therapeutic approaches.* New York: Springer.

Wood, D., Del Nouvo, A., Bucky, S. F., Schein, S., & Michalik, M. (1979). Psychodrama with an alcohol abuser population. *Group Psychotherapy, Psychodrama, & Sociometry, 32*, 75–88.

Yablonsky, L., & Manzella, L. (1991). Psychodrama as an integral part of a therapeutic community. *Journal of Group Psychotherapy, Psychodrama & Sociometry,*
44(3), 121–125.

C. Outpatient Group Psychotherapy

Aronson, M. L. (1990). Integrating Moreno's psychodrama and psychoanalytic
group therapy. *Journal of Group Psychotherapy, Psychodrama & Sociometry,*
42(4), 199–203.

Beagan, D. (1985). Spontaneity and creativity in the N[ational]H[ealth]S[service]:
Starting a new group psychodrama with adult day patients. *British Journal of*
Occupational Therapy, 48(12), 370–374.

Blatner, H. (1968). Goal-orientation and action-orientation as two criteria for
patient selection in group psychotherapy. *Voices, 4*(3), 90–95.

Collison, C. R., & Miller, S. L. (1985). The role of family reenactment in group psychotherapy. *Perspectives in Psychiatric Care, 23*(2), 74–78.

Emunah, R. (1983). Drama therapy with adult psychiatric patients. *The Arts In*
Psychotherapy, 10, 77–84.

Kole, D. (1967). The spectrogram in psychodrama. *Group Psychotherapy, 20*(1–2),
53–61.

Mintz, E. E. (1974). On the dramatization of psychoanalytic interpretations. In L.
R. Wolberg & M. L. Aronson (Eds.), *Group therapy, 1974.* New York: Stratton
Intercontinental Medical Book Corp.

Naar, R. (1982). *A primer of group psychotherapy.* New York: Human Sciences Press.
(Especially pp. 177–203).

Nicholas, M. W. (1984). *Change in the context of group therapy.* New York:
Brunner/Mazel.

Olsson, P. A. (1989). Psychodrama and group therapy approaches to alexithymia.
In D. A. Halperin (Ed.), *Group psychodynamics: New paradigms and new per-*
spectives (pp 168–180). Chicago: Year Book Medical.

Shaffer, J. B., & Galinsky, M. D. (1974). *Models of group therapy and sensitivity train-*
ing (pp. 108–127). Englewood Cliffs, NJ: Prentice-Hall.

D. Family Therapy

Blatner, A. (1994). Psychodramatic methods in family therapy. In C. E. Schaefer &
L. Carey (Eds.), *Family play therapy* (pp. 235– 246). Northvale, NJ: Jason
Aronson.

Chasin, R., & Roth, S. (1994). Entering one another's worlds of meaning and
imagination: Dramatic enactment and narrative couple therapy. In M. F.
Hoyt (Ed.), *Constructive Therapies.* New York: Guilford.

Chasin, R., Roth, S., & Bograd, M. (1989). Action methods in systemic therapy:
Dramatizing ideal futures and reformed pasts with couples. *Family Process,*
28(1), 121–135.

Compernolle, T. (1981). J. L. Moreno: An unrecognized pioneer of family therapy. *Family Process, 20,* 331–335.

Drake, B. (1975). Psychoanalytically oriented psychodrama with multiple family groups. *American Journal of Orthopsychiatry, 45*(2), 260–261.

Duhl, F. J., Kantor, D., & Duhl, B. S. (1973). Learning, space and action in family therapy: A primer of sculpture. In D. A. Bloch (Ed.), *Techniques of family therapy.* New York: Grune and Stratton.

Guldner, C. A. (1982). Multiple family psychodramatic therapy. *Journal of Group Psychotherapy, Psychodrama, & Sociometry, 35*(2), 47–56.

Hollander, C. E. (1983). Comparative family systems of Moreno and Bowen. *Journal of Group Psychotherapy, Psychodrama & Sociometry, 36*(1), 1–12.

Hollander, S. (1981). Spontaneity, sociometry, and the warming up process in family therapy. *Journal of Group Psychotherapy, Psychodrama, & Sociometry, 34,* 44–53.

Holmes, P. (1993). The roots of enactment: The process in psychodrama, family therapy and psychoanalysis. *Journal of Group Psychotherapy, Psychodrama & Sociometry, 45*(4), 149–162.

Lee, R. H. (1986). The family therapy trainer as coaching double. *Journal of Group Psychotherapy, Psychodrama & Sociometry, 39*(2), 52–57.

Perrott, L. (1986). Using psychodramatic techniques in structural family therapy. *Contemporary Family Therapy, 8*(4), 279–290.

Remer, R. (1986). Use of psychodramatic intervention with families: Change on multiple levels. *Journal of Group Psychotherapy, Psychodrama, & Sociometry, 39*(1), 13–30.

Rozema, H. J., & Gray, M. A. (1987). Stimulus activities for family communication. *Journal of Group Psychotherapy, Psychodrama, & Sociometry, 40*(1), 37–42.

Seeman, H., & Wiener, D. J. (1985). Comparing and using psychodrama with family therapy: Some cautions. *Journal of Group Psychotherapy, Psychodrama, & Sociometry, 37*(4), 143–157.

McKelvie, W. H. (1987). Kinetic family sculpture: Experiencing family change through time. *Individual Psychology: Journal of Adlerian Theory, Research & Practice, 43*(2), 160–173.

E. Child Psychotherapy and "In The Home"

Barsky, M., & Mozenter, G. (1976). The use of creative drama in a children's group. *International Journal of Group Psychotherapy, 26,* 10–14.

Carpenter, P., & Sandberg, S. (1973). "The things inside": Psychodrama with delinquent adolescents. *Psychotherapy: Theory, Research and Practice, 10*(3), 245–247.

Chasin, R., & White, T. (1989). The child in family therapy: Guidelines for active engagement across the age span. In L. Combrinck-Graham (Ed.), *Children in family conflicts* (pp. 5–25). New York: Guilford.

Creekmore, N. N., & Madan, A. J. (1981). The use of sociodrama as a therapeutic technique with behavior disordered children. *Behavioral Disorders, 7*(1), 28–33.

Goodrich, J., & Goodrich, W. (1986). Drama therapy with a learning disabled, personality disordered adolescent. *The Arts in Psychotherapy, 13,* 285–291.

Irwin, E. C., & Curry, N. E. (1993). Role play. In C. E. Schaefer (Ed.), *The therapeutic powers of play.* Northvale, NJ: Jason Aronson.

Levenson, R. L., Jr., & Herman, J. (1991). Role playing in child psychotherapy. *Psychotherapy: Theory, Research, & Practice, 28,* 660–666. Also reprinted in C.E. Schaefer (Ed.), *Play therapy techniques.* Northvale, NJ: Jason Aronson, 1993.

Shearon, E. M. (1978). Psychodrama with children. *Group Psychotherapy, Psychodrama, & Sociometry, 33,* 142–155.

F. Adolescents and Delinquency

Altman, K. P. (1985). The role-taking interview: An assessment technique for adolescents. *Adolescence, 20*(80), 845–851.

Carpenter, P., & Sandberg, S. (1985). Further psychodrama with delinquent adolescents. *Adolescence, 20*(79), 599–604.

Corder, B. F., & Whiteside, R. (1994). Involving parents in structured therapy groups for adolescents. *Journal of Child & Adolescent Group Therapy, 4*(3), 157–167.

Dushman, R. D., & Bressler, M. J. (1991). Psychodrama in an adolescent chemical dependency treatment program. *Individual Psychology, 47*(4), 515–520.

Emunah, R. (1990). Expression and expansion in adolescence: The significance of creative arts therapy. *The Arts in Psychotherapy, 17,* 101–107.

Guldner, C. A. (1990). Family therapy with adolescents. *Journal of Group Psychotherapy, Psychodrama & Sociometry, 43*(3), 142–150.

Holmes, P. (1984). Boundaries or chaos: An outpatient psychodrama group for adolescents. *Journal of Adolescence, 7*(4), 387–400.

Knittel, M. (1990). Strategies for directing psychodrama with the adolescent. *Journal of Group Psychotherapy, Psychodrama & Sociometry, 43*(3), 116–120.

Leveton, E. (1984). *Adolescent crisis.* New York: Springer. Especially pp. 77–97.

Olsson, P. A., & Myers, I. L. (1972). Nonverbal techniques in an adolescent group. *International Journal of Group Psychotherapy, 22*(2), 186–191.

Saroyan, J. S. (1990). The use of music therapy on an adolescent psychiatric unit. *Journal of Group Psychotherapy, Psychodrama & Sociometry, 43*(3), 139–141.

Sasson, F. (1990). Psychodrama with adolescents: Management techniques that work. *Journal of Group Psychotherapy, Psychodrama & Sociometry, 43*(3), 121–127.

Warzak, W. J., & Page, T. J. (1990). Teaching refusal skills to sexually active adolescents. *Journal of Behavior Therapy & Experimental Psychiatry, 21*(2), 133–139.

Weil, F., Pascal, M., Kaddar, Y., & Luboshitzky, D. (1990). The place of verbal games in the framework of inpatient group psychotherapy with late adolescents. *Journal of Group Psychotherapy, Psychodrama & Sociometry, 43*(3), 128–138.

G. Mental Retardation

Bailey, S. D. (1993). *Wings to fly: Bringing theatre arts to students with special needs.* Rockville, MD: Woodbine House.

Buchan, L. G. (1972). *Roleplaying and the educable mentally retarded.* Belmont, CA: Fearon.

Chesner, A. (1995). *Dramatherapy for people with learning disabilities: A world of difference.* London: Jessica Kingsley.

Klepac, R. L. (1978). Through the looking glass: Sociodrama and mentally retarded individuals. *Mental Retardation, 16*(5), 343–345.

Newburger, H. (1967). Psychodrama treatment with the brain damaged. *Group Psychotherapy, 20*(3), 129–130.

Pankratz, L., & Buchan, G. (1966). Techniques of warm-ups in psychodrama with the retarded. *Mental Retardation, 4*(5), 12–16.

Taylor, J. F. (1969). Role-playing with borderline and mildly retarded children in an institutional setting. *Exceptional Children, 36,* 206–208.

H. Other Disabilities

Aach, S. (1976). Drama: A means of self-expression for the visually impaired child. *New Outlook for the Blind 70*(7), 282–285.

Altman, K. P. (1981). Psychodrama with blind psychiatric patients. *Journal of Visual Impairment & Blindness, 75*(4), 153 156.

Clayton, L., & Robinson, L. D. (1971). Psychodrama with deaf people. *American Annals of the Deaf, 116*(4), 415–419.

Swink, D. F. (1983). The use of psychodrama with deaf people. *Journal of Group Psychotherapy, Psychodrama & Sociometry, 36*(1), 23–29.

Schlanger, P. H., & Birkmann, M. H. (1978). Role playing used to elicit language from hearing-impaired children. *Group Psychotherapy, Psychodrama & Sociometry, 31,* 136–143.

Wolpe, Z. (1957). Play therapy, psychodrama, and parent counseling. In L. E. Travis (Ed.), *Handbook of speech pathology* (pp. 1006–1015). New York: Appleton-Century-Crofts.

I. Education

Amies, B., Warren, B., & Watling, R. (1986). *Social drama: Towards a therapeutic curriculum.* London: John Clare Books.

Bell, S. (1981). Sociodrama as an instructional approach for teaching about exceptional children and youth. *Journal for Special Educators, 17*(4), 371–375.

Blatner, A., & Blatner, A. (1988). Applying sociodramatic methods in education. In *The art of play: An adult's guide to reclaiming imagination and spontaneity* (pp. 142–151, 188–189). New York: Human Sciences Press.

Blatner, A. (1995). Drama in education as mental hygiene: A child psychiatrist's perspective. *Youth Theatre Journal, 9,* 92–96.

Courtney, R. (1980). *The dramatic curriculum.* New York: Drama Book Specialists.

Duveen, J., & Solomon, J. (1994). The great evolution trial: Use of role-play in the classroom. *Journal of Research in Science Teaching, 31*(5): 575–582.

Goleman, D. (1995). *Emotional intelligence.* New York: Bantam.

Haas, R. B. (1949). *Psychodrama and sociodrama in American education.* Beacon, NY: Beacon House.

Hollander, C. E. (1978). Psychodrama, role playing and sociometry: Living and learning processes. In D. Kurpius (Ed.), *Learning: Making learning environments more effective* (pp. 168– 241). Muncie, IN: Accelerated Development.

Kritzerow, P. (1990). Active learning in the classroom: The use of group role plays. *Teaching Sociology, 18*(2), 223–225.

Lee, T. (1991). The sociodramatist and sociometrist in the primary school. *Journal of Group Psychotherapy, Psychodrama & Sociometry, 43*(4), 191–196.

Maier, H. W. (1991). Role playing: Structures and educational objectives. *Journal of Child and Youth Care, 6*(4), 145–150.

Mathis, J. A., Fairchild, L., & Cannon, T. M. (1980). Psychodrama and sociodrama in primary and secondary education. *Psychology in the Schools, 17*(1), 96–101.

Milroy, E. (1982). *Role-play: A practical guide.* Aberdeen, Scotland: Aberdeen University Press.

Nieminen, S. (1986). Using psychodramatic techniques as a means of preventive mental health work in Finland. *School Psychology International, 7*(2), 94–97.

Pearson-Davis, S. (1989). Drama in the curriculum for troubled young people. *Journal of Group Psychotherapy, Psychodrama & Sociometry, 41*(4), 161–174.

Shaftel, F., & Shaftel, G. (1982). *Role-playing in the curriculum* (2nd ed.). Englewood Cliffs, NJ: Prentice-Hall. A revised edition of the authors' *Role Playing for Social Values,* 1967.

Shearon, E. M., & Shearon, W. (1973). Some uses of psychodrama in education. *Group Psychotherapy & Psychodrama, 26*(3–4), 47–53.

Stanford, G., & Roark, A. (1975). Role playing and action methods in the classroom. *Group Psychotherapy & Psychodrama, 28,* 33–49.

Sturkie, J., & Cassady, M. (1992). *Acting it out junior.* San Jose, CA: Resource Publications.

Van Mentz, M. (1983). *The effective use of role-play: A handbook for teachers and trainers.* London: Kogan Page.

Warren, B. (1995). *Creating a theatre in your classroom.* York, Canada: Captus Press.

J. Professional Training

Barton, D., & Crowder, M. K. (1975). The use of role playing techniques as an instructional aid in teaching about dying, death and bereavement. *Omega, 6*(3), 243–250.

Beglen, G. G. (1983). The use of psychodramatic and sociometric techniques in the in-service training of residential treatment child care staff. *Journal of Group Psychotherapy, Psychodrama, & Sociometry, 36*(1), 13–22.

Costa, J., & Walsh, S. (1991). A psychodrama group for professional clinicians. *British Journal of Psychodrama, 6*(1), 24–37.

Drew, N. (1990). Psychodrama in nursing education. *Journal of Group Psychotherapy, Psychodrama & Sociometry, 43*(2), 54–62.

Holmes, P. (1991). "Dont tell us—show us": The use of role play in the teaching of psychoanalytic theory. *British Journal of Psychodrama, 6*(1), 38–46.

Kipper, D. A., & Ben-Ely, Z. (1979). The effectiveness of the psychodramatic double method, the reflection method, and lecturing in the training of empathy. *Journal of Clinical Psychology, 35*(2), 370–375.

Kranz, P., & Huston, K. (1984). The use of psychodrama to facilitate supervisee development in Master's level counseling students. *Journal of Group Psychotherapy, Psychodrama, & Sociometry, 37*(3), 126–134.

Mansfield, F. (1991). Supervised role play in the teaching of the process of consultation. *Medical Education, 25*(6), 485–490.

Reed, E. J. (1984). Using psychodrama with critical care nurses. *Dimensions of Critical Care Nursing, 3*(2), 110–114.

Rosnow R. L. (1990). Teaching research ethics through role play and discussion. *Teaching of Psychology, 17*(3), 179–181.

Thacker, A. K. (1984). Using psychodrama to reduce "burnout" or role fatigue in the helping professions. *Journal of Group Psychotherapy, Psychodrama & Sociometry, 37*(1), 14–26.

Vander May, J., & Peake, T. (1980). Psychodrama as a psychotherapy supervision technique. *Group Psychotherapy, Psychodrama & Sociometry, 33*, 25–32.

Wolff, T. K., & Miller, D. A. (1993). Using roleplaying to teach the psychiatric interview. *Journal of Group Psychotherapy, Psychodrama & Sociometry, 46*(2), 43–51.

K. Industry, Business, and Organizational Development

Brewer, U. (1993). Using the role reversal technique in an industrial setting. *Journal of Group Psychotherapy, Psychodrama & Sociometry, 46*(2), 73–74.

Eitington, J. E. (1989). Role playing. In *The Winning Trainer* (2nd Ed.) (pp. 67–93). Houston: Gulf Publishing.

Greenberg J., & Eskew D. E. (1993). The role of role playing in organizational research. *Journal of Management, 19*(2), 221–241.

Hoffman, C. C., Wilcox, L., Gomez, E., & Hollander, C. (1992). Sociometric applications in a corporate environment. *Journal of Group Psychotherapy, Psychodrama & Sociometry, 45*(1), 3–16.

Lippitt, R., & Hubbell, A. (1956). Role playing for personnel and guidance workers: Review of the literature. *Group Psychotherapy, 9*(2), 89–114.

Shaw, M. E., Corsini, R., Blake, R., & Mouton, J. (1980). *Role playing: A practical manual for group facilitators.* San Diego, CA: University Associates. Excellent bibliography, oriented mainly to business and organizational audiences. This is a reworking of the 1961 edition entitled *Role-playing in Business and Industry,* with Corsini as the first author.

Swink, D. F. (1993). Role-play your way to learning. *Training and Development, 47*(5), 91–97.

Torrance, E. P., & Wright, J. A. (1987). Sociometric audience technique as a device for maximizing creativity in problem solving in large groups. *The Creative Child and Adult Quarterly, 12*(3), 147–151.

Wohlking, W., & Weiner, H. (1971). Structured and spontaneous role playing: Contrast and comparison. In W. Wohlking (Ed.), *Role playing: Its application in management development* (pp. 1–11). New York: Cornell University Press.

L. Religion

Carvalho, E. S. (1986). Christian reconciliation: A psychodramatic contribution. *Journal of Psychology & Christianity, 5*(1), 5–10.

Johnson, P. E. (1959). Interpersonal psychology of religion: Moreno and Buber. *Group Psychotherapy, 12,* 211–217.

Kraus, C. (1984). Psychodrama for fallen gods: A review of Morenean theology. *Journal of Group Psychotherapy, Psychodrama & Sociometry, 37*(2), 47–64.

Moreno, J. L. (1948). Experimental theology. *Sociatry, 2*(1–2), 93–98.

Nolte, J., Smallwood, C., & Weistart, J. (1975). Role reversal with God. *Group Psychotherapy & Psychodrama, 28,* 70–76.

Pitzele, P. (1995). *Our fathers' wells: A personal encounter with the myth of Genesis.* San Francisco: HarperCollins.

Pitzele, P. (1996). *Scripture windows: Theory and practice of Biblical psychodrama.* Los Angeles: Torah Aura Productions.

M. Criminal Justice System

Barocas, H. (1972). Psychodrama techniques in training police in family crisis intervention training. *Group Psychotherapy and Psychodrama, 25,* 30–31.

Buchanan, D. R. (1981). Action methods for the criminal justice system. *Federal Probation, 45,* 17–25.

Melnick, M. (1984). Skills through drama: The use of professional theater techniques in the treatment and education of prison and ex-offender populations. *Journal of Group Psychotherapy, Psychodrama, & Sociometry, 37*(3), 104–116.

Schramski, T. G., & Harvey, D. R. (1983). The impact of psychodrama and role playing in the correctional environment. *International Journal of Offender Therapy & Comparative Criminology, 27*(3), 243–254.

Stallone, T. M. (1993). The effects of psychodrama on inmates within a structured residential behavior modification program. *Journal of Group Psychotherapy, Psychodrama & Sociometry, 46*(2), 24–31.

Swink, D. F., Siegel, J., & Spodak, B. (1984). Saint Elizabeths Hospital Action Training Lab for Police. *Journal of Group Psychotherapy, Psychodrama, & Sociometry, 37*(3), 94–103.

N. With the Elderly

Altman, K. P. (1983). Psychodrama with the institutionalized elderly: A method for role re-engagement. *Journal of Group Psychotherapy, Psychodrama, & Sociometry, 36*(3), 87–96.

Buchanan, D. R. (1982). Psychodrama: A humanistic approach to psychiatric treatment for the elderly. *Hospital & Community Psychiatry, 33*(3), 220–223.

Carman, M., & Nordin, S. (1984). Psychodrama: A therapeutic modality for the elderly in nursing homes. *Clinical Gerontologist, 3*(Fall), 15–24.

Johnson, D. R. (1986). The developmental method in drama therapy: Group treatment with the elderly. *Arts in Psychotherapy, 13*(1), 17–33.

Martin, R. B., & Stepath, S. A. (1993). Psychodrama and reminiscence for the geriatric psychiatric patient. *Journal of Group Psychotherapy, Psychodrama & Sociometry, 45*(4), 139–148.

Mazor, R. (1982). Drama therapy for the elderly in a day care center. *Hospital & Community Psychiatry, 33*, 577–579.

Nordin, S. R. (1987). Psychodrama with the elderly. *Journal of Group Psychotherapy, Psychodrama, & Sociometry, 40*(2), 51–61.

Remer, R., Morse, H. B., Popma, J., & Jones, S. M. (1993). Spontaneity training and psychodrama with Alzheimer's patients. *Journal of Group Psychotherapy, Psychodrama & Sociometry, 45*(4), 131–138.

Sandel, S. L., & Johnson D. R. (1987). *Waiting at the gate: Creativity and hope in the nursing home.* New York: Haworth.

Schloss, G. A. (1988). Growing old and growing: Psychodrama with the elderly. In R. W. MacLennan, S. Saul, & M. B. Weiner (Eds.), *Group psychotherapies for the elderly* (pp. 343–358). Madison CT: International Universities Press.

Telander, M., Quinlan, F., & Verson, K. (1987). *Acting up! An innovative approach to creative drama for older adults.* Morton Grove, IL: Coach House Press.

Weisberg, N., & Wilder, R. (Eds.). (1986). *Drama with older adults: Therapeutic interventions.* New Haven: National Association of Drama Therapists.

Wiener, R., & Traynor, J. (1988). The use of sociodrama in staff training in working with older people. *Practice, 1*(4), 332–338.

O. Other Conditions

Callahan, M. L. (1989). Psychodrama and the treatment of bulimia. In L. M. Hornyak & K. Baker (Eds.), *Experiential therapies for eating disorders* (pp. 101–120). New York: Guilford.

Corti, P., & Casson, J. (1990) Dramatherapy into psychodrama: An account of a therapy group for women survivors of sexual abuse. *British Journal of Psychodrama, 5*(2), 37–53.

Hudgins, M. K. (1989). Experiencing the self through psychodrama and gestalt therapy in anorexia nervosa. In L. M. Harnyk & E. K. Baker (Eds.), *Experiental therapies for eating disorders.* New York: Guilford.

Jay, S. (1992). Eating feelings: Working with women who have bulimia. *British Journal of Psychodrama, 7*(2), 5–18.

Raaz, N., Carlson-Sabelli, L., & Sabelli, H. C. (1993). Psychodrama in the treatment of multiple personality disorder: A process-theory perspective. In E. S. Kluft (Ed.), *Expressive and functional therapies in the treatment of MPD* (pp. 169–188). Springfield, IL: Charles C. Thomas.

9

Theoretical Issues

The practice of psychodrama is based on a rich complex of theoretical understandings, although these do not constitute a single, separate theory as such. In fact, I challenge the appropriateness of seeking a unified theory—as psychodynamic psychology attempted to do a generation ago, when psychotherapy was fragmented into numerous major "schools of thought" and hundreds of minor therapies. Instead, psychodrama should be recognized as being a methodology which is embedded within an integrated field of psychotherapy. In turn, psychotherapy is itself embedded within a comprehensive, holistic view of psychology. This wider context includes a number of fields which have their own understandings and which can further the appreciation of the richness of the foundations of psychodrama.

Although psychodrama does not have to be viewed as having a separate theory, it nevertheless does have a number of core themes. In these, it not only draws from the greater field of psychology and psychotherapy, but also contributes to our views of human nature.

METATHEORETICAL CONSIDERATIONS

Metatheory is theorizing about theory itself, and in this case, the question is, should there be a special theory of psychodrama? My answer, as noted earlier, is no. Indeed, I question the very tradition of theory building that evolved within psychology in this century, a tradition which tended to offer competitive systems rather than adding new understandings to an integrative general framework. The historical and cultural trends which led to this misguided use of the intellect arose from the confusion of the natures of the behavioral sciences with the natural sciences, and ignored the essential qualitative difference in the types of complexity involved in the two types of science. A careful examination of this difference goes beyond the scope of this chapter, but its conclusion is simply that psychotherapists need to entertain a more fluid mode of theorizing which can include different frames of reference.

Medicine, which involves hundreds of theories, all quite compatible, each addressing a particular dynamic in an incredibly complex systems, presents an analogy. Medical theories are constantly being elaborated, revised, and sometimes discarded and replaced. Certainly they are not held as an ideology. Psychology also addresses phenomena which involve many different levels of organization and types of systems. Thus, psychotherapy should be eclectic and integrative, addressing both neurophysiology on one hand and social and cultural psychology on the other (Lazarus & Beutler, 1992).

It is quite possible to formulate a person's problem and understand many relevant dynamics without having to maintain an allegiance to any single theory. Some people's problems may be better explained using certain ideas derived from Adler or Reich while others' issues may be illuminated most effectively using ideas taken from Jung or Freud.

Note that I am not suggesting that a psychotherapist become atheoretical. That would be an abdication of the challenge of understanding at an abstract level, and of continuously developing the complexity of one's model of human nature. Actually, I'm encouraging a truly professional and highly rigorous committment to learning and reading and creating one's own schema from many sources. It is quite possible, but only with a willingness to relinquish one's hold on to a single explanatory schema. There isn't one in medicine, and there doesn't need to be one in psychology.

From a multidimensional understanding of psychology, an equally multimodal approach to treatment may be rationally formulated. No one would want a physician who believed in using only one type of treatment, excluding all others. Similarly, there are times in working with patients when it is appropriate to meet with the family, or in a group setting. At other times a change in frequency or length of session might be indicated. Similarly, therapy may appropriately include various approaches, using action some times, and simple discussion at others, depending on the needs of the patient (Blatner, 1969-1970).

INTERDISCIPLINARY FOUNDATIONS

To appreciate the depth and richness of psychodrama, one must learn about many different associated activities. To begin with, when used in a psychotherapeutic context, as mentioned above, its application rests on the theory of psychotherapy itself, and the rationale for a variety of treatment techniques. These, in turn, rest on a foundation of understandings about the nature of learning, conditioning, catharsis, conflict resolution, creativity, insight, the influence of social networks and culture, the power of imagery and language, and other fundamental dynamics in change, sickness, and healing.

Since psychodrama most often is a group method, much of the theory related to group therapy applies also to the management of psychodrama groups. A good deal of psychoanalytic theory can be used without having to also apply the classical analytic methods. And the rich theories of Gestalt therapy, Transactional Analysis, and many other approaches to group work also help explain why psychodrama is a useful approach.

Beyond the group therapy literature, the understanding of group dynamics as developed by many workers other than Moreno, such as Kurt Lewin and pioneers in the fields of organizational development, all add to the theory of psychodrama (Moreno, 1953). It should be noted that simulations—whether astronaut training or military war games—are an extension of the basic ideas about role playing, and the theories associated with skill development and problem solving also have relevance to the issues discussed in this book.

Shifting to another source, in many ways the rationale for play therapy with children also applies to the use of psychodrama. Theories on the nature of learning in children, theories of education, and, especially, theories of experiential learning, such as Richard Courtney's (1990, 1995) work on drama in education are part of this field. Beyond this is all the work that's been done on the place of play and imagination not just in child development, but in adulthood, in old age, for recreation, and as an important element of culture itself (Blatner, 1995; Blatner & Blatner, 1988).

These fields merge with another domain, the study of the more complex sublimation of the play impulse in ritual and drama (Fryba, 1972; Harmeling, 1950). Academic work has been done on the dynamics of imagination, play, and symbolization in ritual studies, a field that integrates anthropology, comparative religion, mythology, art history and theater. And of course, the history of the theatre, and the extensive writings on the theoretical foundations of drama therapy, all apply also to psychodrama.

Psychodrama is certainly an expressive therapy, and many elements in the theoretical bases of the other creative arts therapies— the use of art, music, dance, movement, poetry, and drama in treatment—also apply to the understanding of how enactment in a multidimensional, space-time process can deepen and extend the therapeutic process tremendously (Blatner, 1992). Related, too, are the theoretical justifications for the use of devices such as puppets, masks, and videoplayback.

Psychodrama is a very social approach, not just because it uses other people and addresses the interpersonal field with more methodological richness than any other type of treatment, but also because its focus is as much on the social field as it is on individual psychodynamics. It is important to recognize that both the depth and subtleties of individual experience and the complexities of social interactions may be amply explored using psychodramatic methods. Thus, many of the theoretical foundations of social psychology, role theory, the dramaturgical approach in sociology, and applied or clinical sociology also support the rationale for the use of action methods.

Certain contemporary trends in psychology and psychotherapy also find a major vehicle for implementation in psychodrama, especially those of narrative psychology, constructivism, intersubjectivity, hermeneutics, personal mythology, feminist theory, and other postmodern developments. Psychodramatic elements held common with neurolinguistic programming, George Kelly's "personal construct theory," and numerous other theoretical and practical systems have been noted in the current literature (Bonney & Scott, 1983; Buchanan & Little, 1983).

A relevant bibliography of all these theoretical foundations of psychodrama, then, would also need to include scores if not hundreds of citations relating to each of these fields.

MORENIAN THEORY IN BRIEF

Having presented some considerations on metatheory and the interdisciplinary connections which support the use of psychodrama, let us return to a consideration of the essential ideas involved in this approach. Psychchodrama may be understood most simply in terms of the interaction of four basic ideas: creativity, spontaneity, playfulness, and drama.

Moreno noted that a significant dynamic in the problems of individuals and groups with problems was a diminishing of creativity. And creativity cannot be forced—it generally doesn't arise out of sitting and thinking about the problem. Rather, creative breakthroughs come when people get involved, actively communicate, experiment. Experimentation, indeed, is the function of a laboratory, and psychodrama may be considered a kind of social psychological laboratory. Its various elements (as described in the first chapter) are the living equivalent of the physical scientist's glassware, chemicals, and electronic equipment (Moreno, 1956; Kottler, 1994, p. 273).

In this "laboratory," it is necessary to create the circumstances so that if an "experiment" doesn't work, it doesn't blow up the laboratory and kill all the people. The social equivalent to this safety factor is the fail-safe context of play. Play is not to be thought of as mere frivolity, the opposite of seriousness, but rather a special frame of mind in which actions don't generate ultimate consequences—in other words, the realm of pretend. Children naturally

have a capacity for play, and adults sublimate.this archetypal inclination in the social institutions of ritual and drama. Psychodrama
harnesses this innate capacity in the service of healing.

In a safe context, then, people are invited to improvise, because
it is through spontaneity that creativity can best be generated. And
Moreno found that *drama*, that is, the enactment of problematical
situations, simulating or role playing them, offered a particularly
rich vehicle for exploring the attitudinal and emotional roots of
these problems and for finding more constructive alternatives.
Drama is unique in its capacity to integrate imagination and physical action with emotion, intuition, and reasoning, to provide an
experiential as well as intellectual way to learn and grow.
Furthermore, the various psychodramatic techniques may then be
understood as specific laboratory instruments for achieving a wide
range of goals. (In this analogy, psychoanalysis might also be
viewed as being a kind of laboratory, only it has a much narrower
range of equipment and available procedures. And this analogy
can then be extended to offer a rationale for integrating psychodramatic methods with other therapeutic approaches.)

ROLE DYNAMICS

Another theoretical foundation of psychodrama is Moreno's role
theory. Partly influenced by Moreno and also by a number of
other original thinkers in sociology and social psychology, social
role theory has also emerged as a sub-field which uses the role
concept for understanding human interactions. Moreno's special
contribution and insight is that people not only play many roles,
but also are capable of bringing a degree of self-reflection to the
process (Moreno, 1961). Further, this observing function itself is a
kind of "managing" meta-role which can be cultivated (Blatner,
1991). Clayton (1994) and others in Australia use role theory in an
innovative fashion that helps people expand and work with their
identities.

I have gone a another step further and suggest that the role concept, which was derived originally from the theater, may serve as
the basis for a practical language for applied individual and social

psychology and psychotherapy. I've systematized Morenian role theory and named this general theoretical approach *role dynamics*. Talking about problems and situations in terms of the roles being played is very useful because the terminology is relatively familiar and non-stigmatizing, that is, less suggestive of being viewed as sick or abnormal. Furthermore, the language serves as a metaphor, evoking images of events as interactions in a play (Blatner, 1988, Chapter 10). This viewpoint then makes it easier to suggest that the person mentally step back, think like a director or playwright, and wonder how else the scene might be played. Role dynamics, then, fosters an active and more creative type of imaginative thinking.

One of the more intriguing theoretical implications of role dynamics is that the drive to expand the role repertoire may be recognized as being as fundamental a discovery of a motivating force as Freud's identification of sexuality, Adler's noting the seeking of a feeling of being effective, or Jung's proposed process of *individuation*—finding a holistic balance among the various aspects of the psyche. This view rests on the observation that people operate along many simultaneous dimensions of activity and cognition, or, stated simply, people play many roles (Moreno, 1961).

Furthermore, from a role dynamics standpoint, psychopathology reflects not only a distortion of one of these aspects of personality, but often represents a compensatory expression of one facet of the personality primarily due to a lack of development of another. For example, a person with few creative opportunities, or little validation for building skills in the realm of imagination and feelings, tends to become overintellectualized. The intellectualization is a *vacuum activity* (a term borrowed from ethology, referring to the time- filling behavior of animals when their normal outlets are frustrated, often by being in a cage).

Psychotherapy and education viewed from the position of role theory would emphasize the training of the person's capacity in a variety of roles that can balance and complement each other. The normal function of play in childhood is to at least symbolically enact a wide variety of roles that then become a core of identifications and ego strengths (Sarbin, 1943). For example, the child must play at being a mother or father before he or she can convert internalized nurturing behaviors given by the parents into an active sense of nurturing others.

In addition to helping people have insight into the presence and the nature of various complexes or parts of themselves which may have remained out of immediate consciousness, psychodrama offers ways to help them find more effective ways to play out their lives in a more aware and matured fashion. The phases of this process may include discovery, identification of the key attitudes, clarification and renegotiation of the beliefs on which those attitudes are based, remaking decisions, and practice of the new, more finely discriminated or redirected attitudes.

EXPANSION OF THE ROLE REPERTOIRE

Psychodrama is more effective than simply verbal methods for going through the process because it anchors the insights and emotions in experience, in the more emotional, imaginal and intuitive parts of the mind. Physical action generates a more experiential and participatory type of learning, which makes it a vitalizing component a total psychotherapeutic program (Anzieu, 1984). Some specific ways in which developing a wider role repertoire may function are:

1. *The sense of choice* is increased, as there are more behavioral roles with which one is familiar.

2. *The importance of many different aspects of life* is validated through role-taking behaviors. Dimensions such as play, dance, achievement, competition, and imagination are valued.

3. *Identification.* Practice in taking other roles builds an increased capacity for empathy. Meerloo (1966) writes, "Partaking in the psyche of the other means using the vicarious signs of preverbal communication. Moreno, the founder of modern group therapy, calls this mutual partaking and emotional communicative understanding from afar 'telic sensitivity' and 'telic-reciprocity.'"

4. *Experiencing the sense of self.* Taking active and creatively spontaneous roles in many dimensions fulfills an extremely important function: that of validating the sense of one's own vitality, will, authenticity, feelings, imagery, and, in short, the sense of being deeply alive, of being a "self."

5. *Flexibility.* Role-taking behavior, if reinforced, helps people to allow themselves to develop a sense of mastery in many different role situations: father, lover, daughter, judge, student, friend, teacher, police officer. In turn, the components of each role can be applied more easily in new situations where synthesis is required.

CONTRIBUTIONS TO PSYCHODYNAMICS

The theory implicit in psychodrama complements and enriches the mainstream of theory in psychology and psychotherapy in a variety of specific ways. The most unique aspects of psychodrama are discussed in this section.

Vitality as a Core Dynamic. Excitement, interest, and vitality are key emotional states, to be valued and promoted. These are among the basic positive affects, and deserve their own explication, as has been done for such affects as shame, anger, and fear. A corollary to promoting positive affect is Moreno's orientation to "expanding wellness" rather than merely attempting to directly counter the symptoms of psychopathology.

Self-expression is recognized as being a very more important process. The term replaces the negatively toned "exhibitionism," which gives all artistic and dramatic productivity a suggestion of frustrated sexuality. Psychodrama thus offers a specific methodology which supports the implications of Jung's and Rank's theories about art.

Creativity is itself given a central place in psychology, referring not simply to art or science, but to the activities of everyday life, in relationships, in societal institutions, and in personal and spiritual development. The exercise of creativity is a cheerful and courageous way of synthesizing the postmodernist, deconstructionist philosophy with the best of modernity and traditionalism (McKissack, 1992). Faced with the uncertainties that contemporary global civilization generates, we are called on to dare to create a better world in the face of being unable to rely on any fixed authority. In their emphasis on creativity, the principles of psychodrama also carry forth a constructivist and existentialist philosophy, expressing in operationalized form the best insights of these attempts to address the dilemmas of modern life.

A metaphor for self-reflection. The use of drama serves not only as a technique, but more, as a metaphor which suggests an imagined double role for people—as both the actor and the playwright/director of their own life's dramas. This image makes it easier for clients in psychotherapy or young people in the process of learning to step back from their involvements and reflect on their behavior and the assumptions which motivate those reactions.

The importance of play and spontaneity. Psychodrama supports playfulness not only as a context for improvisation, but also as an important dimension of vitality. The stand holding the urn with Moreno's ashes has the inscription, "Here lies the man who brought laughter and play back into psychiatry." Also, spontaneity is recognized as an important quality which must be cultivated as a deep skill and value in the soul. Like Jung, Moreno intuited the unconscious as not only being a repository for repressed and disowned complexes of thoughts and feelings, but also a potential source of wisdom and creativity. To mobilize its forces, plunging forward in the activity of improvisation reflects a respect for and receptivity to the deeper flows of images and insights. One of Moreno's most significant insights was that the best way to foster creativity was to promote spontaneity (Karp, 1994).

A method for empathy. The idea of role reversal gives clients in therapy and students in school a method for understanding others; understanding proceeds not from mere exhortation but rather from cultivating a skill that tends to draw people out of their mental habits of egocentricity and promote a greater degree of Alfred Adler's goal of "community feeling" (Adler, 1939). Most therapies don't emphasize the importance of appreciating the other person's viewpoint, but psychodrama places this procedure at the heart of the method and as an important element in the theory of full heal-ing.

A pluralistic model of personality. The role theory implicit in psy-chodrama suggests a view of the person as having many parts within their self. Thus, it allows people to entertain their own mixed and sometimes contradictory feelings without having to feel abnormal. Authenticity often involves the expression of a more complex reaction. The attempt to impose an artificially "con-sistent" persona can be draining, and the expressing of the view-points of several different roles can feel more genuine.

A more socially conscious psychology. Psychodrama is a powerful bridge between individual and social psychology and helps to redirect people towards becoming conscious of their "social being-ness." This again serves as a method for countering what Wallach and Wallach (1983) called "psychology's sanction for selfishness." Further, it is an approach which offers a wealth of component ideas and techniques for exploring the interpersonal field, exam-ining the nature of *tele* (Moreno's term for interpersonal prefer-ence) as well as a number of other types of group dynamics, sub-sumed under Moreno's general method of sociometry (Blatner, 1988, Chapters 12 & 13.)

Everyone in the group a cotherapist. Moreno's approach to therapy struggles against the natural tendencies to establish the director as the sole authority and to redistribute the locus of healing among all participants in the process. By learning the techniques, group members are empowered to more actively guide the pursuit of the group's task.

Imagination as a dimension of healing. The concept of *surplus reali-ty* invites people to appreciate the significance of the imaginal in life, the psychological "truth" of what not only may have never happened, but *could* never happen. Yet these events—a dialogue with an ancestor or God, an encounter with an unborn child or oneself in the past or future, a replaying of what would have been the ideal transformation of a past event—if enacted with the wit-nessing and consensual validation of others, have the potential to be occasions for discovery and healing (Blomkvist & Rützel, 1994).

Catharsis as an agent of healing. Psychodrama is particularly help-ful in evoking catharsis, which serves to anchor the protagonist experientially in a more conscious owning of previously repressed feelings. This in turn allows him to more holistically introduce corrective images and empowering experiences, to say, as if speaking to the inner child, "Yes, I fully appreciate your pain and I can use my present awareness to protect you from now on." Unless there has been a real catharsis, the inner child won't believe superficial reassurances, and will counter with, "You don't really know the full extent of my feelings, so I can't really trust you." The dynamics of catharsis were once an important part of therapy, but have become generally eclipsed (Jackson, 1994). An understanding of the function of catharsis is an important tool in the psychodramatist's kit (Ginn, 1973; Kellermann, 1984; Blatner, 1985).

Addressing past, present, and future. Psychodramas may reenact past events, explore future possibilities, and broaden awareness in the here-and-now. Goals may be clarified and made more specific, and—using the future projection technique—enacted, in order to neutralize fears and rehearse required skills (Yablonsky, 1954). And, as with Gestalt therapy, these methods may be used to expand a sense of awareness and involvement in the present moment.

Sociatry. Moreno also envisioned a broader view of the use of psychodrama, one which included the entire society, offering methods for intensifying involvement and expanding effectiveness in a variety of contexts that went beyond the formal medical model. He sought to revitalize the function of theatre so that it serves to integrate people within a community, adding to methods for team and community building, making learning more relevant and enjoyable in school, and fulfilling many purposes.

FACILITATING PROBLEM-SOLVING

Whether in psychotherapy or a role-playing session in business or education, whether in a group, family, or with an individual, there are certain obvious stages in problem solving which may be facilitated by the use of psychodramatic methods.

Identifying the nature of the problem is often difficult if the people involved tend to speak in terms of generalizations. Enactment results in a much greater degree of specificity and also an opportunity to clarify the influence of the participants' nonverbal behaviors.

Problems are usually related to implicit and possibly unconscious assumptions or attitudes which need to be discovered and brought into awareness. This is the heart of much that is written about psychotherapy—but also is the object of organizational consultations or even cultural criticism. Problem solving simply needs to take place at a deeper level. Psychodramatic methods are especially helpful in bringing out the emotional levels of a problem. Through dramatization, with the use of supportive doubling, amplification and many other techniques, the protagonist is enabled to engage the problem on an experiential as well as cognitive level.

Yet for a true understanding of a problem, it is necessary for the parties to consider the viewpoints and feelings of the other people involved. Role reversal is a powerful method for helping people to use their intuitive and imaginative capacity as a bridge to becoming more empathic.

When all the factors affecting the situation have been clarified, psychodramatic methods may then aid also in seeking more constructive solutions. Alternatives may be tried out, rehearsed, and the effects of varying styles or approaches can be assessed. The group setting is excellent for getting feedback, and a playful, supportive context allows for a more spontaneous and creative level of participation. From a behavioristic approach, effective responses are modeled and when learned, reinforced, while ineffective adaptations become immediately apparent and are gradually extinguished (Sturm, 1970). Further, the group's support provides a corrective emotional experience.

INTEGRATION WITH OTHER PSYCHOTHERAPEUTIC APPROACHES

As noted at the beginning of this chapter, I consider the various theoretical systems of psychotherapy and their practical methodologies as being essentially compatible with each other. The different approaches address some facets of human experience more than others, and so a flexible application of several different methods may be required in the individualized treatment of each case.

Without explicitly saying so, a number of other therapies already utilize certain elements either historically derived from psychodrama or developed independently, yet rely on some similar principles. The role playing used in assertion and social skills training may be viewed as behavioristic, but is really no different than what Moreno called "role training." Family therapists often behave more like psychodrama directors than do traditional individual or group therapists, and their techniques of "circular interviewing," side taking, and family sculpture are further derivatives. The guided imagery in psychosynthesis or other imagination therapies are based on principles similar to those of psychodrama. I encourage the concretization of imagined scenes in order to further anchor their dynamics in experience. The activities of bioenergeic analysis may often be used in conjunction with psychodramatic work, and other types of body therapies similarly are synergistic. Albert Pesso's movement approach uses a method that is very much like psychodrama (Pesso & Crandall, 1991). I discuss this theme of integrations of psychodrama with other therapies in greater depth in my *Foundations of Psychodrama* (Blatner, 1988).

SUMMARY

Psychodrama is more of a praxis than a separate school of thought (Blatner, 1992). A praxis is a complex of both technique and the principles which underlie their application. The theoretical foundation of psychodrama is that it is a methodology which is best understood within the context of a broader and more integrative theory of therapy, and this in turn is to be viewed within the greater context of a multidimensional psychology.

In keeping with his time, Moreno expounded his own theories of psychodrama in an unsystematic fashion, and the result was certainly incomplete. Bischof (1964) has an excellent review of Moreno's wealth of valuable ideas. Over the last generation, many have continued to develop and integrate Moreno's theoretical concepts with other aspects of the developing behavioral sciences. This chapter suggests some of those more recent developments.

REFERENCES / RECOMMENDED READINGS

Adler, A. (1939). *Social interest: A challenge to mankind.* New York: G. P. Putnam's Sons.

Anzieu, Didier. (1984). Analytic psychodrama and physical exercises. In *The group and the unconscious* (pp. 43–67). (Translated from the French by B. Kilborne.) London: Routledge & Kegan Paul.

Bischof, L. J. (1964). Moreno. In, *Interpreting personality theories* (pp. 355–420). New York: Harper & Row.

Blatner, A. (H. A.) (1969–70). Theoretical aspects of psychodrama—general comments. *Bulletin de Psychologie, 23*(13–16), 957–968.

Blatner, A. (1985). The dynamics of catharsis. *Journal of Group Psychotherapy, Psychodrama, & Sociometry, 37*(4), 157–166.

Blatner, A. (1988). *Foundations of psychodrama: History, theory, and practice.* New York: Springer.

Blatner, A. (1991). Role dynamics: A comprehensive theory of psychology. *Journal of Group Psychotherapy, Psychodrama & Sociometry, 44*(1), 33–40.

Blatner, A. (1992). Theoretical principles underlying creative arts therapies. *The Arts in Psychotherapy, 18*(4), 405–409.

Blatner, A. (1995). Drama in education as mental hygiene: A child psychiatrist's perspective. *Youth Theatre Journal, 9,* 92–96.

Blatner, A., & Blatner, A. (1988). *The art of play: An adults' guide to imagination and spontaneity.* New York: Human Sciences Press.

Blomkvist, L. D., & Rützel, T. (1994). Surplus reality and beyond. In P. Holmes, M. Karp, & M. Watson (Eds.), *Psychodrama since Moreno: Innovations in theory and practice* (pp. 235–257). London: Routledge.

Bonney, W. C., and Scott, K. H. (1983). An exploration of the origin of role formation via psychodrama and personal construct theories. *Journal of Group Psychotherapy, Psychodrama, & Sociometry, 36*(2), 47–54.

Buchanan, D. R., and Little, D. (1983). Neuro-linguistic programming and psychodrama: Theroretical and clinical similarities. *Journal of Group Psychotherapy, Psychodrama, & Sociometry, 36*(3), 114–122.

Clayton, M. (1994). Role theory and its applications in clinical practice. In P. Holmes, M. Karp, & M. Watson (Eds.), *Psychodrama since Moreno: Innovations in theory and practice* (pp. 121–144). London: Routledge.

Courtney, R. (1990). *Drama and intelligence: A cognitive theory.* Montreal: McGill-Queen's University Press.

Courtney, R. (1995). *Drama and feeling: An aesthetic theory.* Montreal: McGill-Queen's University Press.

Fryba, M. (1972). Psychodrama elements in psychosis treatment by shamans of Sri Lanka. In M. Pines & L. Rafaelsen (Eds.), *The individual and the group: Boundaries and interrelations: Vol. 2. Practice* (pp. 333–339). New York: Plenum.

Ginn, I.B. (1973). Catharsis: Its occurrence in Aristotle, psychodrama, and psychoanalysis. *Group Psychotherapy & Psychodrama, 26*(2), 7–22.

Greenberg, I., and Bassin, A. (1976). Reality therapy and psychodrama. In A. Bassin, T. Bratter, and R. Rachin (Eds.), *The reality therapy reader* (pp. 231–240). New York: Harper & Row.

Harmeling, P. C. (1950). Therapeutic theatre of Alaska Eskimos. *Group Psychotherapy, 3*(1–2), 74–75.

Jackson, S. W. (1994). Catharsis and abreaction in the history of psychological healing. *Psychiatric Clinics of North America, 17*(3), 471–491.

Jacobs, A. (1977). Psychodrama and TA. In M. James (Ed.), *Techniques in transactional analysis for therapists and counselors* (pp. 239–249). Reading, MA: Addison-Wesley.

Karp, M. (1994). Spontaneity and creativity: The river of freedom. In P. Holmes, M. Karp, & M. Watson (Eds.), *Psychodrama since Moreno: Innovations in theory and practice* (pp. 39–60). London: Routledge.

Kellermann, P. F. (1984). The place of catharsis in psychodrama. *Journal of Group Psychotherapy, Psychodrama & Sociometry, 37*(1), 1–13.

Kelly, G. R. (1982). Theoretical applications of symbolic interactionism and psychodrama. *Journal of Group Psychotherapy, Psychodrama, & Sociometry, 35*(1), 39–45.

Kottler, J.A. (1994). *Advanced group leadership.* Pacific Grove, CA: Brooks/Cole.

Landy, R. (1990). The concept of role in drama therapy. *The Arts in Psychotherapy, 17,* 223–230.

Lazarus, A. A., & Beutler, L. E. (1992). The future of technical eclecticism. *Psychotherapy: Theory, Research, Practice, Training, 29*(1), 11–18.

McKissack, I. (December 1992). Psychodrama in the postmodern world. *Australian & New Zealand Psychodrama Association Journal, 1,* 27–30.

Meerloo, J.A.M. (1966). Why do we sympathize with each other? *Archives of General Psychiatry, 15,* 390–397.

Moreno, J. L. (1953). How Kurt Lewin's "Research Center for Group Dynamics" started. *Sociometry, 16*(1), 101–104.

Moreno, J. L. (1956). Psychotherapy: Present and future. In, F. Fromm-Reichmann & J. L. Moreno (Eds.), *Progress in psychotherapy* Vol. 1 (pp. 327–333). New York: Grune and Stratton.

Moreno, J. L. (1961). The role concept: A bridge between psychiatry and sociology. *American Journal of Psychiatry, 118,* 518–523.

Naar, R. (1977). A psychodramatic intervention with a T.A. framework in individual and group psychotherapy. *Group Psychotherapy, Psychodrama & Sociometry,, 30,* 127–134.

Orcutt, T. L. (1977). Roles and rules: The kinship and territoriality of psychodrama and Gestalt therapy. *Group Psychotherapy, Psychodrama, & Sociometry, 30,* 97–107.

Pesso, A., & Crandall, J. (Eds.). (1991). *Moving psychotherapy.* Cambridge, MA: Brookline.

Sarbin, T. R. (1943). The concept of role-taking. *Sociometry, 6,* 273–285.

Seeman, H. (1982). A methodology for existential psychotherapy: Psychodrama. *Journal of Group Psychotherapy, Psychodrama, & Sociometry, 35*(2), 70–82.

Shearon, E. M. (1978). Aspects of persuasion in psychodrama. *Group Psychotherapy, Psychodrama, & Sociometry, 31,* 96–108.

Shearon, E. M. (1981). Comparison of Rogers' self theory and Moreno's spontaneity theory. *Journal of Group Psychotherapy, Psychodrama, & Sociometry, 34,* 112–133.

Sturm, I. E. (1970). A behavioral outline of psychodrama. *Psychotherapy: Theory, Research and Practice, 7*(4), 245–247.

Wallach, M.A., & Wallach, L. (1983). *Psychology's sanction for selfishness: The error of egoism in theory and therapy.* San Francisco: W. H. Freeman & Co.

Worell, J., & Remer, P. (1992). *Feminist perspectives in therapy: An empowerment model for women.* New York: Wiley.

Whitmont, E. C. (1984). Recent influences on the practice of Jungian analysis. In M. Stein (Ed.), *Jungian Analysis* (pp. 346–360). Boulder, CO: Shambhala.

Yablonsky, L. (1954). The future-projection technique. *Group Psychotherapy, 7,* 303–306.

10

The Training of the Psychodramatist

Directing psychodrama requires a substantial degree of training, because the method is powerful—and, in untrained hands, potentially dangerous. It may be likened to surgery in that its practice requires both mastery of a specialized technique and grounding in a broader professional knowledge. Kellermann (1992b) points out that a director needs to be competent as an understanding analyst, a healing therapist, an aesthetic dramatic producer, and a flexible group leader. In turn, these four roles involve a further variety of more specific abilities.

In conducting classical psychodrama, directors must be discriminating in selecting protagonists, and as with surgery, must make sure the setting is supportive and the psychosocial equivalent of a recovery room is available (as is discussed more fully in the chapter on pitfalls). On the other hand, a number of psychodramatic techniques, such as role reversal, may be integrated into many types of therapy, and their application may be likened to the use of minor surgical techniques which are part of any family practitioner's practice.

Directing psychodrama requires more than mere knowledge of the techniques. One of the problems in any field is the fact that there are many people who claim a level of competence that they do not in fact have. Also, it is not apparent to the general population (or to a good many therapists) exactly what psychodrama consists of. Many self-proclaimed directors have assembled a grab-bag of structured experiences, creative drama or theatre games techniques and other active exercises which they then call "psy-chodrama." Others have attended one or a few workshops and, under the illusion that directing seems simple enough, introduce the method in their groups. However, all too often these novices don't know how to manage the powerful emotions that are evoked. The recipients of this treatment in turn blame and deval-ue the psychodramatic method itself rather than the overreaching of the group leader. ·

Unless the appropriate standards for directing are widely known, consumers often cannot discriminate the well-trained practitioner from the amateur. Unfortunately, professionals are often tempted to think that the mere possession of a degree allows them to engage in practices which are, in fact, beyond their actual competence. And since psychodrama can seem to be easy from the point of view of some naive audience members, they may feel safe in presuming that they can direct also.

Becoming a psychodramatist is far more demanding than it might appear, because it requires a mastery of personal and pro-fessional abilities:

- psychodramatic techniques as described in this book
- experience directing under supervision and revising one's approach with appropriate feedback
- development of personal spontaneity, authenticity, open-ness, creative flexibility, humility, responsibility, and caring
- well-grounded knowledge of the principles of human devel-opment throughout the life cycle, varieties of psychosocial problems (psychopathology), methods of diagnosis, and an appreciation of the full range of available treatment approaches
- appreciation of group dynamics, including Moreno's own method of sociometry whereby people can be helped to give themselves feedback in groups regarding patterns of attrac-tion and repulsion

- understanding of the principles underlying psychotherapy
- appreciation of drama that includes recognition of the power of its methodology, and aesthetic sensibility regarding staging, ritual, and timing
- understanding of and commitment to the ethics of therapy and group leadership
- dedication to a philosophy of creativity, spontaneity, and encounter which includes the spiritual dimensions of life

For these reasons, psychodrama should be recognized as being as complex a subspecialty of psychotherapy as neurosurgery is a subspecialty of medicine. Those who wish to do more than integrate some of these techniques into their own practice should realize that a commitment to several hundred hours of further training may be demanded.

CERTIFIED TRAINING

The field of psychodrama has become professionalized, which means that its recognized practitioners have dedicated themselves to an ongoing development of their abilities and knowledge. Like most professions, it has established standards for differentiating those who have fulfilled a recognized course of training from those whose "expertise" is merely self-proclaimed. Thus, in the mid-1970s the American Board of Examiners in Psychodrama, Sociometry and Group Psychotherapy and was formed and established two levels of competence: Certified Practitioner (CP) and Trainer, Educator & Practitioner (TEP). Certified Practitioners are recognized as being capable of directing psychodrama at any degree of depth; TEPs are recognized as capable of teaching others to direct psychodramas.

The board has developed criteria for certification, has established examination procedures, and makes available materials which explain these requirements. For those interested in pursuing subspecialty training in psychodrama, please write:

The American Board of Examiners in Psychodrama,
Sociometry and Group Psychotherapy
P.O. Box 15572
Washington, DC 20003-0572
Telephone: (202) 483-0514

As a psychotherapeutic specialty, psychodrama requires first that a certified practitioner complete a program of training in one of the recognized fields of psychotherapy—psychiatry, psychology, social work, psychiatric nursing, or counseling, obtaining at least a Master's degree. The prerequisite training should provide a basic knowledge of diagnosis and treatment, although it is expected that psychodramatists will continue to engage in an ongoing process of professional and personal self- improvement.

The board also makes available a directory of certified professionals, so practitioners can more easily be located. As of this writing, there are over a hundred certified trainers (TEPs) and over two hundred certified practitioners in the USA, and a number in other countries who have been certified by the American board.

Psychodrama is becoming widespread internationally, with an estimated ten thousand practitioners and perhaps one thousand trainers. There are over twenty other national organizations of psychodramatists and less-organized networks of professionals in many other countries. Some of these organizations have established their own accreditation procedures. However, arrangements regarding reciprocity of certification are still being negotiated.

In the United States, the American Society for Group Psychotherapy and Psychodrama (also known as ASGPP) is the organization founded by Moreno himself. The ASGPP now holds national and regional conferences, provides a subscription to a national journal, the *Journal of Group Psychotherapy, Psychodrama & Sociometry*, and offers a number of other membership benefits.

For information regarding conferences, help in networking with practitioners in your area (or country, if you are outside of the United States), write:

The American Society for Group
Psychotherapy & Psychodrama
301 North Harrison St, Suite 508,
Princeton, NJ 08540
Telephone: (609) 452-1339

The ASGPP, incidentally, was the first organization of group psychotherapists, established in 1942, some few months before the American Group Psychotherapy Association (AGPA) was established by Samuel Slavson, a psychoanalytically-oriented group worker who was a rival of Moreno's. Because psychoanalysis established a hegemony among the psychotherapies during the middle of this century, the AGPA became the more widely known of the two organizations. But in the last decade, it has expanded beyond the boundaries of psychoanalysis and included representatives from family therapy, gestalt therapy and psychodrama as part of its annual programs.

Moreno was also the founder of the International Association for Group Psychotherapy (IAGP)—the first international group therapy organization—which hosts an annual meeting every three years. It has subgroups of analytic, psychodramatic, and other types of approaches. Information regarding membership may be obtained by writing the cochairperson for the section on psychodrama: David Kipper, PhD, Action Methods Associates, Ltd., 444 N. Michigan Ave., Suite 810, Chicago, IL 60611, or Grete Leutz, M.D., Moreno Institut, Uhlandstrasse 8, Uberlingen/Bodensee D88662, Germany.

THE ELEMENTS OF TRAINING

Learning to direct psychodrama involves both didactic and experiential components. Much of the rest of this chapter will primarily discuss training for those who would apply psychodrama as a therapeutic method. However, for those who wish to use psychodrama in nontherapeutic contexts, modifying it as role playing or sociodrama, adequate training—and caution—are still necessary. In using role playing in the classroom or in a business, the director needs to know how to develop and sustain the warming-up process. Knowing psychodramatic methods alone, however, can't make a person a competent teacher, group leader, or organizational consultant. Each of these roles has its own set of basic skills to which the knowledge of psychodrama can serve as a complement.

In addition to the information in this book, the reader is urged to seek out other descriptions of techniques and further theoretical discussions. Many books and articles in the field are listed listed in the bibliography at the end of this volume. I wrote *Foundations of Psychodrama* (1988) as a complement to this present book. It addresses in greater depth a number of psychodrama's underlying principles and ways to integrate psychodrama with various theories.

The elements of training that will be discussed include experiential learning, personal development, group dynamics, spontaneity training, role expansion, and associated approaches.

Experiential Learning

The learning of psychodrama requires a knack—that is, an integration of intuition, emotion, imagination, rational cognition, and physical activity—which can only be acquired through a process of holistic involvement. A student of psychodrama must experience the process in all available roles: auxiliary ego, audience, director, and especially, protagonist. In this respect the learning is more like the training of a psychoanalyst than the training of a surgeon. Only through the repeated experience of being the protagonist can a person learn some of the nuances of feeling which then develop the requisite sensitivity in a would-be director.

Training in psychodrama is primarily experiential, with an overlay of didactic instruction and adjunctive reading. Students begin to direct small enactments and circumscribed role-playing activities under supervision as soon as they are able. Also, they are encouraged to introduce psychodramatic methods as complements to their other activities as therapists in individual, family, or group treatment (Stein & Callahan, 1982). Just as clients in therapy must engage a kind of risk taking in order to relearn new lessons and skills in life, so, too, must therapists have a sense of adventure in acquiring the skills of directing. The sense of competence is, like true insight, a "felt sense," achieved through an integrated process in which bodily experience, muscular action, feeling pulled or pushed, the actual "doing" of self-expression (as differentiated from merely talking about it, or even vividly imagining it), all deepen the shift in cognition.

In the course of training, there are a number of ways that the student of psychodrama can be aided by the teacher (Goldman, Morrison & Schramski, 1982; Nolte & Hale, 1976). Theories of psychodrama can help the apprentice director bring out the group's main concern and relate it to the work of the protagonist (Buchanan, 1980). But perhaps the most important experience is working under supervision. Students benefit greatly from having an opportunity to "process" what has been done as a director with a trainer. Kellermann (1992a) reviews the various issues which must be addressed in this type of pedagogic debriefing.

Anyone who wishes to achieve competence in directing must develop a willingness to take risks—the risks of being a protagonist repeatedly, speaking up in the group, daring to critique authority, affirming individual inclinations, and especially to direct imperfectly and be the recipient of criticism—and in so doing, exercise the more demanding dimensions of spontaneity. Becoming a protagonist not only provides a powerful experience of therapy, but it also helps to sensitize the student to the role of the patient in psychodrama. The future director learns from the inside, so to speak, which of the acting director's maneuvers are most helpful, and which are most distracting and/or misleading. The student identifies with and internalizes the helpful behaviors, learning through modeling by the trainer even from within the quasi-hypnotic experience of enactment.

Personal Development

It must be acknowledged that every professional, every trainer, every practioner continues to struggle with challenges. Most professionals in training (and ever after) continue to address and work through at least some degree of residual reaction patterns based on previous family experiences, friendship and primary romantic relationships, continuing frictions with parents, partners, co-workers, and children, spiritual conflicts, dealing with addictive tendencies, self-management, life planning, role balance, and other issues. I am not implying that only those who have fully resolved all life issues should dare to direct a psychodrama. I doubt that any of us ever reach that possibly illusory endpoint. However, directing does require the achievement of psychological-mindedness, insight, and openness to evaluating least a fair proportion of one's own weaknesses. If blocks occur, then, the director can at least consider that they may be expressions of his or her own psychodynamic "blind spots," and will not be too proud or defensive to ask for help or consultation.

A basic principle for the practice of psychotherapy is that therapists must become alert to the way their own problems can interfere with their helping of others. Directors of psychodrama, whether in training or fully certified, must keep in mind the inevitability of encountering situations that "push their buttons," evoke what in psychoanalysis is generally called countertransferences, subconscious reaction patterns that can block optimal work with a protagonist.

Perhaps the best way to learn to help others is to become familiar with the process of self-discovery, which involves learning how to become sensitive to one's own tendencies to error. Direction can be flawed by patterns of misinterpretation of others' behaviors; limitations of possible responses; false beliefs about oneself, others, the nature of life, or the best way to cope with the world; tendencies to bias or distortion regarding certain situations or ideas; unconscious reaction patterns to certain people; and so forth. The student of psychodrama, like any therapist, must become aware of his or her transferences, or proclivities to react not to who the other person really is, but rather to a person whose image or memory is evoked by the other person. These distortions must be cleared through the sometimes painful process of personal therapeutic exploration.

Students of psychodrama who are not seeing a psychotherapist to explore their own personal issues should at least participate in an ongoing series of personal growth experiences. The purpose should include not only the correction of personality traits that might interfere with the practice of psychotherapy, but equally important, the acquisition of some strategies and a motivation to continue one's own self-reflective adventure on a lifelong basis.

Group Dynamics

Being part of a group, whether it be an actual therapy group, a personal growth group, or a training group, offers opportunities to learn about one's own interpersonal interactions and, at an experiential level, one also learns about a number of Moreno's principles of sociometry. Often the ongoing dynamics of the group's interaction will be more relevant to the learning of each participant than observing or participating in a protagonist-centered classical psychodrama. And using psychodramatic methods such as doubling and role reversal to address group phenomena can deepen the experience tremendously.

Learning experientially and didactically can be synergistic. Ancillary reading of books and articles on group process (e.g., Corey & Corey [1992], Ettin [1992], or Nicholas [1984] is highly recommended. It's also helpful to get involved in some task-oriented groups in which the challenge goes beyond mere insight. Much can be learned about oneself and group dynamics through events which involve taking responsibility, delegating authority, managing, dealing with disappointments, learning to give and receive constructive criticism, allowing oneself to be vulnerable, and other interpersonal challenges in group endeavors.

Spontaneity Training

The capacity to warm oneself up to spontaneity is an important skill in directing psychodrama. The director must become open and receptive to inspiration, intuition, and creativity. This requires practice, as much as any other skill. Most people are somewhat inhibited, timid and stilted, and learning how to counter the subtle and often not-so-subtle conditioning of a culture that generally feels threatened by spontaneity. Teaching and preaching, selling and mediating, shifting between the confident helper and the humble student are all components of the psychodrama director's role. Initiative, comfort in taking charge, and the ability to project one's voice can be cultivated.

The kinds of activities that promote spontaneity development include theatre games, the kinds of warm-ups described in Chapter 4 or in the books and articles in the references of that chapter, and the activities described in *The Art of Play*, (Blatner & Blatner, 1988). Also, the activities associated with the other creative arts therapies are often spontaneity based, and invite an expansion of roles into new territories.

Role Expansion

A related mode of learning involves the student's development of role-taking skills in general. The basic idea is to learn to think like an actor rather than a textbook, to exert the "muscles of imagination" in wondering what it might be like to be in another person's situation. Actually enacting those unfamiliar roles becomes a powerful exercise which builds empathy and understanding (Blatner, 1985a; Blatner & Blatner, 1988). Role-taking skills grow with practice, and that practice can often be structured so that it's playful and fun.

Directors must also appreciate the depth and variety of dynamic and social issues which affect minorities and other subgroups whose life situation hasn't become part of the general cultural awareness. Some therapists deal with addicts, criminals, the homeless, the elderly, the terminally ill, people who are HIV positive or with AIDS, and and part of their training should then include the exploration of roles which many feel abhorrent or frightening. Yet this kind of role-taking also helps trainees reconnect with what Jungians call the *shadow complexes*, those dynamics which have been most rejected and possibly even repressed as "not-me." This kind of work, thus, not only is personally therapeutic, but helps to sensitize directors to themes which might otherwise cause "blind spots" or countertransferences (Blatner, 1985a).

I have found it especially helpful to become familiar with the varieties of self-deception and interpersonal manipulations. The different *defense mechanisms*, as they are called in psychoanalysis, can be appreciated as inner dramatic maneuvers, little subjective performances which serve to restore the individual's sense of control or self-esteem. Don't just learn them from the textbooks, but role play these avoidant techniques. They are subconscious, magical, somewhat primitive forms of thinking which can be expressed not only in descriptive prose, but also in the form of dialogue—the language of the self-system discussed in Chapter 3. In fact, these cognitive transformations are often performed on a preverbal or nonverbal level, but they nevertheless have a verbal equivalent. A sullen withdrawal may have no conscious equivalent, but it functions *as if* to say, "I'm not going to budge. You should reach out to me," or "Leave me alone, everything you do just makes me feel worse."

Learn also how these stances can be expressed in bodily postures, character styles, and even through the clichés and norms of the culture. These constitute a great portion of the "hidden" levels of feeling and communication. This knowledge may be used by auxiliaries in the role of double to portray the deeper truths which in real life too often remain unspoken and thus inaccessible to reevaluation and healing.

Related Therapeutic Approaches

Beyond learning a basic approach to psychotherapy, which includes the acquisition of an appreciation for the fundamentals of psychodynamic theory, psychosocial development, diagnosis, psychopathology, and at least one mainstream method of treatment, it is also helpful for a student of psychodrama to learn about those therapeutic approaches that are particularly related to psychodrama.

From the 1950s through the 1970s, group psychotherapy was dominated by the hegemony of psychoanalysis, but gradually, since the mid-1960s, alternative approaches, some of which have been influenced directly or indirectly by Moreno's ideas, have gained recognition. During the 1980s, there have been increasing interconnections between mainstream group psychotherapy and psychodrama. This point deserves emphasis: There is a great potential for the integration of psychodramatic methods and principles with other approaches. Knowing about Morenian approaches can deepen, intensify and complement psychodynamic group work and in turn, the practice of psychodrama can be enriched by the best insights of the various other innovators in the psychodynamic approaches. Cross-fertilization is especially productive in the subfields discussed below.

Conjoint family therapy has been a natural area of complementarity. Most family therapists behave in a fashion that is closer to a psychodrama director than do most group therapists. One of the reason this book's title uses the term, "psychodramatic methods" rather than "psychodrama" is that I want to counter the cliché that psychodrama is necessarily a "group" approach. It may be that the modification and applications of Morenian techniques will occur in more active and intensive work with families, couples, and even individuals.

Furthermore, the systems orientation of family therapy theory is a mode of thought similar to Moreno's sociometric ideas. And this approach extends beyond simple family dynamics to include multiple generations, extended family, friends and neighbors, relevant social agencies, and other areas in the social network.

Humanistic and existential approaches to psychotherapy share some important viewpoints with Morenean thought and should be included in the development of an overall perspective toward psychology (Seeman, 1982).

The *cognitive* therapies, including cognitive-behavioral therapy and some related forms, such as Albert Ellis' *rational- emotive therapy,* involve the process of reviewing beliefs and modes of thinking. Cognitive and cognitive behavioral therapies, developed mainly in the 1970s by Aaron Beck and others, is becoming one of the fastest-growing general modalities in therapy in the 1990s (Beck, 1995). Knowing about these approaches can help psychodramatists to better deal with their protagonists' beliefs, as discussed in the chapter on action.

Another related modality in psychotherapy is the utilization of the power of imagery and visualization. This capacity has become recognized as a vehicle for accessing the emotions and reactions of the preverbal psychological functions. Furthermore, the theory underlying these so-called *right brain therapies* also bolsters the rationale for psychodrama, which, as I like to emphasize, integrates imagination as well as action.

The creative arts therapies also utilize the patients' imagery, and add to imagery self-expression in aesthetic forms which becomes a form of sublimation and empowerment even as it is helping the conscious mind to understand deeper and more subtle dimensions of feeling (Blatner, 1987). Art, music, dance, poetry, and a variety of drama therapy techniques are all potentially powerful sources for expanding the psychodramatist's repertoire. The techniques involved serve as natural vehicles for both the warming-up and integration (see Creamer, 1983, and especially McNiff, 1986).

Gestalt therapy was methodologically derived in part from psychodrama, especially regarding the use of the technique of the empty chair. This rich approach invites an existential and vivid way to access the realm of awareness in the present moment. It is one of the most important complements to the use of psychodrama, and many practitioners freely synthesize both methods.

The *body therapies* recognize the importance of the muscular patterns of tension and habitual usage. Bioenergetic analysis, Alexander Lowen's derivative of Wilhelm Reich's early ideas about character and "body armoring," is perhaps the best known of these approaches (Lowen, 1995). Yet there are elements of this concept in Gestalt therapy and other active treatment methods. Some bioenergetic techniques can be adapted to help patients deal with blocked emotions during psychodramatic explorations.

Working with nonverbal communications is an important dimension of psychodrama. In order to bring out the unspoken expressions of emotion, however, the practitioner must first be sensitive to the wide variety of ways that people knowingly or (more often) unknowingly give each other messages. Related also is a knowledge of patterns of verbal communications, the fields of practical semantics and linguistics that can help the student to understand the common problems of miscommunication that are so prevalent in pathological family interactions (Blatner, 1985b).

In addition, the student of psychodrama and psychotherapy should learn about those fields related to psychodrama theoretically: drama therapy, drama in education, constructivism, feminism, and others (see Chapter 9). And finally, the psychodramatist should be conversant with current cultural issues and the stresses of our changing world. Issues related to shifting patterns in relations between the sexes, relations with parents and children, the nature of success and philosophies of life, the spiritual journey and religious crises, challenges in educational and vocational choices— these and many other themes are evolving along with new forms of technology and socioeconomic organizations. Political issues relating to ecology, human rights, and the arms race are also factors of increasing relevance to people's lives, and these "sociodramatic" issues often lead to meaningful psychodramas regarding personal values and choices.

It must be emphasized that there are many occasions in which psychodrama or action approaches are irrelevant or even contraindicated. The freedom to refrain from doing drama is as important as the not infrequent and highly desirable surgeon's consultation at which it is decided that an operation is not indicated. Psychodrama should be viewed as an optional set of tools, not a single approach for all patients.

For example, psychodramatists, as psychotherapists, should become familiar with the current general status of biological psychiatry, that is, the indications and benefits (as well as the limitations and side effects) of the latest psychotropic medications, which are as much a part of a comprehensive treatment as antibiotics. There are many situations in which they are not needed— and indeed, times when they're overprescribed—but a competent therapist is able to use—via referral when necessary—all modes of treatment.

SUMMARY

The student of psychodrama must balance several aspects of learning:

1. the *knowledge* that comes with reading and classroom work

2. the *understanding* that comes with experiencing a variety of situations through the exercise of role reversal, as auxiliary, as protagonist, and simply in play

3. the *competence* that comes with practice to the point of mastery

4. the *wisdom* that comes from integrating into the learning process one's own personal therapeutic journey, and consists of the growing capacity to liberate and access one's own higher self.

REFERENCES / RECOMMENDED READINGS

Beck, A. T., & Weishaar, M. E. (1995). Cognitive therapy. In R. J. Corsini & D. Wedding (Eds.), *Current psychotherapies* (5th ed.) (pp. 229–261). Itasca, IL: F. E. Peacock.

Blatner, A. (1985a). Further role explorations. In *Role Development* (pp. 55–58). San Marcos, TX: Author.

Blatner, A. (1985b). Becoming aware of nonverbal communication. In *Role Development* (pp. 47–54). San Marcos, TX: Author.

Blatner, A. (1987). The function of the creative therapies—A preface. In M. R. Morrison (Ed.), *Poetry as therapy* (pp. 17–19). New York: Human Sciences Press.

Blatner, A., & Blatner, A. (1988). *The art of play: An adult's guide to reclaiming imagination and spontaneity.* New York: Human Sciences Press.

Buchanan, D. R. (1980). The central concern model: A framework for structuring psychodramatic production. *Group Psychotherapy, Psychodrama, & Sociometry, 33,* 47–62.

Corey, M. S., & Corey, G. (1992). *Groups: Process and practice.* (4th ed.). Pacific Grove, CA: Brooks/Cole.

Creamer, N. (1983). The silent language: Basic principles of movement/dance therapy for the non-movement therapist. *Journal of Group Psychotherapy, Psychodrama & Sociometry, 36*(2), 55–60.

Ellis, A. (1979). Rational-emotive therapy. In R. J. Corsini (Ed.), *Current psychotherapies* (2nd ed.)(pp. 185–229). Itasca, IL: F. E. Peacock.

Ettin, M. F. (1992). *Foundations and applications of group psychotherapy: A sphere of influence.* Boston: Allyn & Bacon.

Feder, E., and Feder, B. (1981). *The expressive arts therapies.* Englewood Cliffs, NJ: Prentice-Hall.

Goldman, E. E., Morrison, D. S., & Schramski, T. G. (1982). Codirecting therapy: A method for psychodramatist training. *Journal of Group Psychotherapy, Psychodrama, & Sociometry, 35*(2), 65–69.

Kellermann, P. F. (1992a). Processing in psychodrama. *Journal of Group Psychotherapy, Psychodrama & Sociometry, 45*(2), 63–73.

Kellermann, P.F. (1992b). The psychodramatist. *Journal of Group Psychotherapy, Psychodrama & Sociometry, 45*(2), 74–88.

Lowen, A. (1995). Bioenergetic analysis. In R. J. Corsini & D. Wedding (Eds.), *Current psychotherapies* (5th ed.)(pp. 409–418). Itasca, IL: F. E. Peacock.

McNiff, S. (1986). *Educating the creative arts therapist: A profile of the profession.* Springfield, IL: Charles C Thomas.

Nicholas, M. W. (1984). *Change in the context of group therapy.* New York: Brunner/Mazel.

Nolte, J., and Hale, A. E. (1976). The director's soliloquy and the director's double. *Group Psychotherapy and Psychodrama, 29,* 23–32.

Seeman, H. (1982). A methodology for existential psychotherapy: Psychodrama. *Journal of Group Psychotherapy, Psychodrama & Sociometry, 36*(2), 70–82.

Stein, M. B., & Callahan, M. L. (1982). The use of psychodrama in individual psychotherapy. *Journal of Group Psychotherapy, Psychodrama & Sociometry, 36*(3), 118–129.

Zuretti, M. (1982). Teaching the psychodramatic method. In M. Pines & L. Rafaelsen (Eds.), *The individual and the group.* New York: Plenum.

11

A Brief History of Psychodrama

Psychodrama, invented by J. L. Moreno, MD, was a product of philosophical interest in the phenomenon of creativity, in the nature of spontaneous play in experiments with children, in sociological dynamics, and a desire to reform the theatre to make it more involving, real, and meaningful to people. Gradually, from these multidimensional foundations, Moreno began to apply improvisational dramatics in the service of family, group and individual psychotherapy. Moreno's life was eventful and complex, and this chapter will offer only an overview of its high points. A number of articles have been written about him, mentioned at the end of this chapter in the references, but especially notable are Marineau's 1989 biography of Moreno, Moreno's own abridged autobiography edited by his son, Jonathan (Moreno, 1989), and three chapters I wrote in Foundations of Psychodrama which discuss other contributors to the field—noting especially events in the life of his wife, Zerka Toeman Moreno—and offer a consideration of why psychodrama remained a rather minor development in the field of psychotherapy during his lifetime (Blatner, 1988).

Jacob Levy Moreno was born on May 19, 1889, in Bucharest, Rumania. In a number of his own earlier books, he gave the date 1892, and also at times said that he was born on a boat in the Black Sea, but this has since been corrected (Bratescu, 1975). He was the oldest of six children. When he was five years old his family moved to Vienna. Moreno attended the University of Vienna as a student of philosophy and was impressed with the currently popular ideas about creativity, such as those presented by Henri

Bergson. Around 1908, he also became interested in the play of children in the city's parks, and involved himself as a catalyst, discovering that their vitality was enhanced when they improvised in enacting familiar stories rather than following conventional interpretations.

Moreno then went on to medical school at the University of Vienna (circa 1912-1917). During this period, he also explored his ideas of a more creative type of theology, developed his philosophy of encounter, and implemented his ideas in social action. For example, he instituted self-help groups for some of the prostitutes in the city; indeed, this may have been one of the first examples of the use of both self-help groups and of what might today be considered a form of community psychiatry.

Around the end of his medical training Moreno was assigned to be the physician attending a refugee camp in the nearby town of Mittendorf. The patterns of cultural disorganization he noticed there seemed to be partly products of artificial rules. He proposed that opening the governing process more to input from the refugees themselves might make the stress of relocation a bit more humane. This application of his ideas about "encounter" (and he was one of the earliest writers to use this term) to sociological problems was the seed of his later method of sociometry: Interviewing the people at the camp regarding whom they would prefer to have as neighbors, he used feedback to work out more congenial living arrangements. This may seem obvious today, but at the time it was a highly innovative approach, contrasting with the tendencies of administrators to assign living quarters and jobs on an arbitrary or bureaucratic basis.

Vienna in the first few decades of this century was a center of intellectual activity. During and after medical school Moreno plunged into the literary, philosophical, and social milieu of the city. He edited a literary journal, *Daimon*, and included in its contents the writings of such fellow intellectuals as Martin Buber and Max Scheler. Moreno also wrote inspirational poetry and prose. One of his earliest books (later translated from the German as *The Words of the Father*) expressed his view that creativity was something that flowed through every individual and that was renewed in every moment (Blatner, 1985). His earliest books were published anonymously, a symbolic gesture of his inclusive ideals, but later, seeing that there was no advantage to this, he noted his authorship.

Fascinated by the theater, but feeling that it had become a degraded form, Moreno wanted to see more impromptu acting, more vitality. In many ways, he was anticipating the emergence of experimental forms in theater which arose almost a half-century later. He organized a troupe of actors and began to experiment with various types of improvsational drama, such as the "living newspaper." Moreno dates the roots of psychodrama itself to his first public performance in April, 1921. Later he renamed his troupe *Die Stegreiftheatre*—in English, "The Theatre of Spontaneity." The principles governing the troupe's performances were then written in a book with the same title. This experimental "improv" troupe had some good reviews and periods of success. Incidentally, Moreno's fertile mind also produced plans for one of the first "theatres in the round."

During this time, Moreno lived in the Viennese suburb of Voslau and served the community as their public health officer and family physician—and was reputed to be very competent. He was lovingly remembered many years later as "our doctor." Perhaps his role as doctor helped him discover an interesting side effect of his "improv" troupe: the role-taking process was often cathartic and healing for the actors themselves.

Because postwar Vienna suffered from runaway inflation and the society was disorganized, Moreno, unable to sustain his experiments with the drama, decided to emigrate to the United States. Arriving in New York in 1925, he was able to introduce his ideas to the various hospitals and clinics in the area.

Moreno was a man of many talents. He had invented something like a wire recorder, and it was with the sponsorship of a businessman in the United States that he was able to immigrate. Later on, he wrote some of the earliest papers about the possible applications of both audio and video recording in psychotherapy.

In the 1930s, Moreno consulted with prisons, residential treatment centers for delinquent adolescents, and various other facilities. These experiences fitted with his emerging identity as a psychiatrist dedicated to social concerns. He coined the term *group psychotherapy* in 1932, and became one of the pioneers of the promotion of this approach. He continued to develop his theoretical and practical ideas about sociometry, and in 1934 published *Who Shall Survive? A New Approach to the Problem of Human Interrelations.* This book included many of his early ideas about psychodrama, role theory, and social psychology (Hare, 1986, 1992). Sociometry went on to become a significant method in sociology, especially around the mid-1950s, and the journal *Sociometry: A Journal of Interpersonal Relations,* which Moreno initiated, is still published by the American Sociological Association.

In 1936, Moreno opened a sanitarium in Beacon, New York, about 60 miles north of New York City on the Hudson River. He built a theater designed specifically for psychodrama and began to treat patients using that method. Although Moreno has stated that he invented the method earlier, it seems apparent to me that it was during the period of around 1935 through 1945 that he was really developing psychodrama as a form of psychotherapy. The Moreno Sanitarium became his home and the hub of a number of related activities. He also started his own publishing operation, Beacon House, which put out a series of journals, monographs and books on the subjects of psychodrama, sociometry, group psychotherapy, and related topics.

Also around that time Moreno had contacts with a number of other pioneers and believed that he had been influential in the development of their work: Samuel R. Slavson (with whom he developed a major rivalry), Alfred Korzybski (who originated the field of semantics), Kurt Lewin, and a number of Lewin's students in the subsequent years (Berger, 1990; Cramer-Azima, 1990). For these reasons, Moreno felt that he deserved more credit in the ensuing years, especially regarding the origins of the ideas that gave rise to the "T-Group," sensitivity training, and the encounter group movement (Bradford, Gibb, & Benne, 1964).

During the Second World War, Moreno continued to practice, opened an institute for training in New York City, did sociometric studies in schools in the area, and organized the first professional association devoted to group psychotherapy, the American Society of Group Psychotherapy and Psychodrama (ASGPP). After the war, he began to publish other journals, more monographs, books, and articles. At the beginning of the 1940s, he met Zerka Toeman, who became professionally associated with him (Moreno, 1970). They were married in 1949, and together they began to teach and present Moreno's ideas and methods throughout the United States and internationally.

From the period of 1940 through the mid-1960s, psychoanalysis held a hegemony in psychotherapy, but Moreno's action methods served as one of the major alternatives to the relative passivity of traditional psychiatric treatment. Moreno also actively encouraged a wide range of other forms of therapy, using his journals and the professional meetings of the ASGPP as vehicles for the promotion of such approaches as dance therapy, poetry therapy, family therapy, and so forth. In turn, psychodramatic methods have since been integrated into many of the "innovative" approaches that have emerged since the 1960s, such as "family sculpture" (another name for action sociometry), Gestalt therapy, and so on. In addition, psychodramatic elements are used in conjunction with Adlerian therapy and behavior therapy, among others.*

---

*Eric Berne wrote: "In his selection of specific techniques, Dr. Perls shares with other 'active' psychotherapists the 'Moreno problem': The fact that nearly all known 'active' techniques were first tried out by Dr. J. L. Moreno in psychodrama, so that it is difficult to come up with an original idea in this regard." From a review of Gestalt Therapy Verbatim, *American Journal of Psychiatry*, 126(10: 15-20,), April 1970.

A. H. Maslow (the "dean" of American humanistic psychology) wrote, regarding Jane Howard's article on Esalen and other new developments in education and psychotherapy, "I would however like to add one credit-where-credit-is-due footnote. Many of the techniques set forth in the article were originally invented by Dr. Jacob Moreno, who is still functioning vigorously and probably still inventing new techniques and ideas." (Letter to Editors, LIFE Magazine, August 2, 1968).

Dr. William Schutz (a major figure in the American encounter group movement) noted that ". . . Virtually all of the methods that I had proudly compiled or invented [Moreno] had more or less anticipated, in some cases forty years earlier...," "Leuner's original article (on guided fantasy) has appeared in (Moreno's) Journal in about 1932, and he had been using the method periodically since... I invite you to investigate Moreno's work. It is probably not sufficiently acknowledged in this country. Perls' Gestalt Therapy owes a great deal to it. It is imaginative and worth exploring." (*Here Comes Everybody*, Harper & Row, 1971.)

Moreno collaborated with a number of leaders in the field of mental health. He and Zerka were major organizers of the first international conferences of group psychotherapy, along with S. H. Foulkes of Great Britain, S. Lebovici of France, and other eminent figures. Beginning with a group called the International Committee of Group Psychotherapy, the attendees began planning in Paris in 1951, and held periodic meetings through 1973, when the name of the group was changed to the International Association of Group Psychotherapy (IAGP). These conferences were usually attended by over 1,000 participants each time. In the 1960s and early 1970s Moreno also organized a series of International Congresses of Psychodrama and Sociodrama, which reflected the widespread reception of psychodrama. Moreno's books, along with books on psychodrama being produced by writers in other countries, have been translated into many languages.

Moreno's energy, vitality, charisma, and drive were remarkable. He had his faults, too: Like a number of other innovators, he was often insensitive to group and personal politics. Yet the sheer range of interests and the validity of his vision combine to generate a powerful complex of ideas that continue to find increasing appreciation for their relevance to the challenges of today's world.

In May 1974, after a period of gradually declining health, Moreno decided to die and therefore stopped eating. He received visitors who came to pay their respects and died soon after the annual meeting of the ASGPP. Since that time, Zerka Moreno has carried on the work, teaching all over the world, writing, and encouraging others. She has also fostered more democratic participation and control in the ASGPP.

Psychodrama continues to be a significant component of the International Association of Group Psychotherapy. With Moreno's name on its letterhead as the founder, IAGP meetings have been held every three years, most recently the eleventh in Montreal, 1992, and the twelfth in Buenos Aires in 1995. The thirteenth is being planned for 1998 in London. International meetings on psychodrama continue also in such locations as England, Australia, Italy, Japan, and Jerusalem with significant activity in Scandinavia, Germany, and emerging in eastern Europe.

In addition to the continuing expansion of psychodrama internationally, there has, in addition, been a growth of national associations and journals. In the United States and elsewhere, there has been a move towards professional certification boards, as described in the previous chapter on training. As the cost-containment crisis continues in the health care fields, the use of psychodrama in hospital therapy may decline somewhat, but its use will increase in day treatment. Also, I envision more use of this method in its modified forms of sociodrama and action techniques in other social institutions, thus implementing Moreno's "sociotherapeutic" goals of bringing these methods and principles to the wider context of our culture. Psychodrama will be used more and more in the service of preventive mental hygiene and community building, and even for the more global goals of fostering the capacity for communications, problem solving and self-awareness.

MORENO'S CONTRIBUTIONS

Certainly, as discussed above, Moreno was one of the most energetic pioneers of group psychotherapy in general, and psychodrama in particular. He worked toward a general rapprochment of the social and the individual dimensions of psychology. His role theory has a great potential as the basis for a more integrative theory of psychology, and his many techniques have helped to make the field of psychotherapy more eclectic and dynamic—in the sense of being able to achieve in a much shorter time what used to require months or even years of more verbal, nondirective talk therapy.

But beyond this, and still generally unappreciated, is the sheer richness of his philosophical and psychological observations. These continue to have great relevance, perhaps even more now than in his own time, because the challenge in our era is to find the courage to take initiative, to become involved, to apply in a collective fashion that quality of spontaneity he said was so important. Holmes, Karp, and Watson (1994) comment on the "matrix" of psychodrama and how Moreno's many concepts may be viewed in terms of how they address both the psychospiritual and the conscious-unconscious dimensions.

The many contributions mentioned in the chapter on theory have yet to be deeply understood and appreciated by most social scientists or psychotherapists. Moreno's emphasis on creativity is particularly relevant in addressing the challenges of our postmodern world. But, further, his deeper philosophical ideas lend a measure of depth and suggest the possibility of *operationalizing methods* to a number of other contemporary intellectual trends (Blatner, 1985; Blatner & Blatner, 1988; Lindqvist, 1994). One of the most prominent of his themes is a return to a more spiritual sensibility, and in closing I would suggest that psychodramatic methods have great promise for helping people integrate the most essential procedures in psychotherapy with other aspects of transpersonal psychology. The synthesis of a spiritual, social, and individual perspective with a *praxis*, a complex of techniques and principles, then, explains the opening line to Moreno's *Who Shall Survive?* (1934): "A true therapeutic procedure cannot have less an objective than the whole of mankind" (p. 3).

REFERENCES / RECOMMENDED READINGS

Berger, M. M. (1990). J. L. Moreno's autobiography: More than meets the eye. *Journal of Group Psychotherapy, Psychodrama & Sociometry, 42*(4), 213–221.

Blatner, A. (1985). Moreno's "process philosophy." *Journal of Group Psychotherapy, Psychodrama & Sociometry, 38*(3), 133–136.

Blatner, A. (1988). *Foundations of psychodrama: History, theory, and practice* (especially pp. 13–42, 191–198). New York: Springer.

Blatner, A., & Blatner, A. (1988). The metaphysics of creativity as reflected in Moreno's "metapraxie" and the mystical tradition. *Journal of Group Psychotherapy, Psychodrama & Sociometry, 40*(4), 155–163.

Blatner, A. (1995). Images in psychiatry: J. L. Moreno. *American Journal of Psychiatry, 152*(11), 1664.

Blatner, A. (1996). Moreno's *idée fixe. Journal of Group Psychotherapy, Psychodrama & Sociometry, 48* (4), 155–158.

Borgatta, E. F., Boguslaw, R., & Haskell, M. (1975). On the work of Jacob L. Moreno. *Sociometry, 38*(1), 148–161.

Bradford, L., Gibb, J. R., and Benne, K. D. (1964). *T-Group theory and laboratory method: Innovations in re-education.* New York: Wiley.

Bratescu, G. (1975). The date and birthplace of J. L. Moreno. *Group Psychotherapy, Psychodrama & Sociometry, 28,* 2–4.

Buchanan, D. R. (1981). Forty-one years of psychodrama at St. Elizabeths Hospital. *Journal of Group Psychotherapy, Psychodrama & Sociometry, 34,* 134–147.

Corsini, R. J. (1955). Historic background of group psychotherapy. *Group Psychotherapy, 8*(3), 219–225.

Cramer-Azima, F. (1990). Moreno—A personal reflection. *Journal of Group Psychotherapy, Psychodrama & Sociometry, 42*(4), 222–224.

Fox, J. (1978). Moreno and his theatre. *Journal of Group Psychotherapy, Psychodrama & Sociometry, 31,* 109–116.

Hare, A. P. (1986). Moreno's contribution to social psychology. *Journal of Group Psychotherapy, Psychodrama & Sociometry, 39*(3), 85–94.

Hare, A. P. (1992). Moreno's sociometric study at the Hudson School for Girls. *Journal of Group Psychotherapy, Psychodrama & Sociometry, 45*(1), 24–39.

Holmes, P., Karp, M., & Watson, M. (Eds.). (1994). The matrix of psychodrama. In, *Psychodrama since Moreno: Innovations in theory and practice* (pp. 113–116). London: Routledge.

Horley, J. & Strickland, L. H. (1984). A note on Jacob Moreno's contribution to the development of social network analysis. *Journal of Community Psychology, 12*(3), 291–293.

Kraus, C., & Clouse, J. (Spring, 1986). Report from the J. L. Moreno collection. *Journal of Group Psychotherapy, Psychodrama & Sociometry, 39*(1), 41–44. (Collection in the rare books and manuscripts department, F. A. Countway Library of Medicine in Boston.)

Lindqvist, M. (1994). Religion and the spirit: The cosmic circus. In P. Holmes, M. Karp, & M. Watson (Eds.), *Psychodrama since Moreno: Innovations in theory and practice* (pp. 191–209). London: Routledge.

Leutz, G. A. (1978). Recent developments of psychodrama in Western Europe. *Group Psychotherapy, Psychodrama, & Sociometry, 31,* 168–173.

Marineau, R. F. (1989). *Jacob Levi Moreno, 1889-1974.* London: Routledge.

Marineau, R. F. (1990). *J.L. Moreno, sa vie, son oeuvre.* Montreal: Editions Saint-Martin. (In French, expanded, has extra photos.)

Marineau, R.F. (1994). Bucharest and Vienna: The cradles of Moreno's contributions. In P. Holmes, M.Karp, & M.Watson (Eds.), *Psychodrama since Moreno: Innovations in theory and practice* (pp. 81–94). London: Routledge.

Meiers, J. (1949). Origins and development of group psychotherapy: Historical survey, 1930-1945. *Sociometry, 8*(4), 499–530.

Moreno, J. D. (Ed.). (1989). The autobiography of J.L. Moreno, M.D.: Parts 1 and 2. *Journal of Group Psychotherapy, Psychodrama & Sociometry, 42*(1,2), 3–52, 59–125.

Moreno, J. L. (1934). *Who shall survive? A new approach to the problem of human interrelations.* Washington, DC: Nervous & Mental Disease Publishing. In 1953, this was revised and expanded, and the subtitle changed to *Foundations of sociometry, group psychotherapy, and sociodrama.* Beacon, NY: Beacon House. It was republished by ASGPP in 1993.

Moreno, J. L. (1969). The Viennese origins of the encounter movement. *Group Psychotherapy, 22*(3 4), 7–16.

Moreno, J. L. (1970). Is God a single person? My first encounter with a muse of high order, Zerka. *Group Psychotherapy, 23*(3–4), 75–78.

Moreno, Z. T. (1967). The seminal mind of J. L. Moreno and his influence upon the present generation. *Group Psychotherapy, 20*(3– 4), 218–229.

Moreno, Z. T. (1976). In memoriam: Jacob L(evy) Moreno. *Group Psychotherapy, Psychodrama & Sociometry, 29,* 130–135.

Renouvier, P. (1955). The group psychotherapy movement and J. L. Moreno. *Group Psychotherapy, 11*(1–2), 69–88.

Sacks, J. M. (1977). Reminiscence of J. L. Moreno. *Group, 1*(3), 194–200.

Treadwell, T., & Treadwell, J. (1972). The pioneer of the group encounter movement. *Group Psychotherapy, 25*(1–2), 16–26.

Weiner, H. B. (1968). J. L. Moreno—Mr. Group Psychotherapy. *Group Psychotherapy, 21*(3–4), 144–150.

Wolberg, A. R. (1976). The contributions of Jacob Moreno. In L. R. Wolberg & M. L. Aronson (Eds.), *Group therapy, 1976—An overview* (pp. 1–15). New York: Stratton Intercontinental Medical Book Corp. (There are some other fine articles that are also relevant in this book.)

Whitaker, C. (1988). Foreword. In. J. Fox (Ed.), *The essential Moreno* (vii–ix). New York: Springer.

Yablonsky, L. (1975). Psychodrama lives. *Human Behavior, 4,* 25–29.

Bibliography

One of the goals of this book is to promote scholarship, the reading of books and articles and further research and writing in the field. To this end I've sought to provide updated resources in each edition. Because of the recent efforts of Sacks, Bilaniuk and Gendron (1995), I've felt I could emphasize the more current items in the literature, and have therefore omitted a number of older references that were in previous editions.

The following references cover the more general issues in the field, and are meant to supplement the more topic-centered references at the ends of each of the previous chapters—and especially the various types of applications at the end of Chapter 8.

I have also included a number of books on drama therapy because of the relevance of underlying theory and principles of treatment. Furthermore, I have inserted two appendixes, noting (a) major books written by psychodramatists in other countries, (b) some journals in other countries, and (c) the addresses of the publishers who have a significant number of major texts on subjects related to this field.

AMERICAN JOURNALS

Most of the articles in the psychodrama literature are to be found in the journals that Moreno started, but some of these have changed their name several times.

Sociometry: A Journal of Interpersonal Relations, Vols. 1–18, 1937–1956. The early volumes contain some of Moreno's basic ideas and include articles on activities related to psychodrama, the expressive arts in therapy, family therapy, and other areas aside from just sociometry. However, in 1956, this journal was turned over to the American Sociological Association and became a more academic and formal social science journal.

Moreno continued to publish on sociometric and other topics, though, and intermittently produced:

International Journal of Sociometry, Vols. 1–5, 1956–1968.
Handbook of International Sociometry, Vols. 6–8, 1971–1973.

His second major journal (after *Sociometry*) eventually became the major, ongoing professional vehicle for psychodrama. Its first title was *Sociatry* (subtitled: *A Journal of Group and Intergroup Therapy*), Volumes 1–3 were published from 1947–1950. Later titles were *Group Psychotherapy* (Vols. 4–22, 1951–1970) and *Group Psychotherapy and Psychodrama* (Vols. 23–28, 1970–1975).

Following Moreno's death in 1974, the journal was edited by a committee of leaders in the field of psychodrama and renamed *Group Psychotherapy, Psychodrama, and Sociometry* (Vols. 29–33, 1976–1980).

As the American Society for Group Psychotherapy and Psychodrama became more organized, it contracted with the Helen Dwight Reid Educational Foundation (HELDREF) to publish its journal, beginning in 1980. In 1981 the name became *Journal of Group Psychotherapy, Psychodrama, & Sociometry* (Vols. 34+, 1981 through the present). For subscription information or to submit an article for publication, write to:

Journal of Group Psychotherapy, Psychodrama & Sociometry
HELDREF Publications
1319 Eighteenth Street, NW
Washington, DC 20036-1802

GENERAL BIBLIOGRAPHY

Badaines, A. (1988). Psychodrama. in J. Rowan & W. Dryden (Eds.), *Innovative Therapy in Britain*. Open University Press.

Barragar Dunne, P. (1992). *The narrative therapist and the arts: Expanding possibilities through drama, movement, puppets, masks and drawings*. Los Angeles: Drama Therapy Institute/ Possibilities Press, 1315 Westwood Blvd, Los Angeles, CA 90024-4901.

Bentley, E. (1977). Theatre and therapy. In W. Anderson (Ed.), *Therapy and the arts* (pp. 29–50). New York: Harper/Colophon.

Bischof, L. J. (1964). *Interpreting personality theories* (pp. 355–420). New York: Harper & Row.

Bilaniuk, M. T. (1990). *Bibliography of Psychodrama, 1980-1990*. Toronto: Author. (See also Sacks, Bilaniuk, & Gendron, 1995.)

Blatner, H. A. (Ed.) (1968). *Practical aspects of psychodrama*. Belmont, CA: Author. (Out of print. May be available at some libraries.) (*N.B.: In 1977 H. A. Blatner changed his name to A. Blatner, so these items are placed in chronological rather than alphabetical order*.)

Blatner, H. A. (Ed.) (1970). *Psychodrama, role-playing and action methods: Theory and practice*. Thetford, England: Author. (This was a revision and expansion of the previous book, also now out of print.)

Blatner, H. A. (1973). *Acting-In: Practical applications of psychodramatic methods* (1st ed.). New York: Springer. (Blue cover; 1988, 2nd ed., revised and updated, purple cover.)

Blatner, A. (1985). *Creating your living: Applications of psychodramatic methods in everyday life*. San Marcos, TX: Author. Out of print. Being revised and expanded for republication.

Blatner, A. (in preparation). *Role dynamics: An integrative language for psychology*.

Blatner, A., & Blatner, A. (1988). *The Art of Play: An adult's guide to reclaiming imagination and spontaneity*. New York: Human Sciences.

Blatner, A. with Blatner, A. (1988). *Foundations of psychodrama: History, theory, and practice*. New York: Springer.

Blatner, A. (1995). Psychodramatic methods in psychotherapy. *Psychiatric Times, 12*(5), 20.

Blatner, A. (1995). Psychodrama. In R. J. Corsini and D. Wedding (Eds.), *Current Psychotherapies* (5th ed., pp. 399–408.). Itasca, IL: Peacock. (Also in 4th ed., 1989.)

Boal, A. (1985). *Theatre of the oppressed*. New York: Theatre Communications Group. (Applications of Morenean-like ideas and methods in Latin America.)

Boies, K. G. (1973). Role playing as a behavior change technique: Review of the empirical literature. In I. M. Marks et. al. (Eds.), *Psychotherapy and behavior change, 1972* (pp. 372–379). Chicago: Aldine.

Bouquet, C. M. (1982). Theory of the scene. In M. Pines and L. Rafaelsen (Eds.), *The individual and the group* (pp. 179–186). New York: Plenum.

Brazier, D. (1991). *A guide to psychodrama*. London: Association for Humanistic Psychology in Britain.

Buchanan, D. R. (1984). Psychodrama. In T. B. Karasu (Ed.), *The psychiatric therapies, Part 2: the psychosocial therapies* (pp. 783–799). Washington, DC: American Psychiatric Association.

Buchanan, D. R., & Taylor, J. A. (1986). Jungian typology of professional psychodramatists: Myers-Briggs type indicator analysis of certified psychodramatists. *Psychological Reports, 58*, 391–400.

Clayton, G. M. (1991). *Directing psychodrama: A training companion.* Available from ICA Centre. 167 Hawthorne Rd., Caulfield, Victoria, Australia 3162. Other small books available by Dr Clayton:

(1992). *Enhancing life & relationships: Role training.*
(1993). *Living pictures of the self: Role theory.*
(1994). *Effective group leadership.*

Cohen, R. G., & Lipkin, G. B. (1979). Psychodrama. In *Therapeutic group work for health professionals* (pp. 179–217). New York: Springer.

Corey, G. (1994). Psychodrama, Chapter 8. In *Theory and practice of group counseling* (4th ed., pp. 206–235). Pacific Grove, CA: Brooks/Cole. Also good chapters in 2nd ed (1985) and 3rd ed. (1990).

Corsini, R. J., and Putzey, L. J. (1956). The historic background of group psychotherapy. *Group Psychotherapy, 9,* 177–249. A 1700- item bibliography including items dating from 1906-1955.

Corsini, R. J. (1967). *Role playing in psychotherapy.* Chicago: Aldine. Has annotated bibliography.

Davies, M. H. (1988). Psychodrama group therapy. In M. Aveline & W.Dryden (Eds.), *Group Therapy in Britain* (pp. 88–114). Open University Press.

Dayton, T. (1994). *The Drama Within: Psychodrama and experiential therapy.* Deerfield Beach, FL: Health Communications Inc.

Emunah, R. (1994). *Acting for real. Drama therapy process and technique.* New York: Brunner/Mazel. Definitive text!

Farmer, C. (1995). *Psychodrama and systemic therapy.* London: Karnac.

Feldhendler, D. (1994). Augusto Boal and Jacob L. Moreno: Theatre and therapy. In M. Schutzman & J. Cohen-Cruz (Eds.), *Playing Boal: Theatre, therapy, activism* (pp. 87–109). London: Routledge.

Fine, L. J. (1979). Psychodrama. In R. J. Corsini (Ed.), *Current psychotherapies* (2nd ed., pp. 428–459). Itasca, IL: Peacock.

Fleshman, B., & Fryrear, J. (1981). *The arts in therapy.* Chicago: Nelson Hall.

Fox, J. (Ed.). (1987). *The essential Moreno: Writings on psychodrama, group method, and spontaneity.* New York: Springer.

Fox, J. (1994). *Acts of service: Spontaneity, commitment, tradition in the nonscripted theatre.* Available from Tusitala Publishing, 137 Hasbrouck Rd., New Paltz, NY 12561.

Fuhlrodt, R. L. (Ed.). (1990). *Psychodrama: Its application to ACOA and substance abuse treatment.* Available from Perrin & Treggett Books, 3130 Rt 10 W, Denville, NJ 07834.

Gale, D. (1990). *What is psychodrama? A personal and practical guide.* Loughton, England: Gale Centre Publications.

Gendron, J. (1980). *Moreno: The roots and the branches; and bibliography of psychodrama, 1972–1980.* Beacon, NY: Beacon House.

Gold, M. (1991). *The fictional family in drama, education, and group work.* Springfield, IL: Charles C. Thomas.

Goldman, E. E., & Morrison, D. S. (1984). *Psychodrama: Experience and process.* Eldemar Corp. (5812 N. 12th St. # 32, Phoenix, AZ 85014)

Goldman, E. E., Morrison, D. C., & Goldman, M. S. (1987). *Psychodrama: A Training Videotape.* Phoenix, AZ: Eldemar Corp.

Grainger, R. (1990). *Drama & Healing: The roots of drama therapy.* London: Jessica Kingsley.

Greenberg, I. A. (1968). *Psychodrama and audience attitude change.* Beverly Hills: Behavioral Studies Press.

Greenberg, I. A. (Ed.). (1974). *Psychodrama: Theory and therapy.* New York: Behavioral Publications.

Greenberg, I. A. (Ed.). (1977). *Group hypnotherapy and hypnodrama* (pp. 231–303). Chicago: Nelson-Hall.

Greenberg, I. A. (1986). Psychodrama. In I. L. Kutash & A. Wolf (Eds.), *Psychotherapist's casebook* (pp 392–412). San Francisco: Jossey-Bass.

Gregoric, L., & Gregoric, M. (1981). Sociodrama: Video in social action. In J. L. Fryrear & B. Fleshman (Eds.), *Videotherapy in mental health* (pp. 244–256). Springfield, IL: Charles C Thomas.

Haas, R. B. (1949). *Psychodrama and sociodrama in American education.* Beacon, NY: Beacon House.

Haas, R. B., & Moreno, J. L. (1961). Psychodrama as a projective technique. In H. H. Anderson and G. L. Anderson (Eds.) An *introduction to projective techniques* (pp 662–675). Englewood Cliffs, NJ: Prentice-Hall.

Hale, A. E. (1981; 1985). *Conducting clinical sociometric explorations: A manual for psychodramatists and sociometrists.* A revised, expanded edition is due out by 1996 from Royal Publishing, 2757 Richelieu Ave., Roanoke, VA 24014. A classic.

Hare, A. P. (1985). *Social interaction as drama.* Beverly Hills: Sage.

Hare, A. P. (1986). Bibliography of the work of J. L. Moreno. *Journal of Group Psychotherapy, Psychodrama, and Sociometry, 39*(3), 95–128.

Haskell, M. R. (1975). *Socioanalysis: Self direction via sociometry and psychodrama.* Long Beach: Role Training Associates (1750 E. Ocean Blvd., Long Beach, CA 90802).

Haskell, R. J., Pearl, C. E., & Haskell, M. R. (1986). *A world in microcosm: Psychodrama and related subjects.* Previously entitled *Sociometry through group interaction psychotherapy.* Long Beach, CA: Role Training Associates.

Heilveil, I. (1983). *Video in mental health practice* (pp. 60–67). New York: Springer.

Heisey, M. J. (1982). *Clinical case studies in psychodrama.* Washington, DC: University Press of America.

Holmes, P. (1992). *The inner world outside: Object relations theory and psychodrama.* New York: Routledge.

Holmes, P., & Karp, M. (Eds.) (1991). *Psychodrama: inspiration & technique.* New York: Routledge.

Holmes, P., Karp, M., & Watson, M. (Eds.). (1994). *Psychodrama since Moreno: Innovations in theory and practice.* London & New York: Tavistock/Routledge. Important collection of articles by current leaders in the field.

Hudgins, M. K. (1996). *The therapeutic spiral model: An experiential approach to trauma.* New York: Guilford. Other monographs on psychodrama by Hudgins (1991-1995) are available from the Center for Experiential Learning. Madison, WI.

Irwin, E. C., & Portner, E. (Eds.) (1984). *The scope of drama therapy: Proceedings from the first annual drama therapy conference.* New Haven, CT: National Association for Drama Therapy.

Jennings, S. (1973). *Remedial drama.* London: Pitman. (U.S. publication, 1974, and revised 2nd ed., 1982. New York: Theatre Arts Books.)

Jennings, S. (Ed.). (1987). *Dramatherapy: Theory and practice for teachers and clinicians.* Cambridge, MA: Brookline.

Jennings, S. (1990). *Dramatherapy with families, groups and individuals: Waiting in the wings.* London: Jessica Kingsley.

Jennings, S. (Ed.). (1992). *Dramatherapy theory and practice 2.* London: Routledge.

Jennings, S., & Minde, A. (1993). *Art therapy and dramatherapy: Masks of the soul.* London: Jessica Kingsley.

Jennings, S. (1994a). *Introduction to dramatherapy.* London: Jessica Kingsley.

Jennings, S. (Ed.). (1995). *Dramatherapy with children and adolescents.* London & New York: Routledge.

Jennings, S., Cattanach, A., Mitchell, S., Meldrum, B., & Chesner, A. (1994). *Handbook of Dramatherapy.* London: Routledge.

Kipper, D. A. (1986). *Psychotherapy through clinical role playing.* New York: Brunner/Mazel.

Kipper, D. A. (1992). Psychodrama: Group psychotherapy through role playing. *International Journal of Group Psychotherapy, 42*(4), 495–521.

Kellermann, P. F. (1992). *Focus on psychodrama: The therapeutic aspects of psychodrama.* London: Jessica Kingsley.

Kumar, V. K., & Treadwell, T. W. (1985). *Practical sociometry for psychodramatists.* West Chester, PA: Authors.

Landy, R. J. (1993). *Persona and performance: The meaning of role in drama, therapy, and everyday life.* New York: Guilford.

Landy, R. J. (1994). *Drama therapy: Concepts and Practices.* (2nd Ed.) Springfield, IL: Charles C Thomas. (1st ed., 1986).

Langley, D. (1983). *Dramatherapy and psychiatry.* London: Croom Helm.

Lebovici, S. (1974). A combination of psychodrama and psychoanalysis. In S. de Schill (Ed.), *The challenge for group psychotherapy: Present and future* (pp. 286–315). New York: International Universities Press.

Lee, R. H. (1981). Video as adjunct to psychodrama and role playing. In J. L. Fryrear & B. Fleshman (Eds.), *Videotherapy in mental health.* Springfield, IL: Charles C Thomas.

Leveton, E. (1992). *A clinician's guide to psychodrama.* New York: Springer. This is a second edition of her 1977 book titled: *Psychodrama for the timid clinician,* also from Springer.

Link, A. (1992). *Mirrors from the heart: Emotional identity and expression through drama.* Ontario, Canada: Elora.

Marineau, R. F. (1989). *Jacob Levi Moreno, 1889–1974.* (A Biography) New York: Routledge. (A 1990 edition in French published in Quebec has even more information and photos.)

Martin, R. B. (1991). The assessment of involvement in role playing. *Journal of Clinical Psychology, 47,* 587–596.

McReynolds, P., & DeVoge, S. (1977). Use of improvisational techniques in assessment. In P. McReynolds (Ed.), *Advances in psychology: Vol.4. Assessment.* San Francisco: Jossey-Bass.

Miller, M. M. (1971). *Psychodrama: The self on stage.* Washington, DC: The New School of Psychotherapy.

Mitchell, S. (Ed.) (1995). *Dramatherapy: Clinical studies.* London & Bristol, PA: Jessica Kingsley.

J. L. MORENO

For research on Moreno and his works, his papers are located at the Moreno Collection, Countway Medical Library, 10 Shattuck St., Boston, MA 02115 (Telephone: (617) 432-4888).

Moreno, J. L. (Jacob Levi). Note: The originator of psychodrama was a prolific writer, publishing scores of articles and monographs on the subject, only a few of which we need mention here. A complete listing of his works has been noted by Hare (1986) (q.v.). Moreno also wrote numerous articles on group psychotherapy and sociometry and related subjects. His books and articles have been translated into many languages. You will notice that most of his books were published by Beacon House, which was Moreno's own publishing house, named in honor of his home and sanitarium in Beacon, New York. Until his death, he also supervised the publication of the major journals devoted to psychodrama, sociometry, and group psychotherapy. Some of his better known and more substantial writings are listed here.

Moreno, J. L. (1921). *The Words of the Father,* first published anonymously in Vienna; inspirational poetry and some exposition of Moreno's philosophical-theological ideas. (Also entitled *The psychodrama of God: A new hypothesis of the self.)* Reissued in 1971. Beacon, NY: Beacon House.

Moreno, J. L. (1923). *The theater of spontaneity.* First published in Potsdam with the title, *Das Stegreiftheatre,* and translated and published by Beacon House in 1947 and 1973. Reprinted again in 1983.

Moreno, J. L. (1934). *Who shall survive? A new approach to the problem of human interrelations.* Washington, DC: Nervous & Mental Disease Publishing. In 1953, this was revised and expanded, and the subtitle changed to *Foundations of sociometry, group psychotherapy, and sociodrama.* Beacon, NY: Beacon House. It was republished by the ASGPP in 1993.

Moreno, J. L. (1946). *Psychodrama: Vol. 1.* Beacon, NY: Beacon House. Reprinted numerous times since then. Republished by ASGPP in 1993.

Moreno, J. L. (Ed.). (1946). *Group Psychotherapy: A symposium.* Beacon, NY: Beacon House.

Moreno, J. L. (1951). (Ed.) *Sociometry: Experimental method and the science of society.* Beacon, NY: Beacon House.

Moreno, J. L. (1956). *Sociometry and the science of man.* Beacon, NY: Beacon House.

Moreno, J. L. (Ed.). (1956-1960). *Progress in psychotherapy (Vols. 1–5).* New York: Grune & Stratton. Coedited with Frieda Fromm-Reichmann (Vol. 1), and then Jules Masserman (Vols. 2–5), both of whom were the first names on the books. This series of five books contains a number of important articles on psychodrama by Moreno and others.

Moreno, J. L. (1960). *The sociometry reader.* Glencoe, IL: The Free Press. Coedited with Helen Hall Jennings and others.

Moreno, J. L. (1963). Reflections on my method of group psychotherapy and psychodrama. *CIBA Symposium, 2(4),* 148–157. (Reprinted in 1974 in H. Greenwald (Ed.), *Active Psychotherapy.* New York: Jason Aronson.) (This book was reissued in 1984.)

Moreno, J. L. (1971). Psychodrama. In H. I. Kaplan & B. J. Sadock (Eds.), *Comprehensive group psychotherapy* (pp. 460–500). Baltimore: Williams & Wilkins.

Moreno, J. L. (1972). The religion of God-Father. In P. E. Johnson (Ed.), *Healer of the mind: A psychiatrist's search for faith* (pp. 197–215). Nashville, TN: Abington.

Moreno, J. L. (1987). *The essential Moreno.* (See Fox, 1987).

Moreno, J. L., & Elefthery, D. G. (1975). An introduction to group psychodrama. In George Gazda (Ed.), *Basic approaches to group psychotherapy and group counseling* (2nd. Ed.). Springfield, IL: Charles C Thomas.

Moreno, J. L., Friedemann, A., Battegay, R., & Moreno, Z. (Eds.). (1966). *International handbook of group psychotherapy.* New York: Philosophical Library.

Moreno, J. L., & Moreno, Z. T. (1959). *Psychodrama, Vol. 2.* Beacon, NY: Beacon House.

Moreno, J. L., & Moreno, Z. T. (l969). *Psychodrama, Vol. 3.* Beacon, NY: Beacon House.

Moreno, J. L., & Zeleny, L. D. (1958). Role theory and sociodrama. In J. S. Roucek, *Contemporary Sociology* (pp. 642–654). New York: Philosophical Library.

Moreno, J. D. (Ed.). (1989). The autobiography of J. L. Moreno, M.D.: Part 1. *Journal of Group Psychotherapy, Psychodrama & Sociometry, 42*(1), 3–52; Part 2: *42*(2), 59–125. Abridged, edited by his son, Jonathan.

Moreno, Z. T. (1959). A survey of psychodramatic techniques. *Group Psychotherapy, 12,* 5–14.

Moreno, Z. T. (1965). Psychodramatic rules, techniques, and adjunctive methods. *Group Psychotherapy, 18*(1–2), 73–86.

Moreno, Z. T. (1978). Psychodrama. In H. Mullan & M. Rosenbaum (Eds.), *Group psychotherapy* (2nd ed., pp. 352–376). New York: Free Press.

Moreno, Z. T. (1983). Psychodrama. In H. I. Kaplan & B. J. Sadock (Eds.), *Comprehensive group psychotherapy* (2nd ed., pp. 158–166). Baltimore: Williams & Wilkins.

Moreno, Z. T. (1987). Psychodrama, role theory, and the concept of the social atom. In J. Zeig (Ed.), *The evolution of psychotherapy* (pp. 341–358). New York: Brunner/Mazel. Also excerpted in *JGPPS, 42*(3), 1989.

Murray, N. (1976). Psychodrama—post Moreno. In A. Wolberg & M. Aronson (Eds.), *Group therapy, 1976—An overview* (pp. 16–20). New York: Stratton Intercontinental Medical Book Corp.

Naar, R. (1990). Psychodrama in short-term psychotherapy. In R. A. Wells & V. J. Giannetti (Eds.), *Handbook of the brief psychotherapies* (pp 583–600). New York: Plenum.

Olsson, P. A. (1980). Psychodrama and literature in evaluation and treatment. In H. S. Moffic and G. L. Adams (Eds.), *A clinician's manual on mental health care: A multidisciplinary approach* (pp. 130–138). Menlo Park, CA: Addison-Wesley.

Olsson, P. A., & Barth, P. A. (1983). New uses of psychodrama. *Journal of Operational Psychiatry, 14*(2), 95–101.

Pearlman, W. D. (1995). *Characters of the sacred: The world of archetypal drama.* Placitas, NM: Duende Press.

Polansky, N. A. (1982). Ego functions in psychodrama. In *Integrated ego psychology* (pp. 270–293). New York: Aldine.

Portner, E. (Ed.). (1986). *Drama therapy in print: A bibliography.* New Haven, CT: National Association for Drama Therapy.

Sacks, J. M. (1974). The psychodramatic approach. In D. S. Milman & G. D. Goldman (Eds.) *Group process today: Evaluation and perspectives* (pp. 137–145). Springfield, IL: Charles C Thomas.

Sacks, J. M. (1981). Drama therapy with the acting out patient. In G. Schattner & R. Courtney (Eds.), *Drama in therapy. Vol. 2: Adults* (pp. 35–56). New York: Drama Book Specialists.

Sacks, J. M. (1988). Psychodramatic techniques in work with borderline patients. In N. Slavinska-Holy (Ed.), *Borderline and narcissistic patients in therapy* (pp. 343–358). Madison, CT: International Universities Press.

Sacks, J. M. (1990). Psychodrama. In I. L. Kutash & A. Wolf (Eds.), *The group psychotherapist's handbook: Contemporary theory & technique* (pp 211–230). New York: Columbia University Press.

Sacks, J. M. (1993). Psychodrama. In H. I. Kaplan & B. J. Sadock (Eds.), *Comprehensive group psychotherapy* (6th ed., pp. 214–228). Baltimore: Williams & Wilkins.

Sacks, J. M., Bilaniuk, M. & Gendron, J. M. (1995). *Bibliography of psychodrama: Inception to date.* Over 2,000 items, this 130 page book has an extensive index of 30 pages, and is also available on either MacIntosh or IBM-compatible computer diskette. Available from Dr James M. Sacks, Psychodrama Center of New York, 71 Washington Pl., New York, NY 10011-9184 for $35.

Salas, J. (1993). *Improvising real life: Personal story to playback theatre.* Dubuque, IA: Kendall/Hunt.

Salas, J., & Swallow, J. (1994). *Tracing our roots, finding our place.* Video of playback theatre regarding the history of psychodrama. Videotape, $35.00. McLean, VA: American Society for Group Psychotherapy & Psychodrama.

Schattner, G., & Courtney, R. (Eds.) (1981). *Drama in therapy Vol. 1: Children; Vol. 2: Adults.* New York: Drama Book Specialists. Excellent anthology with many relevant articles.

Seabourne, B. (1985). *Practical aspects of psychodrama.* St Louis: Author. Papers first privately produced in 1960s and included in Blatner's 1968 and 1970 books (q.v.). May be obtained by writing to author at 546 Oakwood, St. Louis, 63119.

Siroka, R. W., Siroka, E., & Schloss, G. (Eds.) (1971). *Sensitivity training and group encounter—An introduction.* New York: Grosset & Dunlap. Includes a section on psychodrama.

Starr, A. (1977). *Rehearsal for living: Psychodrama.* Chicago: Nelson-Hall.

Stietzel, L. D., & Hughey, A. R. (1994). *Empowerment through spontaneity: A taste of psychodrama.* San Jose, CA: Associates for Community Interaction, 5667 Snell Ave. #178, San Jose, CA 95123.

Sternberg, P., & Garcia, A. (1989). *Sociodrama: Who's in your shoes?* Westport, CT: Praeger.

Swink, D. F., & Buchanan, D. R. (1984). The effects of sociodramatic goal-oriented role play and non-goal-oriented role play on locus of control. *Journal of Clinical Psychology, 40*(5), 1178–1183.

Torrance, E. P. (1978). Sociodrama and the creative process (#14). In Frederic Flach (Ed.), *Creative Psychiatry.* Geigy Pharmaceuticals.

Torrance, E. P., Murdock, M., & Fletcher, D. (1995). *Role playing: Creative problem solving in action.* Clubview, South Africa: Benedic Books.

Treadwell, T. W. (Ed.). (1974). *Confrontation and training via the group process—The action techniques.* New York: Simon & Schuster.

Vander May, J. H. (1981). *Psychodrama a deux.* Author: 6207 Eastridge Dr, Hudsonville MI 49426.

Warner, G. D. (1978-1986). *Psychodrama training tips.* Vols. 1 & 2. Published by author, but now out of print.

Weiner, H. B. (1975). Living experiences with death—A journeyman's view through psychodrama. *Omega, 6*(3), 251–274.

Weiner, H. B. (1981). Return from splendid isolation. In G. Schattner & R. Courtney (Eds.), *Drama in therapy* (pp. 129–156). New York: Drama Book Specialists.

Williams, A. (1989). *The passionate technique: Strategic psychodrama with individuals, families, and groups.* New York: Tavistock/Routledge.

Williams, A. (1991). *Forbidden agendas: Strategic action in groups.* New York: Tavistock/Routledge.

Yablonsky, L. (1972). Psychodrama and role training. In L. N. Solomon & B. Berzon (Eds.). *New perspectives on encounter groups* (pp. 255–265). San Francisco: Jossey-Bass.

Yablonsky, L. (1992). *Psychodrama: Resolving emotional problems through role-playing.* New York: Brunner/Mazel. This major book in the field was first published by Basic Books in 1976, and then again in 1981 by Gardner Press.

Appendix A: Addresses of Major Publishers of Books on Psychodrama

Blatner (1973, 1988, 1996), Fox (1987), Leveton (1992): Springer Publishing Co., 536 Broadway, New York, NY 10012-3955.
(Phone: (212) 431-4370)

Blatner & Blatner (1996), Emunah (1994), Kipper (1986), Yablonsky (1976/92): Brunner/Mazel Publishers, 19 Union Square West, New York, NY 10003. (Phone: (800) 825-3089)

Holmes (1992), Holmes & Karp (1992), Holmes, Karp & Watson (1994), Jennings (1995), Marineau (1989), Williams (1989, 1991): Routledge Publishing Co., 29 West 35th Street, New York, NY 10001. (Phone: (800) 634-7064)

Jennings (1990, 1994), Kellermann (1991), Landy (1996), others, Jessica Kingsley Publishers, 1900 Frost Road, Suite 101, Bristol, PA 19007-1598, (Phone: (800) 821-8312) (In England: 116 Pentonville Rd., London N1 9JB)

Appendix B: Major Books in Other Languages

Aguiar, M. (Ed.) (1989). *O Psicodramaturgo J.L. Moreno (1889- 1989)*. Sao Paulo: Casa do Psicologo, Revista Brasiliera de Psicodramae. A celebration of the centennial of Moreno's birth.

Anzieu, D. (1979). *Le psychodrame analytique chez l'enfant et l'adolescent* (2nd ed.). Paris: Presses Universitaires de France.

Boria, G. (1983). *Tele: Manuale di psicodramma classico*. Milano: Franco Angeli.

Buer, F. (1989). *Moreno's therapeutische philosophie*. Opladen, Germany: Leske & Budrich.

Le groupe d'études de Psychologie de l'Université de Paris (Eds.). (1969-1970). Le Psychodrame. *Bulletin de psychologie*, 285(13-16), 713-999. Special issue on psychodrama.

Bustos, D. (1985). New directions in psychodramatic psychotherapy: Individual, couple, and group in social function. La Plata, Argentina: Editorial Momento. Spanish.

Dias, V. (1987). *Psicodrama: Teoria e Prática*. S. Paulo: Editora Agora.

de Leonardis, P. (1994). *Lo scarto del cavallo: Lo psicodramma come intervento sui piccoli gruppi*. Milano: Franco Angeli.

Leutz, G. A. (1974). *Psychodrama: Theorie und practice*. Berlin: Springer Verlag. (Reissued, 1986).

Leutz, G. A., & Petzold, H. (Eds.). (1970). *Zeistchrift fur praktische psychologie*, 5(8). Special issue on psychodrama.

Leutz, G. A., & Oberborbeck, K. (Eds.). (1980). Psychodrama. *Gruppenpsychotherapie und Gruppendynamik*, 19(3-4). Entire issue.

Leutz, G. A. (1985). *Mettre sa vie en scene: Le psychodrame*. Paris: Editions Desclee de Brouwer.

Marineau, René. (1989). J. L. Moreno, sa vie, son oeuvre. Montreal: Editions Saint-Martin.

Marschall, B. (1988). *"Ich bin der Mythe": Von der Segreifbühne zum Psychodrama Jakob Levy Morenos.* Wien: Böhlau Verlag.

Matsumura, K. (1986). Spontaneity. *The Journal of the Science of Relationships,* 14(1), 30-40. Tokyo, Japan.

Menegazzo, C. M. (1981). *Magia, mito, y psicodrama.* Buenos Aires: Editorial Paidos.

Monteiro, R. (Ed.)(1993). *Tecnicas fundamentais do psicodrama.* São Paulo: Editora Brasiliense.

Nikolić, S. (1983). *Scenska Ekspresija.* Zagreb: Naprijed. Extensive bibliography, emphasizing psychoanalytic psychodrama.

Pavlovsy, E., et al. (1979). *Psicodrama cuando y por que dramatizar.* Madrid: Fundamentos.

Petzold, H., and Mathias, U. (1982). *Rollenentwicklung und Identitat.* Paderborn, Germany: Junfermann.

Petzold, H. (Ed.). (1985). *Dramatische therapie.* (German) Stuttgart: Hippokrates Verlag. Contains many references of articles in German and French.

Roine, Eva. (1992). *Psykodrama [Psychodrama: Playing the Lead in Your Own Life]* (2nd Ed.). Available from Author: Norwegian Psychodrama Institute, 42 Fr.Stangst., 0264 Oslo 2, Norway. First edition (1978).

Rojas-Bermúdez, J.G. (1977). *Introdução ao Psicodrama.* (2nd Ed.) São Paulo: Editora Mestre de Jou.

Rojas-Bermúdez, J.G. (1984). *Que es el sicodrama?* (4th Ed.). Buenos Aires: Editorial Celcius. (1st ed., 1966).

Schutzenberger, A. (1975). *Introduction au jeu de rôle [Introduction to role playing]* Toulouse, France: Edouard Privat.

Schutzenberger, A., & Weil, P. (1977). *Psicodrama triadico.* Belo Horizonte, Brazil: Interlivros.

Soeiro, A.C. (1976). *Psicodrama e Psicoterapia.* São Paulo: Editora Natura.

Widlocher, D. (1979). *Le psychodrame chez l'enfant.* Paris: Presses Universitaires de France.

APPENDIX C: Journals

Psychodrama Journals in Other Countries

Australia & New Zealand Psychodrama Association Journal. Editor: Christine Hosking, ICA Centre, 167 Hawthorn Rd, Caulfield, Victoria 3162, Australia.

Revista Brasileira de Psicodrama. Rua Cardoso de Almeida, N°23-cj. 106, CEP 05013-000 Perdizes, São Paulo-SP, Brazil.

The Journal of the British Psychodrama Association. c/o Peter Haworth, BPA, 8 Rahere Rd, Cowley, Oxford OX4 3Q6, England.

PsychoDrama: Zeitschrift für Theorie und Praxis. Editor: Ulf Klein. Moreno Institut, Schickhardstr. 49, D-7000 Stuttgart 1, Germany.

Psicodrama: Revista da Sociedade Portuguesa de Psicodrama. Director: António Roma Torres. Rua dos Bragas, 54 - 1°Dt°, 4000 Porto, Portugal.

Drama Therapy Journals

The Arts in Psychotherapy. Elsevier Science, Inc. 660 White Plains Rd., Tarrytown, NY 10591-5153.

The British Journal of Dramatherapy. c/o British Association for Dramatherapy: 5 Sunnydale Village, Durlston Rd, Swanage, Dorset, BH19 2HY, England.

Appendix D: International Directory of Psychodrama Training Institutes

(Compiled May 1997)

This is the first international listing of the *major trainers of psychodrama* to appear in any published book. Because of space restrictions, I have included a limited number of items per country other than the English-speaking countries. The point is to promote international exchanges of trainers, students and professional literature. I have made extensive efforts to present correct information but, even so, I apologise for having left out people or training centers who may feel they should have been included. Of course, I shall be open to corrections for future editions. Please note my address: 103 Crystal Springs Drive, Sun City, Georgetown, TX 78628-4502, USA email: ablatner@aol.com

UNITED KINGDOM

British Psychodrama Assocation(BPA)
contact: Peter Haworth, BPA, 8 Rahere Road, Cowley, Oxford OX4 3QG
(Oxford Psychodrama Group - same address - contact Susie Taylor)

Holwell Centre for Psychodrama and Sociodrama
contact: Marcia Karp and Ken Sprague, Holwell Centre, East Down, Barnstaple, North Devon EX31 4NZ

London Centre for Psychodrama and Group Analytic Psychotherapy
contact: James Bamber, 115 Ladbroke Grove, London W11 1PG
Jinnie Jefferies, 115 Audley Rd, Richmond, Surrey TW10 6EY

South Devon College of Arts and Technology
Dept of Music and Theatre Arts
contact: Dorothy Langley, Newton Road, Torquay, Devon TQ2 5BY

Northern School of Psychodrama
contact: The Registrar
Hampden House, 2-4 Palatine Road, Withington, Manchester M20 3JA

Paul Holmes
87 Carleton Road, London N7 0EZ

Sue Jennings
67b, Westmoreland Terrace, London SW1V 4AH

British Association for Dramatherapy
contact: Di Grimshaw, 114a, Highgate Road, London NW5 1PB

IRELAND

Catherine Murray, Newtown House Centre, Doneraile, County Cork.

AUSTRALIA

Australian College of Psychodrama
contact: Dr G. Max Clayton, 167 Hawthorn Road, Caulfield, Victoria 3162

Melbourne Centre for Psychodrama
contact: Teena Lee, 20, Banksia St, Burwood, Victoria 3125

Psychodrama Training Institute of New South Wales
contact: Joyce Williams, 6 National St, Rozelle, NSW 2039

Psychodrama Training Institute of South Australia
contact: Robert Brodie, PO Box 232, Daw Park, South Australia 5041

Psychodrama Training Institute of the ACT
contact: Annette Fisher, PO Box 307, Woden, ACT 2606

Psychodrama Training Institute of Western Australia
contact: Tom Wilson, 563 William St, Mount Lawley, WA 6050

Queensland Training Institute of Psychodrama
contact: Brigid Hirschfeld, 45 Clarence St, Coorparoo, QLD 4151
(ANZPA Newsletter - same address - contact: Peter Howie)

School in Contemporary Psychodrama
contact: Carlos A. Raimundo, 140a Victoria Rd, Gladesville, NSW 2111

Dr Ari Badaines, 5 Fern Place, Bondi Junction, NSW 2022
Dr Effie Best, 35 Hurtle Square, Adelaide, SA 5000

Sue Daniel, 6 Quamby Ave, South Yarra, Victoria 3141

Lynette Clayton, 2/211 Park St, Subiaco, WA 6008

Anthony Williams, Dept of Psychology, La Trobe University, 46 Young St, Kew, Victoria 3101

Joyce Williams, 6, National St, Balmain, NSW 2041

NEW ZEALAND

Auckland Training Centre for Psychodrama
contact: Evan Sherrard, PO Box 26-380, Epsom, Auckland 10030

ATCP(Waikato Branch)
contact: Don Reekie, 12, Alpha St, Cambridge

Christchurch Institute for Training in Psychodrama
contact: Dr Robert Crawford, 79, Bealey Ave, Christchurch 1

CITP(Dunedin Branch)
contact: Leslie Johnson, Cameron Centre, PO Box 374, Dunedin

Wellington Psychodrama Training Institute
contact: Bev Hosking, PO Box 5302, Lambton Quay, Wellington 2

Estelle Mendelsohn, 92 Otitoki Bay Rd, Titirangi, Auckland 7

CANADA

René Marineau, 1270 Grande Rivière Norde, Yamachiche G0X 3L0

Tobi Klein, MSW 3526 Avenue Grey, Montreal, Quebec H4A 3N6

UNITED STATES OF AMERICA

In the USA there are over one hundred certified trainers of psychodrama, and over two hundred certified practitioners. Their names and addresses can be obtained by writing for a copy of the most current directory from:

The American Board of Examiners in Psychodrama, Sociometry and Group Psychotherapy, PO Box 15572, Washington DC 20003-0572
(tel: 202-483-0514)

American Society of Group Psychotherapy and Psychodrama
301 North Harrison St, Suite 508, Princeton, NJ 08540
(tel: 609-452-1339; fax 609-936-1659)

For further information, please consult the Bibliography

BELGIUM

CFIP-Verveine, Groupe de Formation au Psychodrame
contact: Pierre Fontaine and Chantal Nève: Av. Gribaumont 153, 1200
Bruxelles

Bernard Robinson, Chausée de Verviers 18, 4910 Theux

Ferdinand Cuvelier, Relatie Studio, Voskenslaan 167, 9000 Gent

Maria Christine DuPont, St. Lievenspoortstraar 275, B9000 Gent

G. Vanhout, H. Dunantlaan 2, B 9000 Gent

Institute of Developmental Psychotherapy, University of Ghent
contact: Leni Verhofstadt-Denève, Bergwegel 74, 9820 Merelbeke

Roland Geeraert, Ave des Volontaires 41, 1040 Bruxelles

Monique and Rudolf Bernet, rue du Centry 85, 1390 Grez-Doiceau

THE NETHERLANDS

Psychologisch Centrum T.O.P.
contact: Lex Mulder, Langedijk 29, 4142 LD Leerdam

School voor Psychodrama
contact: Renée Oudijk, Stationsdwarsstraat 14, 6131 BA Sittard

Centre for Psychodrama Education
contact: Adeline Salomé-Finkelstein, Huyghens 17-19, 6824 JB Arnhem

Joke Meilo, Pernambucolaan 19, 2051 LV Overveen

Jan Lap and Marjorie Streur, 'Het Dean-His', Vresselseweg 57, 5491 PB ST.
Odenrode

Ria Linssen-Houben, Multatulisstraat 1, 6006 MP Weert

Vereniging voor Psychodrama
contact: Ebba de Niet, Nyensteinheerd 36, NL-9736 fc Groningen

NORWAY

Norwegian Psychodrama Institute, Gronnegt. 10, 0350 Oslo

Eva Roine, Fredrik Stangsgt. 42, 0264 Oslo

Jana Segula, Balders Gate 7b, 0263 Oslo

Mildred Valvik, Thallesveien 43c, 8010 Bodo

Kari Skaatun, Orsnesallene 2c, 3120 Tonsberg

Melinda Ashley Meyer, Lallakroken 8A, N 0259 Oslo

SWEDEN

Svenska Morenoinstitutet
contact: Leif-Dag Blomkvist, G:a Radstugevagen 26, S-602 24 Norrkoping

Inara Erdmanis, Surbrunnsgatan 6EP, S-114 21 Stockholm

Kerstin Jurdell, Wollmar Yxkullsgatan 37, S-116 50 Stockholm

Eva-Karin Ström, Baggeby Torg 1, S-181 35 Lidingö

Lena Sjöberg, Starrangsringen 44, S-115 50 Stockholm

Psykodramaakadamin
contact: Monika Westberg, Bergholmsvägen 13, S-141 44 Huddinge

Göran Högberg, Maskinistgatan 15, S-117 66 Stockholm

Judit Teszary, Norrbackagatan 43, 3tr, S-113 41 Stockholm

Uppsala Psykodramaforening
contact: Eva Strömberg Fahlström, St. Johannesgatan 2-4tr, S-753 11 Uppsala

Stockholms Psykodramaforening
contact: Lars Tauvon, Sveavägen 52, S-111 34 Stockholm

FINLAND

The Finnish Moreno Institute
contact: Riitta Hiillos-Vuorinen, Ylopistonkatu 10 c 76, 20100 Turku

The Finnish Psychodrama Association
contact: Annelit Frelander, Klaavuntie 7 C 21, 00910 Helsinki

Finnish Psychodrama Association
contact: Paula Jarvinene, Ilmarinkatu 25 I 98, 33500 Tampere

Ilpo Vuorinen, Resurssi, Vadstenankatu 7, 21100 Naantali

Natalia Novitsky, Keijontie 9A, SF-00610 Helsinki

SWITZERLAND

Elisabeth Pfafflin, Bederstr 82, 8002 Zurich

Janet Goldfarb-Dornier, Goldhaldenstrasse 16, CH Zollikon 8702

Gabrielle Wiesmann-Brun, Psychodrama Berne, Melchiorstrasse 23/166, 3027 Bern-Bethlehem

Jörg Burmeister, Besmerstrasse 27, CH-8280, Kreuzlingen

Ellynor and Helmut Barz, Wengi 11, CH 8126 Zumikon

AUSTRIA

Dr Jutta Fürst, A-6060 Hall I.T. Salvatorgasse 2A, Vienna

Karoline Hochreiter, Pelikanstrasse 11, Salzburg A-5020

Austrian Association for Group Psychotherapy and Group Dynamics
contact: Britta Zalodek, Lenaugasse 3, A-1080 Wien

GERMANY

Institut für Psychodrama und Soziometrie
contact: Uwe Seeger, Hardtwald-Klinik II, Hardstrasse 32, D-34596 Bad Zwesten

Moreno Institut für Psychodrama
contact: Gretel Leutz, Uhlandstrasse 8, D-88662 Überlingen

Moreno Institut für Psychotherapie and Socialpädagogik
contact: Winifred Jancovious, Gebelsbergstrasse 9, D-70199 Stuttgart

Psychodrama Institut für Europa
contact: Angela Janouch, Osterstrasse 68, D-32105, Bad Salzuflen

Institut für Tiefenpsychologische Psychodrama-Therapie
contact: Andreas Ploger, Pauwelstrasse, Neu Klinikum, 5100 Aachen

Psychodrama Institut Münster
contact: Martina Rosenbaum, Baaker Mulde 7, D-44879 Bochum

Psychodrama Institut Swesten
contact: Uwe Seeger, Hardtwaldklinkik 2, 3584 Zwesten 1

Institut für Psychodrama
contact: Ella Mae Shearon, An der Rechtschule 3, 50667 Köln

Psychodrama Institut Rheinland
contact; Ernst Diebels or Christian Benz, Neumarktstrasse 36, D-42103 Wuppertal

Szenen-Institut für Psychodrama
contact: Agnes Dudler, Meckenheimer Allee 131, D-53115, Bonn

Ulf Klein, Rambergstrasse 7, D-80799 Munich

FRANCE

Anne Ancelin Schutzenberger, 14 Ave Paul Appell, F 75014 Paris

Ecole Francaise de Psychodrame, 140 bis Rue de Rennes, F 75006 Paris

Institut Francais de Psychodrame et Groupe Analyse
contact: Claude Ouzilou, 12 Rue Emile Deutsch de la Meurthe, 75014 Paris

ARIPP, 6 bis Rue Bachaumont, F 75000 Paris

Psychosomaties, 34 Bo Albert Ier, F-06600 Antibes

PORTUGAL

Sociedade Portuguesa de Psicodrama
contact: Christina Martins, Rua Arnaldo Gama 64, 4000 Oporto

Fernando Santos Vieira, Av. Sao Joao de Deus, 13 C-3 Dto, 1000 Lisboa

Joao Albuquerque, Hospital Julio de Mato, Av. do Brzil No. 53, 1600 Lisboa

Manuela M. Costa, Rua Jose Antunes dos Santos, S-2710 Sintra

SPAIN

Associacion Espanola de Psicodrama
contact: Roberto Inocencio, Pza Cuadro 3, 39400 Cantabria

Jaime G. Rojas-Bermudez, Apartado de Correo 4361, 41080 Sevilla

Instituto de Tecnicas de Grupo y Psicodrama
contact: Pablo Población Knappe, San Martin de Porres 12B, Esc Dcha, Piso
OB, 28035 Madrid

Sociedad Espanola de Psicoterapia y Tecnicas de Grupo
contact: Hanne Campos, San Gervasio 30, 08022 Barcelona

ITALY

Italian Assoc. of Morenian Psychodramatists
contact: Giovanni Boria, Via Cola Montano 18, 20159 Milano

Paolo Carrirolo, via San Gervasio 4, 46100 Mantova

Laura Consolati, via Aleardi 17, 25100 Brescia

Paola de Leonardis, via Quadrio 20, 20154 Milan

Wilma Scategni, via Bagetti 33, 10138 Torino

TURKEY

Ankara Group Psychotherapyand Psychodrama Institute
contact: Haluk Özbay, Adakale Sokak No: 22/16, 0640 Kizilay, Ankara

Abdülkadir Özbek, Gürden sok. No: 6/3, Kavaklidere, Ankara

Istanbul Psychodrama Institute
contact: Deniz Altinay or Nese Karabekir, Valikonagi Cad. No: 173 YKB Vakif
Apt, 80220 Nisantasi, Istanbul

GREECE

Smaroula Pandelis, 7B Kapsali Str, 10674 Athens

Yannis K. Tsegos, Chavaliambi 1, Mavcomihali TT 12972, Athens

Ifigenia Psari, Allamani 45, 43100 Karditsa

Eleni Leventi, Ap Paulou 26, Thessaloniki

HUNGARY

Magyar Pszichodráma Egyesület, 1125 Budapest, Kútvölgyi üt 6

Gabor Pinter, 1025 Budapest, Tömörkeny u. 12/a

Eva Rapcsànyi, 1036 Budapest, Amfiteatrum u.25

Andras Zánkay, 1126 Budapest, Boszormenyi ut 4

Klara Gallus, 1035 Budapest, Vorosvari ut 4

ROMANIA

Dan Prelipceanu, 2 Aleea Bran, Bl.92, Sc.4, Ap.53, R-75158 Bucharest

Delia Marina Podea, Str. D Bolintineanu nr 3, Apt. 4, 2900 Arad

RUSSIA

Elena V. Lopukhina, Novopeschanaya Str. 9, Apt 42, 125057 Moscow

Institute of Group and Family Therapy
contact: Leonid M. Kroll or Ekaterina Mikhailova, Box 85, 103104 Moscow

Nifont B. Dolgopolov, Zandera Str 7-460, 129075 Moscow

Igor M. Kadyrov, Fadeev Str 6/170. 125047 Moscow

Vladimir Romek, Dept of Psychology, Rostov-on-Don State University, PO box 923, Rostov-on-Don 344092

BULGARIA

Psychodrama Centre 'Orpheus'
contact: Galabina Tarashoeva, Sofia 1000, PO Box 335

Alexander Angelov, Sofia 1000, Vitosha Str N42

Georgi Antonov, Sofia 1000, Dandukov Ave N39 ap1

Lubomir Jivkov, Sofia 1000, Bul. Christo Botev 18

Viselka Hrostova, Sofia 1505, Aleko Konstantoniv N 21

ISRAEL

Paul Hare and June Rabson Hare, Dept of Sociology, Ben Gurion University of the Negev, Beer-Sheva

Adina Hurvitz, 27 Arlosorov St, 44453 Kfar Saba

Peter Felix Kellermann, Burla St 23/4, Jerusalem 93714

Elliav Naharin, PO Box 504, Ramat Yishay 30095

Yaacov Naor, 7 Hatzanhanim St, Rehovot 76211

Miri Shoenfeld, Hapalmach Str. 9, Givataim 53406

JAPAN

Tokyo Psychodrama Association
Contact: Yujiro Isoda, Health Service Center, University of Tokyo, 7-8-1 Hongo, Bunkyo-ku, Tokyo 113

Japan Psychodrama Association
Contact: Hajime Mashino, 2-16-9-305 Kokuryo, Chofu, Tokyo 182

Japanese Society for Psychodrama
contact: Akemi Tsuchiya, 13-9-501 Sakuragaoka, Shibuya-ku, Tokyo 150

Nishinippon Psychodrama Society
contact: Susuma Harizuka, Center for Clinical Psychology and Human Development, Kyushu University, 1-6-19 Hakozaki, Kigashi-ku, Fukuoka 812-81

Tomio Miyama, Aichi Gakuin University, Dept of Psychology, 12 Araike, Iwasaki, Nisshincho, Aichi County, Prefect 470-01

Toshio Utena, Action Role Playing Seminar, c/o Hajime Tanabe, Counseling and Consultation Center, University of Tsukuba, 3-29-1 Otsuka, Bunkyo-ku, Tokyo 112

TAIWAN

Chung Ying Chen, Mei Ko Do Psychiatric Clinic, 362 Lien Wu Rd, Taichung

Chiu Ying-Hsiang, Kai-Suan Psychiatric Hospital, 2 FuChen St, Ling-Ya District, Kaohsiung, Taiwan 80240

KOREA

Hun Jin Choi, Dept of Neuropsychiatry, Eulji Medical Hospital, Mockdong 24, Jung Gu, Dea Jeon 310-070

Sung-Hee Cho, Forensic Hospital of Korea, San1, Banggok Li, Bampo-Meon, Gongju si, Chung Nam 315-920

Jung-Il Kim, Ji Am Medical Center, 5th floor, SamSungdong 151-1, Gangnam gu, Seoul

Korean Association of Psychodrama
contact: Sun-Hwa Lee, Student Guidance Center, ChangWon National University, Salim 9 dong, Changwon se, Kyungnam 641-242

Soon-Hwa Kang, Student Guidance Center, Ehwa Women's University, Deahyun dong, Sedaemun gu, Seoul

ARGENTINA

Institute of Psychodrama
contact: Monica Zuretti, Santa Fe 2847, 8 'C', 1425 Buenos Aires

Instituto de Psicodrama J.L. Moreno
contact: Dalmiro Bustos, Honduras 4034 '1', 1180 Buenos Aires

Associacion Argentina de Sicodrama y Sicoterapia de Grupa Avda
contact: Carlos Quinana, Luis Maria Campos 1377, Planta Baja 5, Buenos Aires

Associacion Mendocina de Sicodrama y Sicoterapia de Grup
contact: Jose Vera, Montevideo 444, 5500 Mendoza

Sociedad Argentina de Psicodrama
Thames 620, 1414 Buenos Aires

BRAZIL

Brazilian Federation of Psychodrama
contact: Luis Amadeus Bragante, Rua Cardoso de Almeida 23, 10 Andar,
Conjunto 106, CEP-05013-000 Perdizos, Sao Paulo

Federacion Brasilea de Psicodrama
contact: Oswaldo Politano Junior, Rua Indpendencia 3571, S.J. Rio Preto,
14014-400 Sao Paolo

Moyses Aguiar, Rua Ministro Godoi 502, 05015 Sao Paulo

Geraldo Francisco do Amaral, Rua 114, no. 183 Setor Sul, 74000 Goiania,
G.O.

Vera Cecilia Motta Pereira, Rua di Bianchi Bertoldi 20, 05422 Jardim
Paulistano, Sao Paulo

Luiz Cuschnir, Rua Alfonso de Freitas, 721-Paraiso, CEP 04006-052, Sao Paolo

Index

act completion, act fulfillment, 84, 88, 92
act hunger, xiv, 71, 83–84, 88, 92
acting-in, xiii–xv
action, xiii–xiv, xvi, 68, 146, 167
action techniques, xi, 6, 13–14, 46–47, 62–63, 183
action sociometry, 53
Adler, A., 145, 150, 153
adolescents, 89, 137
affect modulation, 101
alcoholism, 134–135
American Board of Examiners in Psychodrama, Sociometry & Group Psychotherapy, 163–164, 183
American Society for Group Psychotherapy & Psychodrama (ASGPP), 164–165, 180–182, 188
amplification, 5, 31, 75
analogies of psychodrama to
as a laboratory, 148–149
medicine, 145
power tools in carpentry, xvi, 110
surgery, 110
symphony orchestra, xvi
art techniques 51
assertion training, 100
audience, 2, 3, 24–25, 35, 96
autodrama, *see* monodrama
auxiliary, 1, 3, 7–8, 16–27, 68–70, 74–75, 104
trained, 20, 22

auxiliary chair, 23, 53–54
auxiliary ego, *see* auxiliary
awkwardness, 114–115
axiodrama, 133

balcony, 4
behavioral practice, 91, 95–96, 100–102, 156–157
behind-your-back technique, 6, 24, 126
Berne, E., *see* Transactional Analysis
bioenergetic analysis, xvi, 14, 50, 157, 173
black-out technique, 59
business and industry, ix, xi, xv, 119, 131–132, 140–141, 166

catharsis, 64–65, 84, 88–89, 91–92, 95, 112, 103, 106, 146, 154–155, 179
of integration, 95
chair, empty, *see* auxiliary chair
children, xiii, 128, 136–137
chorus, 3, 7, 24
client-centered therapy, 121–122
closure, 9, 107–108
coaching, 99
cognitive therapy, xi, xvi, 81, 101, 173
confrontation, 116–117
countertransference, 45–46, 116, 168, 171
creative arts therapies, 147, 173
creative dramatics, *see* drama

215